Jackson

Revelations

Revelations

DIARIES of WOMEN

EDITED BY

Mary Jane Moffat &
Charlotte Painter

 RANDOM HOUSE, *New York*

*All rights reserved under International and Pan-American
Copyright Conventions. Published in the United States by
Random House, Inc., New York, and simultaneously in Canada
by Random House of Canada Limited, Toronto*

Since this page cannot legibly accommodate all permissions
acknowledgments, they are located on the following pages.

Library of Congress Cataloging in Publication Data

Moffat, Mary Jane, comp.
Revelations: diaries of women.

Bibliography: p.
1. Woman—Biography. I. Painter, Charlotte, joint
comp. II. Title.
CT3202.M618   920.72   74–8040
ISBN 0–394–49128–9

Manufactured in the United States of America

FIRST EDITION

ACKNOWLEDGMENTS

Many persons—friends, students, colleagues, people we've met barely in passing whom we've told about this book—have made useful suggestions about materials for inclusion and have been otherwise of help. We thank them all.

Special thanks to:

Nora Gallagher Stern, our assistant;

and to

Tillie Olsen, John Benton, Brice Howard, Josephine Miles, Diane Middlebrook, Carolyn North Strauss, Judith Rascoe, Carol Rollins, Peggy McKenna, Norma Djerassi, Dale Djerassi, Linda Barnett, Sherry Perkins, Doris Ensign, Bernice Zelditch, Dagmar Morrow, Virginia McKim, Ruth Hart, Constance Houle, Lucy Martell, Virginia Holt, Annette Smith, Giovanna de Angelo, Kathleen Raine, *The Amazon Quarterly*, The Women's History Library, The Arthur and Elizabeth Schlesinger Library on the History of Women in America, Cambridge;

and to our thoughtful families

Tom Voorhees

Michael, Peter and Jack Moffat

Acknowledgments

The National Endowment of the Arts has given support to Charlotte Painter's participation in this project.

A copy of this book is on file at the Women's History Library, 2325 Oak St., Berkeley, California.

Grateful acknowledgement is made to the following for permission to reprint previously published material:

George Allen & Unwin Ltd: Excerpts from *The Pillow Book of Sei Shonagon,* edited by Arthur Waley, (1929)

Jonathan Cape Ltd.: Excerpts from *The Diary of Nellie Ptashkina,* edited by M. Jacques Povolotsky. (1923)

Chatto and Windus Ltd.: Excerpts from *A Life of One's Own* by Joanna Field. (1934)

Clarke, Irwin & Company Limited: Excerpts from *Hundreds and Thousands: The Journals of Emily Carr* by Emily Carr. Copyright © 1966 by Clarke, Irwin & Company Limited.

Thomas Y. Crowell Company and Harper & Row Publishers, Inc.: Excerpts from *George Eliot's Life as Related in Her Letters and Journals,* Volume II, edited by William Cross. (1900)

The Dial Press: Excerpts from *Joshua, First Born* by Frances Karlen Santamaria. Copyright © 1970 by Frances Karlen Santamaria.

Dodd, Mead & Company, Inc.: Excerpts from *The Diary of Alice James,* edited by Leon Edel. Copyright 1934 by Dodd, Mead & Company, Inc., copyright renewed 1961 by Anna R. Burr. Copyright © 1964 by Leon Edel.

Doubleday & Company, Inc.: Excerpts from *The Diary of Selma Lagerlöf* by Selma Lagerlöf, translated by Velma Swanton Howard. Copyright 1936 by Doubleday & Company, Inc. Excerpts from *The Diary of a Young Girl* by Anne Frank. Copyright 1952 by Otto H. Frank.

Acknowledgments

E. P. Dutton & Co., Inc.: Excerpts from Child of the Dark, *The Diary of Carolina Maria de Jesus,* translated by David St. Clair. Copyright © 1962 by E. P. Dutton & Co., Inc. and Souvenir Press Ltd. Excerpts from *The Journal of a Young Artist* by Marie Bashkirtseff, translated by Mary J. Serrano.

Victor Gollancz Ltd.: An excerpt from *The Diary of Tolstoy's Wife 1860–1891* by Sophie A. Tolstoy, translated by Alexander Werth (1928).

Gëbruder Mann Verlag: Käthe Kollwitz. Ich wirken in dieser Zeit. Berlin 1952. *The Diaries and Letters of Käthe Kollwitz,* Chicago 1955.

Harcourt Brace Jovanovich, Inc.: Excerpts from *A Writer's Diary* by Virginia Woolf, copyright 1953, 1954 by Leonard Woolf. Excerpts from *Diary of Anaïs Nin, Volume I,* copyright © 1966 by Anaïs Nin.

Houghton Mifflin Company: Excerpts from *Diary from Dixie* by Mary Boykin Chesnut with an Introduction by Ben Ames Williams. Copyright 1905 by D. Appleton & Company. Copyright 1949 by Houghton Mifflin Company. Excerpts from *An Anthropologist At Work* by Margaret Mead. Copyright © 1959 by Margaret Mead.

International Famous Agency, Inc.: An excerpt from *Confession From the Malaga Madhouse* by Charlotte Painter, Dial Press, Copyright © 1971 by Charlotte Painter.

Alfred A. Knopf, Inc.: Excerpts from *Journal of Katherine Mansfield,* edited by J. Middleton Murry. Copyright 1927 by Alfred A. Knopf, Inc. and renewed 1955 by J. Middleton Murry. Condensation of specified pages from *The Measure of My Days* by Florida Scott-Maxwell. Copyright © 1968 by Florida Scott-Maxwell. Excerpts from *Journal of a Residence on a Georgia Plantation in 1838–39* by Frances Anne Kemble, edited by John A. Scott. Copyright ©1961 by Alfred A. Knopf, Inc.

Macmillan Publishing Co., Inc.: Excerpts from *O Rugged Land of Gold* by Martha Martin. Copyright 1952, 1953 by Macmillan Publishing Company, Inc. Excerpts from *Kotto* by Lafcadio Hearn (1902).

Acknowledgments

Oxford University Press and the Trustees of Dove Cottage: Excerpts from *Journals of Dorothy Wordsworth* edited by Mary Moorman. (1971)

Routledge & Kegan Paul Ltd.: Excerpts from *Dostoevsky As Portrayed by His Wife* by Anna Gragorevna, translated by S. S. Koteliansky

Schocken Books, Inc.: Excerpts from *Hannah Senesh Her Life and Diary* by Hannah Senesh. Copyright © 1966 by Hakibbutz Hameuchad Publishing House Ltd. English edition copyright © 1971 by Nigel Marsh.

Sidgwick & Jackson Ltd: Excerpts from *The Complete Marjory Fleming*, edited by Frank Sidgwick (1934).

The Viking Press, Inc.: Excerpts from *A Prison, A Paradise* by Loran Hurnscot, Copyright © 1958 by Victor Gollancz Ltd.

Yale University Press: Excerpt from *Alphabets and Birthdays* by Gertrude Stein. Copyright © 1957 by Alice B. Toklas. Excerpts from *The George Eliot Letters, Volume 2*, edited by Gordon Haight. (1955)

CONTENTS

Contents

Revelations

FOREWORD

by Mary Jane Moffat

In this collection we offer samples of the diary form by thirty-three women from the early nineteenth century to the recent past. The writers range in age from a seven-year-old Scottish girl to an eighty-year-old Jungian analyst. They come from many countries. All have certain gifts for language and observation. Some of the diaries were secret, even covert, expressing the spontaneous feelings of the moment, intended for no eyes but their authors'. Others carried their diaries or journals further, revising them for publication. We want to show what the form has meant to these women, to suggest why they kept diaries, and to tell you what has made them individually interesting to us.

When we began our reading, we thought we knew exactly what we were looking for. We wanted to know about the inner lives of women. We wanted to read everything we could about those inner lives from primary sources: what women had written about themselves. We wanted to see if it was possible to define the diary, in particular, as a valid literary form, one that for women has often been the only available outlet for honest expression. And we wanted to understand how it was that some women, even within the context of repressive social circumstances, managed to achieve an inner freedom of personal integrity when others remained

3

alienated from their true nature. Was there, we wondered, such a quality as that implied by that quaint nineteenth-century word "character"?

Now, several hundred books of diaries, letters, memoirs and autobiographies later, I'm amused at our naïveté. We discovered a literature by women about their personal feelings that is so vast and varied that many shelves of anthologies would not exhaust the subject. I speak only of writings that have found their way into print. There is an even larger body of unpublished personal writing housed in special collections or in private hands that should be examined before we could presume to make any definitive statement about what has been going on inside women's heads over the centuries.

Even narrowing our focus to diaries, we were surfeited with materials. Many contained interesting passages too difficult to extract without cumbersome explanations. Let it be said that the form, with its repetitions and—in some hands—relentless concentration on the minimal, can be boring, an excellent sedative with no apparent side effects, not even a headache of memory. Many of the diaries we read were of historical interest but cast too little light on the personality of the author. Our own tastes led us to put aside those that posited a self we didn't like or find interesting, and to seek out those that demonstrated character as the ability to make moral distinctions and choices according to a personal code rather than the social or religious codes of the age in which they wrote.

As we read, always wondering what these materials had in common other than that they were written by women, a pattern gradually emerged that led to our arrangement of our final selections under three broad headings: Love, Work and Power. We don't intend these words as they are traditionally understood. What united these disparate lives for us was what we heard as an unconscious call by the women for a redefinition of these concepts into a less divisive, more organic pattern for existence, one where their capacities for both love and work blend, allowing them to be fully human and balanced, true to the power of their individual natures.

Why do women keep diaries? (Or journals or note-books.) Dissatisfaction with the way love and work have been defined for the female is the unconscious impulse that prompts many to pour out their feelings on paper and to acquire the habit of personal accounting on some more or less regular basis. The form has been an important outlet for women partly because it is an analogue to their lives: emotional, fragmentary, interrupted, modest, not to be taken seriously, private, restricted, daily, trivial, formless, concerned with self, as endless as their tasks. Confusion about the conflicting demands of love and work in relationship to the authentic self leads to loneliness, by far the most common emotion expressed in diaries; loneliness stemming either from physical isolation from normal outlets for discourse, as with Anne Frank, or from psychological alienation from one's milieu, as with Fanny Kemble, or from lovelessness, as with George Sand.

The psychic split experienced by women who must forgo love in favor of work is expressed by writers such as young Marie Bashkirtseff, a nineteenth-century artist, whose diary is a plea for the immortality she feared her painting wouldn't bring her; and by Ruth Benedict, whose journal gradually helped her to redefine her early belief that a great love was woman's true work.

One of the saddest motives for diary keeping was that of Alice James, the spinster sister of Henry and William, who had neither a love nor a work-related identity to present to the world as a way she might be understood. But although she was known as an invalid to others, through her diary she retained her sense of significance to herself.

Others kept diaries as an expression of both work and inner power. The diary of Carolina Maria de Jesus led her out of the garbage heaps of São Paulo. Mary Boykin Chesnut was politically powerless to alter the events of the Civil War, but she recorded those events from her own perspective and became a chronicler of her age. Virginia Woolf found among the stray matters she recorded in her diary "diamonds of the dustheap" that were useful to her in her fiction. Dorothy Wordsworth's brother William found diamonds in Dorothy's journal that were useful to him in his poetry; and women such as Joanna Field and Loran Hurnscot used the diary for serious and sustained explorations of their mental processes.

All these motives are apparent in the work of Anaïs Nin, the exemplar of the form, whose early diary-keeping was scorned by her friends and analysts as a nasty self-indulgence but who now is praised for having raised the diary to the realm of art. The persistent theme of the five published volumes of *The Diary of Anaïs Nin* is her struggle to reconcile the conflict between her received definitions of love as a female principle and of work as an exclusively male activity, an aggressive act. To wish to excel as a worker, as an artist, implied a loss of her sense of self as a woman. When she sought outside help, she was told by Otto Rank that "when the neurotic woman gets cured, she becomes a woman. When the neurotic man gets cured, he becomes an artist." René Allendy asked if she had ever wished "to surpass men in their own work, to have more success." She replied that she only wanted to support man, not be one.

For her as for others, the diary became the place where she could escape these definitions and let the real self have its day. She says, "The false person I had created for the enjoyment of my friends, the gaiety, the buoyant, the receptive, the healing person, always on call, always ready with sympathy, had to have its existence somewhere. In the diary I could reestablish the balance. Here I could be depressed, angry, disparaging, discouraged. I could let out my demons."

She tells of a recurrent dream of her diaries burning, which she first interpreted as an anxiety about losing them;

later she understood that "if the diaries burned, I would be left only with this persona, smiling, ever available, ever devoted."* Despite outside pressures to abandon the diary and her own dislike of the self she often encountered on its pages, she persisted. The diary became her life work.

Nin's early rigid definitions of love and work articulate, even exaggerate the unconscious concerns of many of the other diarists. Her steadfastness demonstrates what the diary has accomplished for these women: the courage required to acknowledge one's demons and the slow labor of bringing individuality to the fuller consciousness that honest and regular self-examination implies, are not only attributes of persons of character, they form character.

When Freud was asked what the normal person should be able to do, he replied "to love and to work." We take this statement to mean that neither love nor work should obsess the individual to the exclusion of the other. From a healthy fusion of these two great human capacities will come power, not in the traditional sense of the word as ascendancy or control over others but rather power as energy, emanating from the individual, a source of inner renewal that generates outward and returns to the individual.

We are familiar with the traditional cultural imbalance between work and love, where women have been allowed authority only in the sphere of love while men attend to the work of the world. Such an imbalance results in a warped expression of the individual's potential energy. For women: self-pity, masochism, manipulation, celebration of the torments of the heart, invalidism, madness. For men: slavery, war, corporate profits, destruction of the earth.

The arrangement of our selections from youth to old age is meant to demonstrate how some women have compensated for this imbalance. In the section called Love we see how the

* Anaïs Nin, *The Novel of the Future* (New York, Macmillan, 1968), p. 143.

young girl learns early that love is to be her role but how her lessons often inform her that love is a form of "goodness" that will mean sacrifice of her total identity if she chooses marriage, and lovelessness if she chooses any other occupation. For all the differences in their individual temperaments, social circumstances and historical periods, the girl diarists sound as if they were in conversation with each other, asking the same question, "Who shall I be?" in relationship to love and work. Little Marjory Fleming, with disarming candor, perceived that "goodness" was the way to get a husband, the only acceptable occupation for women in her time. Louisa May Alcott learned the nature of loving goodness through the model of her mother. She regenerated this love not by herself becoming a wife and mother, but by forgoing marriage to work at one of the few other occupations then open to women. Writing was also the ambition of Anne Frank, Nelly Ptaschkina and Hannah Senesh; through their diaries we hear them questioning how this work can be combined with their obligations to the service of love.

We concluded this section with some examples of love as it is experienced by the mature woman. Romantic love as an exacting occupation with formal rules for men as well as women is described by Sei Shonagon, our one departure from diaries of the last two centuries. Although she is separated from us by almost a thousand years, her charming account of how a lover should behave is a wistful expression of what even now women are taught love might be. George Sand shows the wasted energies than can accompany the end of romantic love. Sometimes love appears in ways that women have not been taught to expect, as in Anaïs Nin's relationship with June Miller. Motherhood as not merely a natural loving instinct but rather a learning process in itself is a theme of the diaries of Evelyn Scott, Frances Karlen Santamaria and Charlotte Painter, three women who were able to combine motherhood with their work as writers.

In the section called Work we see in three marriages to

strong and talented male figures, that marriage as traditionally defined is not the natural and fulfilling occupation of every temperament; if the married relationship suited Anna Dostoevsky, with her capacity for patience and self-effacement, it was destructive to the Tolstoys and could not accommodate the strong personalities of Ruth and Stanley Benedict. But the touching diary of an unknown Japanese woman shows us that even an arranged marriage beset by poverty, illness and personal tragedy, can be warm with loving and mutual respect, worthy work for both man and wife, especially in a culture that does not emphasize individual self-fulfillment as an expectation for either sex.

Work for a woman can also be love. Dorothy Wordsworth, talented as she was, probably found greater happiness in performing devoted service to the genius of her brother than she would have as an author in her own right. Teaching as a form of love is exemplified by Sylvia Ashton-Warner, who has said she married her work, although she also married a man who gave her emotional support. George Eliot, Virginia Woolf and Käthe Kollwitz were similarly blessed by relationships with males who saw them not only as wives but as workers.

In the section called Power we have placed women whose character led them to resist the male use of power as slavery, war and political oppression. Fanny Kemble risked and lost her marriage and the experience of mothering through her efforts to persuade her plantation-owner husband to give up his "dreadful possessions." Carolina Maria de Jesus, whose ancestors were Brazilian slaves, was a gadfly to politicians, reminding them at every opportunity that the poor could vote and that she was writing the truth in her diary. Martha Martin found the power within herself to resist the elements and survive a winter alone in the Alaskan wilderness in a rare demonstration of complete female autonomy.

Other women in this section chose not to fight the oppressions of the social or material world but to transcend it through inner journeys. We place Selma Lagerlöf here rather than with the other girl diarists, because her examination of a disturbing imprint upon her adolescent mind helped liberate the imagination that informed her later writing. As adults, Katherine Mansfield, Loran Hurnscot and Joanna Field turned away from their hard-won professional roles to return to the resources of mind and spirit. Joanna Field, in particular, suggests areas women will want to explore once they have achieved equality in the world of work as defined by men. In the early thirties she reflected on the achievements of the suffrage movement: "These people were epoch-makers politically . . . surely the pioneers of the next advance will be dealing with the mind."

The power of the mind is beautifully demonstrated by Florida Scott-Maxwell, who, after years of practice in Jungian psychology, at eighty-two continued her self-questioning, continued to grow. Finally, Emily Carr, her work as an artist curtailed by ill health, shows us a woman facing old age with faith and spirit.

This arrangement is not the only way to view these women. The three concepts of love, work and power thread through all the lives in this volume. We suggest only that these terms need to be redefined. Distinctions need to be made between love as sacrifice or suffering and healthy love; between work as corrupt love and as vocation—the calling or function the individual is born to fulfill; between power as manipulation and power as the energy that comes from a balanced life. The ideal would be such a successful synthesis between love, work and power that a new term emerges to replace all three, as in those primitive languages where single words are poems of connotations. Failing a new vocabulary, we would settle for an expanded definition of love to describe the successful exercise in life of each individual's best capacities.

In honoring these spontaneous feelings of women—who they were on a given day rather than what they remembered (and forgot) in the assessive voice of autobiography—we know full well that diaries yield only partial truths. In his introduc-

tion to Virginia Woolf's *A Writer's Diary*, Leonard Woolf
said he believed it was usually a mistake to publish extracts
from diaries because "the omissions almost always distort or
conceal the true character of the diarist." And as many of the
women in this collection admit, the diary is often turned to
when the writer is unhappy or in a particular kind of mood,
further distorting the picture of that person's life. But we did
not set out to document the full range of women's lives,
rather to reclaim feelings that readers may recognize as their
own.

In making our selections, our intent was not to cite the
many ways that women have been oppressed, although these
writings abound in such evidence. By now it is scarcely news
that women have suffered from injustice throughout history,
that they have been misrepresented or mythologized in literature, that if life has never been easy for most of the human
race, it has always been very hard to be a woman, to earn a
living, to maintain self-respect. But to the extent that the development of the individual can be separated from the demands of society, our concerns have been more with women in
a personal and psychological rather than a political context.

Our own interest in the diary as it relates to the writing
process has left us with a heavier weight of literary figures
than we had originally intended. Absent are the diaries of
women in the suffrage movement (happily, these are increas-
ingly available in other collections), of working (in the traditional definition) women or those speaking for them, of settle-
ment-house leaders, prostitutes, physicians, women in prison.
Nor have we included writings by figures in the contemporary
women's movement. Our supplemental bibliography suggests
areas for further reading.

In a recent course I offered in women's diaries, a student
who had been a secret diary-keeper for years commented, "I
never before realized I was part of a literary tradition." Although earlier taboos are disappearing about what is acceptable
for a woman to feel, and although personal matters that were

never confided even to a close friend are now casual dinner-table conversation, many women still keep diaries. As we continue to speak more openly to each other and to men, breaking the long silence about what a woman's inner life is like, dropping false personas, the need for diaries as an emotional outlet may disappear. But I suspect the form will persist as a way for the individual to explore identity, chart emotional growth, develop character.

This use of the diary may become even more important in the coming years when both sexes face freer choices in the way they will love and work. If our lot is to be prescribed less by gender-defined roles than by who we individually are, the discovery of an authentic self becomes a prime responsibility.

Women are now collectively in process toward a new understanding of who we will be in the future, who we have been in the past. This period in the collective process is not unlike a page from a diary: a moment possessed of its own truth. Our new freedom to become workers is exhilarating. Now, rather than accepting previous definitions of work which is performed to the exclusion of love, we must decide what work is.

In assembling some past moments in the lives of individual women, we are offering what is only a beginning effort to reclaim diaries as a unique literary tradition of honest expression in which we have recognized aspects of ourselves. Jorge Luis Borges says that every writer creates his own precursors; we believe the women writers of the future will stand on the remarkably strong shoulders of women diarists who wrote to please no audience but themselves.

ON KEEPING A DIARY

It makes me laugh to read over this diary. It's so full of contradictions, and one would think I was such an unhappy woman. Yet is there a happier woman than I? It would be hard to find a happier or more friendly marriage than ours. Sometimes, when I am alone in the room, I just laugh with joy, and making the sign of the cross, say to myself, "May God let this last many, many years." I always write in my diary when we quarrel. . . .

Sophie Tolstoy

. . . I have just re-read my year's diary and am much struck by the rapid haphazard gallop at which it swings along, sometimes indeed jerking almost intolerably over the cobbles. Still if it were not written rather faster than the fastest type-writing, if I stopped and took thought, it would never be written at all; and the advantage of the method is that it sweeps up accidentally several stray matters which I should exclude if I hesitated, but which are the diamonds of the dustheap.

Virginia Woolf

On Keeping a Diary

By keeping a diary of what made me happy I had dis-covered that happiness came when I was most widely aware. So I had finally come to the conclusion that my task was to become more and more aware, more and more understanding with an understanding that was not at all the same thing as intellectual comprehension.

Joanna Field

What if, seized without warning by a fatal illness, I should happen to die suddenly! I should not know, perhaps, of my danger; my family would hide it from me; and after my death they would rummage among my papers; they would find my journal, and destroy it after having read it, and soon nothing would be left of me—nothing—nothing—nothing! This is the thought that has always terrified me.

Marie Bashkirtseff

I only regret that everyone wants to deprive me of the journal, which is the only steadfast friend I have, the only one which makes my life bearable; because my happiness with human beings is so precarious, my confiding moods rare, and the least sign of non-interest is enough to silence me. In the journal I am at ease.

Playing so many roles, dutiful daughter, devoted sister, mistress, protector, my father's new found illusion, Henry's needed, all-purpose friend, I had to find one place of truth, one dialogue without falsity. This is the role of the diary.

Anaïs Nin

On Keeping a Diary

What fun it is to generalize in the privacy of a note book. It is as I imagine waltzing on ice might be. A great delicious sweep in one direction, taking you your full strength, and then with no trouble at all, an equally delicious sweep in the opposite direction. My note book does not help me think, but it eases my crabbed heart.

Florida Scott-Maxwell

I haven't written for a few days, because I wanted first of all to think about my diary. It's an odd idea for someone like me to keep a diary; not only because I have never done so before, but because it seems to me that neither I—nor for that matter anyone else—will be interested in the unbosomings of a thirteen-year-old schoolgirl. Still, what does that matter? I want to write, but more than that, I want to bring out all kinds of things that lie buried deep in my heart.

There is a saying that "paper is more patient than man"; it came back to me on one of my slightly melancholy days. . . . Yes, there is no doubt that paper is patient and as I don't intend to show this cardboard-covered notebook . . . to anyone, unless I find a real friend, boy or girl, probably nobody cares. And now I come to the root of the matter, the reason for my diary: it is that I have no such real friend. . . .

Anne Frank

Writing a journal implies that one has ceased to think of the future and has decided to live wholly in the present. It is an announcement to fate that you expect nothing more. It is an assertion that you take each day as it comes and make no connection between today and other days. Writing a journal means that facing your ocean you are afraid to swim across it, so you attempt to drink it drop by drop. It means that you count the last leaves of a tree whose trunk has lost its sap.

When you are in the mood to write a journal the passions have cooled, or else they have so far frozen that they may be examined as safely as ice-bound mountains are explored in the season when no avalanches fall. No one should allow himself to solidify to this extent unless he is in a state of such upheaval that all the fires of his being are in danger of eruption. Then indeed it may be necessary to harden the outer crust in order to check the explosion and save the inner flame from becoming extinct.

George Sand,
Preface to the Piffoël Journal

I used to write diaries when I was young but if I put anything down that was under the skin I was in terror that someone would read it and ridicule me, so I always burnt them up before long . . . I wonder why we are always ashamed of our best parts and try to hide them. We don't mind ridicule of our "silliness" but of our "sobers," oh! . . .

Emily Carr

Everybody reads my journal, but since I have been making sketches of character . . . I keep it under lock and key . . . In my plain speaking and candour, what have I not said, intending no eye save mine to rest upon this page. The things that I cannot tell exactly as they are, I do not intend to tell at all.

Mary Boykin Chesnut

———————————

I am getting fine and supple from the mistakes I've made, but I wish a note book could laugh.

Florida Scott-Maxwell

———————————

. . . Why does a narrative replace a diary. Because it does not.

One day.

One day day before yesterday . . .

There is a difference between omitting and there is a difference between adding . . .

Yesterday today . . .

A diary is not a line a day book . . .

Three days added together . . .

Yesterday evening Bravig and John were here. They will be here again.

Several times other people have been here. There is a difference of opinion as to the desirability of their being here . . .

A diary should simply be.

Yesterday hyacinths and anemones were under-foot at that.

Yesterday at that . . .

This makes a diary.

Who is reputed.

This makes a diary.

Who has had whom.

This makes a diary too tenderly . . .

Nothing has happened today except kindness . . .

Yesterday we turned hyacinths into wisteria.

Today we turned them back to hyacinths from hyacinths to wisteria . . .

Yesterday we had both a ham and a fake bird. It can be very much enjoyed very much enjoyed. Today in the midst in the midst in the midst to know in the midst. . . .

A diary means yes indeed . . .

And now. Today today is celebrated in our annals by perfect satisfaction.

That was just the same as yesterday . . .

Yesterday was a sad day.

Today is a daisy day . . .

Thinking in terms of a diary its origin and its nationality and its return. . . .

A diary should be instantly in recording a telegram. Also in recording a visit also in recording a conversation also in recording embroidery also in recording having wished to buy a basket. That is it . . .

From "A Diary" in *Alphabets and Birthdays*
by Gertrude Stein

PART I   *Love*

MARJORY FLEMING

(1803-1811)

*I*n *the early nineteenth century* a seven-year-old Scottish girl wrote of the difficulties of achieving an ideal of feminine goodness even before she had learned to punctuate. Marjory Fleming's daily diary was a task imposed upon her by Isabella Keith—Isa—her beloved cousin and tutor. Isa corrected Marjory's spelling and character. Pious and virtuous, she was the model of the woman Marjory wished to become.

Fortunately, the real Marjory kept erupting on the pages of her copy book: at such times as that randy moment when her brother was so maddening she called him an "Impudent Bitch." We cannot say if the educative process would have transformed Marjory into a marriageable woman of virtue. She died before her tenth birthday of meningitis, a complication of an attack of measles. Her diary disappeared into the closet of family grief until the 1850's, when it was exploited by H. B. Farnie, who published *Pet Marjorie: A Story of Child Life Fifty Years Ago.* Farnie and later editors glossed the diary with heavy layers of Victorian sentimentality, altering her text and deleting words and phrases they found offensive. Even though censored, Marjory became known around the world. She was the youngest subject in Sir Leslie Stephen's *Dictionary of National Biography.* Mark Twain recognized her spirit and found in her some of the same charm he celebrated in his own rebel, Huckleberry Finn:

Revelations

She was made out of thunder-storms and sunshine, and not even her little perfunctory pieties and shop-made holinesses could squelch her spirits or put out her fires for long. Under pressure of a pestering sense of duty she heaves a shovelful of trade godliness into her journals every little while, but it does not offend, for none of it is her own; it is all borrowed, it is a convention, a custom of her environment, it is the most innocent of hypocrisies; and this tainted butter of hers soon gets to be as delicious to the reader as are the stunning and wordly sincerities she splatters around it every time her pen takes a fresh breath.*

We have preserved the line-for-line reproduction of Marjory's text as it was published by Sedgwick & Jackson Ltd. in 1934. We have omitted Isa Keith's corrections of spelling errors except in the rare case where not to do so would render a line unintelligible.

I confess that I have been
more like a little young
Devil then a creature for
when Isabella went up
to stairs to teach me religion and my multi-
plication and to be good
and all my other lessons
I stamped with my feet
and threw my new hat

* Quoted by Frank Sedgwick in the introduction to *The Complete Marjory Fleming.*

which she made on the
ground and was sulky an
was dreadfuly passionate
but she never whipped me
but gently said Marjory
go into another room and
think what a great crime
you are committing
letting your temper
git the better of you
but I went so sulkely that
the Devil got the better of me
but she never whip
me so that I think I would
be the better of it and the
next time time that I behave
ill I think she should do it . . .

I am now going to tell you
about the horible and wret[ched]
plaege that my multiplication
give me you cant concieve it—
the most Devilish thing is 8 times 8
& 7 times 7 it is what nature itselfe
cant endure . . .

I have a delightl pleasure in
view which is the thoughts of going to Braehead where I will
walk to Craky-hall wich puts
me In mind
that I walked to that delightfull
place with a delightfull
young man beloved by all his

Revelations

friends and espacialy by
me his loveress but I must not
talk any longer about him
for Isa said it is not
proper for to speak of gentalman
but I will never forget him
I hope that at 12 or 13 years old
I will be as learned as Miss Isa
and Nancy Keith for many
girls have not the advan-
tage I have and I am very very
glad that satan has not ge-
ven me boils and many other
Misfortunes . . .

To Day I pronunced a
word which should never
come out of a ladys lips it was
that I called John a Impu-
dent Bitch and Isabella afterwards told
me that I should never say
it even in joke but she kindly
forgave me because I said
that I would not do it again . . .

As this is Sunday I must begin to write serious thoughts
as Isabella bids me. I am
thinking how I should Improve
the many talents I have.
I am very sory I have
threwn them away it is
shoking to think of it when
many have not half

the instruction I have
because Isabella teaches
me to or three hours every
day in reading and
writing and arethmatick
and many other things
and rligion into the bar
gan. On sunday she
teaches me to be virtuous.

This is Saturday, & I
am very glad of it, be-
cause I have play
half of the Day, & I get
mony too, but alas I
owe Isabella 4 pence,
for I am finned 2 pence
whenever I bite my nails
Isa is teaching me
to make *Simecolings nots*
of *interrgations peorids & com*
-moes &c; . . .

Now am I quite
happy : for I am going
tomorrow to a delightfull
place, Breahead by name,
belonging to Mrs Crra-
ford, where their is ducks
cocks hens bublyjocks 2 dogs
2 cats & swine. & which is
delightful; I think
it is shoking to think
that the dog & cat

should bear them &
they are drowned after
all.
I would rather have
a man dog then a women dog because they
do not bear like women
dogs, it is a hard case
it is shoking; . . .
I am going to turn
over a new life &
am going to be a very
good girl & be obedient
to Isa Keith . . .

I will never again trust in
my own power. for I see
that I cannot be good without Gods assistence, I will
never trust in my selfe & it
   Isas health will be
quite ruined by
me it will indeed; . . .

              Spring 1811

Love I think is in the fasion for
every body is marring there
is a new novel published named selfcontroul a very good
maxam forsooth yesterday
a marrade man named M^r
John Balfour Esq^e offered
to kiss me, & offered to marry
me though the man was es-

pused, & his wife was present, &
said he must ask her per
-mission but he did not I
think he was ashamed or con-
founded before 3 gentelman . . .

The weather is very mild
& serene & not like winter
A sailor called here to say
farewell, it must be dread-
full to leave his native country
where he might get a wife
or perhaps me, for I love
him very much & with
all my heart, but O I
forgot Isabella forbid me to
speak about love . . .
. . . Isabella is always reading &
writing in her room & does not
come down for long & I wish every
body would follow her example
& be as good as pious & virtious as
she is & they would get husbands
soon enough, love is a very
papithatick thing as well as
troubelsom & tiresome but O
Isabella forbid me to speak a-
-about it. . . .

LOUISA MAY ALCOTT

(1832-1888)

*L*ouisa May Alcott and her sisters were educated at home by their father, the transcendentalist philosopher whose New England circle included Thoreau and Emerson. The children were required to keep regular journals, and although these were open to the inspection of their parents, they were very frank. Louisa's journal records that the major subject of her education was self-denial. Her model of goodness was her sacrificing mother who became the Marmee of *Little Women*. By the time she was thirteen, she realized that her father's celebration of the glories of the spiritual world and his experiments in running a communal farm were never going to provide the family with even the sparest creature comforts, and that she must not only learn to be good but work to support them.

She sewed, taught school, nursed in the Civil War and finally wrote, like so many hard-working women of her period, not for art but for money. "Whatever suits the customer," she said, for every ten or fifteen dollars she received for a story or an article was immediately translated into a pair of shoes or gloves or a sack of coal to keep the family warm. She ruined her health, often writing fourteen hours a day. When her publisher requested that she write "a girl's book," she commented, "I don't enjoy this sort of thing. Never liked girls or knew many, except my sisters; but our queer plays and experiences may prove interesting, though I doubt it."

Years later she annotated that diary entry with: "Good joke." Because of course *Little Women* was an immediate success and Jo—the first liberated girl in American literature—is still a favorite of girl readers. The author was wise enough to retain the copyright, and for the first time the family's financial security was, if not assured, less perilous. Enough so that Louisa May Alcott could afford to indulge a brief flash of artistic integrity. She wrote, "Girls write to ask who the little women marry, as if that was the only end and aim of a woman's life. I *won't* marry Jo to Laurie to please anyone."

But whatever suits the customer: she invented Professor Bhaer as a husband for Jo. She herself never married. When asked to write an article of advice to girls, she told them of the sweet independence of the spinster's life. But she was not a happy woman. Her expression of love through work was as self-sacrificing as her mother's, and she had too much humor for sainthood. One year when her only birthday remembrance was a book written by her father, she mused, "I never seem to have many presents, as some do, though I give a good many."

These extracts from her childhood diary include annotations Louisa May Alcott made forty years later.

EARLY DIARY KEPT AT FRUITLANDS, 1843
TEN YEARS OLD

September 1st.

I rose at five and had my bath. I love cold water! Then we had our singing-lesson with Mr. Lane. After breakfast I washed dishes, and ran on the hill till nine, and had some thoughts,—it was so beautiful up there. Did my lessons,—

wrote and spelt and did sums; and Mr. Lane read a story, "The Judicious Father": How a rich girl told a poor girl not to look over the fence at the flowers, and was cross to her because she was unhappy. The father heard her do it, and made the girls change clothes. The poor one was glad to do it, and he told her to keep them. But the rich one was very sad; for she had to wear the old ones a week, and after that she was good to shabby girls. I liked it very much, and I shall be kind to poor people.

Father asked us what was God's noblest work. Anna said *men*, but I said *babies*. Men are often bad; babies never are. We had a long talk, and I felt better after it, and *cleared up*.

Sunday, 24th.

Father and Mr. Lane have gone to N.H. to preach. It was very lovely. . . . Anna and I got supper. In the eve I read "Vicar of Wakefield." I was cross to-day, and I cried when I went to bed. I made good resolutions, and felt better in my heart. If I only *kept* all I make, I should be the best girl in the world. But I don't, and so am very bad.

[Poor little sinner! She says the same at fifty.—L.M.A.]

Friday, Nov. 2nd.

Anna and I did the work. In the evening Mr. Lane asked us, "What is man?" These were our answers: A human being; an animal with a mind; a creature; a body; a soul and a mind. After a long talk we went to bed very tired.

[No wonder, after doing the work and worrying their little wits with such lessons.—L.M.A.]

Thursday, 29th.

Eleven years old. It was Father's and my birthday. We had some nice presents. We played in the snow before school. Mother read "Rosamond" when we sewed. Father asked us in the eve what fault troubled us most. I said my bad temper.

I told mother I liked to have her write in my book. She said she would put in more, and she wrote this to help me:—
Dear Louy,—Your handwriting improves very fast. Take pains and do not be in a hurry. I like to have you make observations about our conversations and your own thoughts. It helps you to express them and to understand your little self. Remember, dear girl, that a diary should be an epitome of your life. May it be a record of pure thought and good actions, then you will indeed be the precious child of your loving mother.

Wednesday

—Read Martin Luther. A long letter from Anna [her sister]. She sends me a picture of Jenny Lind, the great singer. She must be a happy girl. I should like to be famous as she is . . .

I wrote in my Imagination Book, and enjoyed it very much. Life is pleasanter than it used to be, and I don't care about dying any more . . . I had a pleasant time with my mind, for it was happy.

[Moods began early.—L.M.A.]

Thursday

—Read the "heart of Mid-Lothian," and had a very happy day. Miss Ford gave us a botany lesson in the woods. I am always good there. In the evening Miss Ford told us about the bones in our bodies, and how they get out of order. I must be careful of mine, I climb and jump and run so much . . .

A Sample of our Lessons.

"What virtues do you wish more of?" asks Mr. L. I answer:—

Patience,	Love,	Silence,
Obedience,	Generosity,	Perseverance,
Industry,	Respect,	Self-denial.

"What vices less of?"

Idleness,	Wilfulness,	Vanity,
Impatience,	Impudence,	Pride,
Selfishness,	Activity,	Love of cats.

Dearest Mother,—I have tried to be more contented, and I think I have been more so. I have been thinking about my little room, which I suppose I never shall have. I should want to be there about all the time, and I should go there and sing and think . . .

Thirteen Years Old.

March, 1846.

I have at last got the little room I have wanted so long, and am very happy about it. It does me good to be alone, and Mother has made it very pretty and neat for me. My work-basket and desk are by the window, and my closet is full of dried herbs that smell very nice. The door that opens into the garden will be very pretty in summer, and I can run off to the woods when I like.

I have made a plan for my life, as I am in my teens, and no more a child. I am old for my age, and don't care much for girl's things. People think I'm wild and queer; but Mother understands and helps me. I have not told any one about my plan; but I'm going to *be* good. I've made so many resolutions, and written sad notes, and cried over my sins, and it doesn't seem to do any good! Now I'm going to *work really*, for I feel a true desire to improve, and be a help and comfort, not a care and sorrow, to my dear mother.

ANNE FRANK
(1929-1944)

*T*he diary of Anne Frank, published as *The Diary of a Young Girl*, was translated into thirty-seven languages, and adapted for the theater and film, and became one of the best-known examples of personal writing in history. Deeply moving as a document illuminating faith in the best of the human spirit during the most inhuman of times, the diary is also of enormous value in understanding the process by which a young girl struggles to bring her individuality to consciousness.

The isolation of The Secret Annexe—the upper floors of the Amsterdam office building where for two years the Frank and Van Daan families hid from the Nazis—led thirteen-year-old Anne to turn to her diary as confidante of the changes her mind and body were undergoing. In this closed atmosphere the process of maturity was tragically intensified. But although her life was in daily jeopardy, she saw her future as one of infinite possibility.

In casting about for the identity of the person she wished to become, she rejected as models the "cramped and narrow" lives of her mother and sister Margot. She prized being a woman and the implications of potential motherhood. She fell "in love" on schedule, learning that she was capable of giving and receiving love. And in rejecting that first adolescent romance, moving instead into friendship, she learned self-esteem. She records that she was a potential wife, mother and, as well, a writer, one who would have "beautiful dresses" and meet "interesting people."

The diary is addressed to an imaginary friend, Kitty. "In order to enhance in my mind's eye the picture of the friend for whom I have waited so long, I don't want to set down a series of bald facts in a diary like most people do, but I want this diary itself to be my friend, and I shall call my friend Kitty."

Sunday, 2 January, 1944

Dear Kitty,

This morning when I had nothing to do I turned over some of the pages of my diary and several times I came across letters dealing with the subject "Mummy" in such a hot-headed way that I was quite shocked, and asked myself: "Anne, is it really you who mentioned hate? Oh, Anne, how could you!" I remained sitting with the open page in my hand, and thought about it and how it came about that I should have been so brimful of rage and really so filled with such a thing as hate that I had to confide it all in you. I have been trying to understand the Anne of a year ago and to excuse her, because my conscience isn't clear as long as I leave you with these accusations, without being able to explain, on looking back, how it happened.

I suffer now—and suffered then—from moods which kept my head under water (so to speak) and only allowed me to see the things subjectively without enabling me to consider quietly the words of the other side, and to answer them as the words of one whom I, with my hotheaded temperament, had offended or made unhappy.

I hid myself within myself, I only considered myself and

quietly wrote down all my joys, sorrows, and contempt in my diary. This diary is of great value to me, because it has become a book of memoirs in many places, but on a good many pages I could certainly put "past and done with."

I used to be furious with Mummy, and still am sometimes. It's true that she doesn't understand me, but I don't understand her either. She did love me very much and she was tender, but as she landed in so many unpleasant situations through me, and was nervous and irritable because of other worries and difficulties, it is certainly understandable that she snapped at me . . .

The period when I caused Mummy to shed tears is over. I have grown wiser and Mummy's nerves are not so much on edge. I usually keep my mouth shut if I get annoyed, and so does she, so we appear to get on much better together. I can't really love Mummy in a dependent childlike way—I just don't have that feeling.

I soothe my conscience now with the thought that it is better for hard words to be on paper than that Mummy should carry them in her heart.

Yours, Anne

Wednesday, 5 January, 1944

Dear Kitty,

I have two things to confess to you today, which will take a long time. But I must tell someone and you are the best one to tell, as I know that, come what may, you always keep a secret.

The first is about Mummy. You know that I've grumbled a lot about Mummy, yet still tried to be nice to her again. Now it is suddenly clear to me what she lacks. Mummy herself has told us that she looked upon us more as her friends than her daughters. Now that is all very fine, but still, a friend can't take a mother's place. I need my mother as an example which I can follow, I want to be able to respect her. I have the feeling that Margot thinks differently about these things and would never be able to understand what I've just told you. And Daddy avoids all arguments about Mummy.

I imagine a mother as a woman who, in the first place, shows great tact, especially towards her children when they reach our age, and who does not laugh at me if I cry about something—not pain, but other things—like "Mums" does . . .

The second is something that is very difficult to tell you, because it is about myself.

Yesterday I read an article about blushing by Sis Heyster. This article might have been addressed to me personally. Although I don't blush very easily, the other things in it certainly all fit me. She writes roughly something like this—that a girl in the years of puberty becomes quiet within and begins to think about the wonders that are happening to her body . . .

I think what is happening to me is so wonderful, and not only what can be seen on my body, but all that is taking place inside. I never discuss myself or any of these things with anybody; that is why I have to talk to myself about them.

Each time I have a period—and that has only been three times—I have the feeling that in spite of all the pain, unpleasantness, and nastiness, I have a sweet secret, and that is why, although it is nothing but a nuisance to me in a way, I always long for the time that I shall feel that secret within me again.

Sis Heyster also writes that girls of this age don't feel quite certain of themselves, and discover that they themselves are individuals with ideas, thoughts, and habits. After I came here, when I was just fourteen, I began to think about myself sooner than most girls, and to know that I am a "person."

Sometimes, when I lie in bed at night, I have a terrible desire to feel my breasts and to listen to the quiet rhythmic beat of my heart.

I already had these kinds of feelings subconsciously before I came here, because I remember that once when I slept with a girl friend I had a strong desire to kiss her, and that I did so. I could not help being terribly inquisitive over her body, for she had always kept it hidden from me. I asked her whether, as a proof of our friendship, we should feel one another's breasts, but she refused. I go into ecstasies every time I see the naked figure of a woman, such as Venus, for example. It strikes me as so wonderful and exquisite that I have difficulty in stopping the tears rolling down my cheeks.

If only I had a girl friend!

Yours, Anne

Thursday, 6 January, 1944

Dear Kitty,

My longing to talk to someone became so intense that somehow or other I took it into my head to choose Peter.

Sometimes if I've been upstairs into Peter's room during the day, it always struck me as very snug, but because Peter is so retiring and would never turn anyone out who became a nuisance, I never dared stay long, because I was afraid he might think me a bore. I tried to think of an excuse to stay in his room and get him talking, without it being too noticeable, and my chance came yesterday. Peter has a mania for cross-word puzzles at the moment and hardly does anything else. I helped him with them and we soon sat opposite each other at his little table, he on the chair and me on the divan.

It gave me a queer feeling each time I looked into his deep blue eyes, and he sat there with that mysterious laugh playing round his lips. I was able to read his inward thoughts.

I could see on his face that look of helplessness and uncertainty as to how to behave, and, at the same time, a trace of his sense of manhood. I noticed his shy manner and it made me feel very gentle; I couldn't refrain from meeting those dark eyes again and again, and with my whole heart I almost beseeched him: oh, tell me, what is going on inside you, oh, can't you look beyond this ridiculous chatter?

But the evening passed and nothing happened, except that I told him about blushing—naturally not what I have written, but just so that he would become more sure of himself as he grew older.

When I lay in bed and thought over the whole situation, I found it far from encouraging, and the idea that I should beg for Peter's patronage was simply repellent. One can do a lot to satisfy one's longings, which certainly sticks out in my case, for I have made up my mind to go and sit with Peter more often and to get him talking somehow or other.

Whatever you do, don't think I'm in love with Peter—not a bit of it! If the Van Daans had had a daughter instead of a son, I should have tried to make friends with her too. . . .

Sunday, 27 February, 1944

Dearest Kitty,

From early in the morning till late at night, I really do hardly anything else but think of Peter. I sleep with his image before my eyes, dream about him and he is still looking at me when I am awake . . .

But how and when will we finally reach each other? I don't know quite how long my common sense will keep this longing under control.

Yours, Anne

Revelations

Dear Kitty,

The weather is lovely, superb, I can't describe it; I'm going up to the attic in a minute.

Now I know why I'm so much more restless than Peter. He has his own room where he can work, dream, think, and sleep. I am shoved about from one corner to another. I hardly spend any time in my "double" room and yet it's something I long for so much. That is the reason too why I so frequently escape to the attic. There, and with you, I can be myself for a while, just a little while . . .

Oh, it is so terribly difficult never to say anything to Peter, but I know that the first to begin must be he; there's so much I want to say and do, I've lived it all in my dreams, it is so hard to find that yet another day has gone by, and none of it comes true! Yes, Kitty, Anne is a crazy child, but I do live in crazy times and under still crazier circumstances.

But, still, the brightest spot of all is that at least I can write down my thoughts and feelings, otherwise I would be absolutely stifled! I wonder what Peter thinks about all these things? I keep hoping that I can talk about it to him one day. There must be something he has guessed about me, because he certainly can't love the outer Anne, which is the one he knows so far . . .

Friday, 28 April, 1944

. . . Oh Peter, what have you done to me? What do you want of me? Where will this lead us? . . . if I were older and he should ask me to marry him, what should I answer? Anne, be honest! You would not be able to marry him, but yet, it would be hard to let him go. Peter hasn't enough character yet . . . he is still a child in his heart of hearts . . .

Am I only fourteen? Am I really still a silly little school-girl? Am I really so inexperienced about everything? . . . I am afraid that in my longing I am giving myself too quickly. How, later on, can it ever go right with other boys? . . .

Sunday morning, 7 May, 1944

Dear Kitty,

Daddy and I had a long talk yesterday afternoon, I cried terribly and he joined in. Do you know what he said to me, Kitty? "I have received many letters in my life, but this is certainly the most unpleasant! You, Anne, who have received such love from your parents, you, who have parents who are always ready to help you, who have always defended you whatever it might be, can you talk of feeling no responsibility towards us? You feel wronged and deserted; no, Anne, you have done us a great injustice!"

. . . Oh, I have failed miserably; this is certainly the worst thing I've ever done in my life . . . Certainly, I have had a lot of unhappiness, but to accuse the good Pim, who had done and still does do everything for—no, that was too low for words . . .

I want to start at the beginning again and it can't be difficult, now that I have Peter . . . he loves me. I love him. I have my books, my storybook and my diary, not utterly stupid, have a cheerful temperament and want to have a good character! . . .

Monday, 8 May, 1944

. . . I can assure you I'm not at all keen of a narrow cramped existence like Mummy and Margot. I'd adore to go to Paris for a year and London for a year to learn the languages and study the history of art. Compare that with

Margot, who wants to be a midwife in Palestine! I always long to see beautiful dresses and interesting people. . . .

Thursday, 11 May, 1944

. . . You've known for a long time that my greatest wish is to become a journalist someday and later on a famous writer . . . Whether I shall succeed or not, I cannot say, but my diary will be a great help. . . .

Friday, 19 May, 1944

. . . All goes well with Peter and me. The poor boy seems to need a little love even more than I do. He blushes every evening when he gets his good-night kiss and simply begs for another . . .

Friday, 9 June, 1944

. . . The whole of the Secret Annexe except Van Daan and Peter have read the trilogy *Hungarian Rhapsody* . . . It is a very interesting book, but in my opinion there is a bit too much about women in it . . .

Wednesday, 14 June, 1944

. . . Peter loves me not as a lover but as a friend and grows more affectionate every day . . . Peter is good and he's a darling, but still there's no denying that there's a lot about him that disappoints me . . . He lets me say a lot of things to him that he would never accept from his mother . . .

Both Peter and I have spent our most meditative years in the "Secret Annexe." We often discuss the future, the past, and the present, but . . . I still seem to miss the real thing and yet I know it's there.

Thursday, 6 July, 1944

Dear Kitty,

It strikes fear to my heart when Peter talks of later being a criminal, or of gambling; although it's meant as a joke, of course, it gives me the feeling that he's afraid of his own weakness . . .

We all live with the object of being happy; our lives are all different and yet the same . . . You must work and do good, not be lazy and gamble, if you wish to earn happiness. Laziness may *appear* attractive, but work *gives* satisfaction.

Poor boy, he's never known what it feels like to make other people happy, and I can't teach him that either . . .

Saturday, 15 July, 1944

. . . I have one outstanding trait in my character, which must strike anyone who knows me for any length of time, and that is my knowledge of myself. I can watch myself and my actions, just like an outsider. The Anne of every day I can face entirely without prejudice, without making excuses for her, and watch what's good and bad about her . . . I understand more and more how true Daddy's words were when he said: "All children must look after their own upbringing." Parents can only give good advice or put them on the right paths, but the final forming of a person's character lies in their own hands . . .

I ponder far more over Peter than Daddy. I know very well that I conquered him instead of him conquering me. I created an image of him in my mind, pictured him as a quiet, sensitive, lovable boy, who needed affection and friendship

. . . I needed a living person to whom I could pour out my heart . . . it automatically developed into an intimacy which, on second thought, I don't think I ought to have allowed . . .

"For in its innermost depths youth is lonelier than old age." I read this saying in some book and I've always remembered it, and found it to be true . . .

Tuesday, 1 August, 1944

Dear Kitty,

"Little bundle of contradictions." That's how I ended my last letter and that's how I'm going to begin this one . . . What does contradiction mean? Like so many words, it can mean two things, contradiction from without and contradiction from within . . .

. . . I have, as it were, a dual personality. One half embodies my exuberant cheerfulness, making fun of everything, my high-spiritedness, and above all, the way I take everything lightly. This includes not taking offense at a flirtation, a kiss, an embrace, a dirty joke. This side is usually lying in wait and pushes away the other which is much better, deeper and purer. You must realize that no one knows Anne's better side and that's why most people find me so insufferable . . .

I'm awfully scared that everyone who knows me as I always am will discover that I have another side, a finer and better side. I'm afraid they'll laugh at me, think I'm ridiculous and sentimental, not take me seriously . . . Sometimes, if I really compel the good Anne to take the stage for a quarter of an hour, she simply shrivels up as soon as she has to speak, and lets Anne number one take over, and before I realize it, she has disappeared . . .

A voice sobs within me: "There you are, that's what's

become of you: you're uncharitable, you look supercilious and peevish, people dislike you and all because you won't listen . . ." Oh, I would like to listen, but it doesn't work; if I'm quiet and serious, everyone thinks it's a new comedy and then I have to get out of it by turning it into a joke, not to mention my own family, who are sure to think I'm ill, make me swallow pills for headaches and nerves, feel my neck and my head to see whether I'm running a temperature, ask if I'm constipated and criticize me for being in a bad mood. I can't keep that up: if I'm watched to that extent, I start by getting snappy, then unhappy, and finally I twist my heart round again, so that the bad is on the outside and the good is on the inside and keep on trying to find a way of becoming what I would so like to be, and I could be, if . . . there weren't any other people living in the world.

Yours, Anne

[This is the last entry. Three days later the occupants of the "Secret Annexe" were arrested. Eight months later Anne died in the concentration camp at Bergen-Belsen.]

MARIE BASHKIRTSEFF

(1860-1884)

*T*he *Journal of Marie Bashkirtseff*, published after her
death from tuberculosis at the age of twenty-four,
caused a literary sensation. One reviewer called her "a horrid
little pig"; another commented that "a human soul has volun-
tarily laid its inmost fibers before us." The editor of the
American edition believed her death was inevitable: "Girls
such as she was never become old women."

   She was born in Russia of noble parentage. Her mother
left her father and raised Marie and her brother in Vienna,
Nice and Paris. She was the darling of her mother and grandparents, who were told by a fortuneteller that she was destined
to become a star. Beautiful as well as talented, she was led by
her ambition for fame into a serious career as a painter. Extra-
ordinarily self-confident of her abilities, even vain, as she admitted, she was often troubled by the conflicting demands of
professional commitment and personal beauty, saying that
what she would wish for a daughter would be to be "beautiful
and stupid, and with some principles, so as not to be lost."

   She kept a journal from an early age, always intending
that it would one day be published, especially if she were to
die young. She fantasied her family finding the journal and
after reading it, having it destroyed, "and in a short time, of
me there would remain nothing . . . This is the thought that
has always terrified me; to live, to be so filled with ambition,

to suffer, to weep, to struggle, and, at the end, oblivion! oblivion! as if I had never existed."

The following extracts concern her early ambition to marry the Duke of H., a man she never met, as one route to fame. After this childhood infatuation, the idea of love seems to have departed her mind: she was to be a worker and her enormous energies often found peculiar outlets, as when she wrote anonymous letters in a chiding tone to literary personages such as Zola and Maupassant. She shared with Alice James (who refused to read Marie's *Journal*) a supreme need to perpetuate herself; somehow, through words, to conquer time.

From the Author's Preface

Of what use were pretense or affectation? Yes, it is evident that I have the desire, if not the hope, of living upon this earth by any means in my power. If I do not die young I hope to live as a great artist, but if I die young, I intend to have my journal, which cannot fail to be interesting, published. Perhaps this idea of publication has already detracted from, if not destroyed, the chief merit that such a work may be said to possess? But, no! for in the first place I had written for a long time without any thought of being read, and then it is precisely because I hope to be read that I am altogether sincere. If this book is not the *exact,* the *absolute,* the *strict,* truth, it has no *raison d'être.* Not only do I always write what I think, but I have not even dreamed, for a single instant, of disguising anything that was to my disadvantage, or that might make me appear ridiculous. Besides, I think myself too admirable for censure. . . .

I was born on the 11th of November, 1860. Only to write it down is frightful. But then I console myself by think-

Revelations

Revelations

ing that I shall be of no age at all when you read this journal. . . .

   After two years of marriage mamma went, with her two children, to live with her parents. I was always with grand-mamma who idolized me. Besides grand-mamma to adore me, there was my aunt . . . who was younger than mamma, but not so pretty; who sacrificed herself to and was sacrificed by everybody.

   . . . It was at Baden that I first became acquainted with the world, and with the refinements of polite society, and that I suffered the tortures of vanity.

   . . . Since I have been able to think, since I was three years old, (I was not weaned until I was three and a half), I have always had aspirations toward greatness of some kind . . . everything I heard from those who surrounded mamma, always bore some reference to this greatness which must one day inevitably come to me.

   . . . Every evening on going to bed I recited . . . the following prayer:

   "My God, grant that I may never have the smallpox; that I may grow up pretty; that I may have a beautiful voice; that I may be happily married. . . ."

   . . . If I should not live long enough to become famous, this journal will be interesting to the psychologist. The record of a woman's life, written down day by day, without any attempt at concealment, as if no one in the world were ever to read it, yet with the purpose of being read, is always interesting; for I am certain that I shall be found sympathetic, and I write down everything, everything, everything. Otherwise why should I write? Besides, it will very soon be seen that I have concealed nothing.

Paris, May 1, 1884

[Marie died the following October.]

48

MARIE BASHKIRTSEFF

January, 1873 (at the age of twelve years).

. . . God grant that the Duke of H—— may be mine!
I will love him and make him happy! I will be happy too. I
will do good to the poor . . .

I was made for triumphs and emotions; the best thing I
can do, therefore, is to become a singer. If the good God
would only *preserve, strengthen,* and *develop* my voice, then I
should enjoy the triumph for which I long. Then I should
enjoy the happiness of being celebrated, and admired; and in
that way the one I love might be mine . . .

I am a modest girl, and I would never give a kiss to any
other man than my husband; I can boast of something that
not every girl of twelve or fourteen years can say, that is, of
never having been kissed, and of never having kissed anyone.
Then, to see a young girl at the highest point of glory to
which a woman can attain, who has loved him from her
childhood with a constant love, simple and modest—all this
will astonish him; he will want to marry me at any cost, and
he will do so through pride. . . .

Friday, December 30.

. . . I must be either the Duchess of H——, and that
is what I most desire (for God knows how ardently I love
him), or become famous on the stage; but this career does not
attract me so much as the other. It is doubtless flattering to
receive the homage of the entire world, from the lowest to the
sovereigns of the earth, but the other!—Yes, I will have him I
love; that is altogether another kind of happiness, and I prefer
it. . . .

Revelations

May 6.

. . . I think if he should ever read this journal, that he will find it stupid,—above all, my confessions of love. I have repeated them so often that they have lost all their force. Ah, when one thinks what a miserable creature man is! Every other animal can, at his will, wear on his face the expression he pleases. He is not obliged to smile if he has a mind to weep. When he does not wish to see his fellows he does not see them. While man is the slave of everything and everybody! And yet I draw this very fate upon myself. I love to visit, and I love to see visitors. . . .

Monday, October 13.

I was looking up my lesson to-day when little Heder, my English governess, said to me: "Do you know that the Duke is going to marry the Duchess M——?" I put the book closer to my face, for I was as red as fire. I felt as if a sharp knife had pierced my heart. I began to tremble so violently that I could scarcely hold the volume. I was afraid I was going to faint, but the book saved me. I pretended to be looking for the place for a few moments, until I grew calmer. I said my lesson in a voice that trembled with emotion. I summoned all my courage—as I had done on a former occasion, when I wished to throw myself over the bridge—and told myself that I must control myself. I wrote a dictation so as not to have to speak. I was rejoiced when I went to the piano; I tried to play, but my fingers were cold and stiff. The Princess came to ask me to teach her to play croquet. "With pleasure," I responded gayly; but my voice still trembled. I ran to dress myself. In a green gown—my hair is the color of gold, and my complexion white and red—I looked as pretty as an angel or a woman. I kept thinking continually, "He is going to marry! Can it be possible? How unhappy I am!" —not unhappy, as formerly, on account of the paper of one room, or the furniture of another, but really unhappy! . . .

Friday, October 17.

I was playing on the piano when the newspapers were brought in. I took up *Galignani's Messenger,* and the first words on which my eyes fell related to the marriage of the Duke of H——. . . .

And I have to take a Latin lesson! Oh, torture! . . .

I shall learn to forget in time, no doubt. To say that my grief will be eternal would be ridiculous—nothing is eternal. But the fact is that, for the present, I can think of nothing else. He does not marry; they marry him. It is all owing to the machinations of his mother. (1880.—*All this on account of a man whom I had seen a dozen times in the street,—whom I did not know, and who did not know that I was in existence.*) Oh, I detest him! I want to see them together. They are at Baden-Baden that I loved so much! Those walks where I used to see him, those kiosks, those shops!

(*All this re-read in 1880 produces no effect on me whatever.*)

Saturday, October 18.

. . . How changed I am since the thirteenth of October,—that fatal day! Suffering is depicted on my countenance. His name is no longer the source of a beneficent warmth . . . This is the greatest misfortune that can happen to a woman; and I have experienced it! Bitter mockery!

I begin to think seriously about my voice. I should so much like to sing. To what end now? . . .

Revelations

Friday, July 16, 1874. [Age fourteen]

In regard to the transference of love, all I possess at present is concentrated on Victor, one of my dogs. I breakfast with him sitting opposite to me, his fine, large head resting on the table. Let us love dogs; let us love only dogs! Men and cats are unworthy creatures . . .

I am going to say once more to the moon: "Moon, O beautiful moon, show me in my sleep the person I am to marry before I die!"

My hair, fastened in a Psyche knot, is redder than ever. In a woolen gown of a peculiar white, well-fitting and graceful, and a lace handkerchief around my neck, I look like one of the portraits of the First Empire; in order to make the picture complete I should be seated under a tree, holding a book in my hand. I love to be alone before a looking-glass, and to admire my hands, so fine and white, and faintly rosy in the palms.

Perhaps it is stupid to praise one's-self in this way, but people who write always describe their heroine; and I am my heroine. . . .

Friday, October 5, 1877. [Age seventeen]

"Did you do that painting by yourself?" M. Julian [her painting teacher] asked me on entering the studio to-day.

"Yes, Monsieur."

I grew as red as if I had told a falsehood.

"Well, I am satisfied with it, very well satisfied with it."

In the studio all distinctions disappear. One has neither name nor family; one is no longer the daughter of one's mother, one is one's-self,—and individual,—and one has before one art, and nothing else. One feels so happy, so free, so proud!

At last I am what I have so long wished to be. I have wished it for so long that I scarcely believe it now to be true.

Apropos, whom do you think I saw in the Champs Elysées today?

None other than the Duke of H—— occupying a *fiacre* all by himself.

The handsome, vigorous young man with yellow locks and a delicate mustache now looks like a big Englishman; his face is very red, and he has little red whiskers that grow from the tip of the ear to the middle of his cheek.

Four years, however, change a man greatly; at the end of half an hour I had ceased to think of him.

Sic transit gloria Ducis. . . .

Wednesday, June 25, 1884. [*Age twenty-four*]

I have just been reading my journal for the years 1875, 1876, and 1877. I find it full of vague aspirations toward some unknown goal. My evenings were spent in wild and despairing attempts to find some outlet for my powers. Should I go to Italy? Remain in Paris? Marry? Paint? What should I strive to become? If I went to Italy, I should no longer be in Paris, and my desire was to be everywhere at once. What a waste of energy was there!

If I had been born a man, I would have conquered Europe. As I was born a woman, I exhausted my energy in tirades against fate, and in eccentricities. There are moments when one believes one's-self capable of all things. "If only I had the time," I wrote, "I would be a sculptor, a writer, a musician!"

. . . How many characters have I been in turn in my childish imagination! First I was a dancer—a famous dancer —worshipped by all St. Petersburg. Every evening I would

53

make them put a low-necked dress on me, and flowers in my hair, and I would dance, very gravely, in the drawing-room, while every one in the house looked on. Then I was the most famous prima donna in the world; I sang and accompanied myself on the harp, and I was carried in triumph, where or by whom I do not know. Then I electrified the people by my eloquence. The Emperor of Russia married me; that he might be able to maintain himself on his throne. I came into personal relations with my people; I explained my political views to them in my speeches, and both people and sovereign were moved to tears.

And then I was in love. The man I loved proved false, and was afterward killed by some accident, generally a fall from his horse, just at the moment when I felt that my love for him was beginning to decrease. When my lovers died I consoled myself, but when they proved false to me I fell into despair and finally died of grief.

In short, I have pictured every human feeling, every earthly pleasure to myself as superior to the reality, and if my dreams are to remain forever unrealized, it is better that I should die.

Why has not my picture been awarded a medal?

The medal! It must be because some of the committee suspected that I had received assistance. It has happened once or twice already that medals have been given to women who, as has afterward been discovered, had received assistance in their work; and when a medal has been once awarded the recipient has the right to exhibit on the following year, and may send the most worthless or insignificant picture if he chooses.

Yet I am young and elegant, and have been praised by the papers! But these people are all alike. Breslau, for instance, said to my model that I would paint a great deal better if I went less into society. They think I go out every evening.

How deceitful appearances are! But to suspect that my picture is not all my own work is too serious a matter; thank Heaven, they have not publicly given utterance to their suspicions, however! Robert-Fleury told me he was surprised that I had not received a medal, for that every time he spoke of me to his colleagues of the committee, they responded, *"It is very good; it is a very interesting picture."*

"What do you suppose they mean when they say that?" he asked me.

Then *it is* this suspicion. . . .

Friday, August 1.

. . . Shall I ever know what it is to love?

For my own part I think love—impossible—to one who looks at human nature through a microscope, as I do. They who see only what they wish to see in those around them are very fortunate.

Shall I tell you something? Well, I am neither an artist, nor a sculptor, nor a musician; neither woman, girl, nor friend. My only purpose in life is to observe, to reflect, and to analyze.

A glance, a face I see by chance, a sound, a pleasure, a pain, is at once weighed, examined, verified, classified, noted. And not until this is accomplished is my mind at rest.

NELLY PTASCHKINA

(1903-1920)

*D*uring *the Russian Revolution,* Nelly Ptaschkina and her family were in constant flight across Russia, suffered harassment by the Bolshevists, brutal searches by the police, and threats of shooting and pillage by the Red and White armies. She recorded not only the political turmoil in her diary but the private feelings of a young girl deciding who she would be in a more peaceful world. The diary, kept in five exercise books, described her life in Moscow, then in Kiev, and thereafter the journey her family made from Kiev to Paris.

In 1918, when she was only fifteen, Nelly had a premonition of her death, imagining herself falling over a precipice "plunging headlong into the chasm." On July 2, 1920, in Chamonix at the foot of Mont Blanc, she mistook some moss for stones, misstepped and fell from an enormous height into the torrent of the Cascade du Dard. Her body was recovered many miles downstream and she was buried in Paris.

Much of her diary, kept with great faithfulness from the age of ten, was lost, but her mother preserved the copy books of her fourteenth and fifteenth years, and published them in Nelly's memory. Her death occurred five days after she had passed her Baccalauréat examination at the Sorbonne in Paris.

January 23, 1918

. . . What is my diary? It is a record of my thoughts and feelings. It was the wish to write them down that gave me the idea of this diary; and this same wish came to me under the influence of Marie Baschkirtsev and Raya [a friend]. It is curious to note that generally speaking they are young people who write diaries, because their inability to concentrate on themselves, the strength of their sensations, their confidence in the beliefs, which they have not yet lost, make them seek an outlet for their emotions. The old, although they may receive vivid impressions, probably regard them in a colder way than we young people, who are only entering upon life. Youth does not know how to concentrate, and, on the other hand, does not want to confide in others. Hence the diary. The old work out everything in themselves.

January 25

. . . The situation is really *terrible!* The decisive days for Russia are at hand, "to be or not to be." My vision is too restricted to be able to picture the whole situation clearly. My home life shelters me and I see reality as something very, very distant . . . I am mentally short-sighted because, after all, I am but a child: this is the first and most important reason, if not the only one. All the same, at odd moments, I clearly realize the full horror of the position in which our country is placed.

January 26

. . . Whatever turns events may take, whatever may happen in Russia, nothing can stop the march of time. The years will pass, I shall grow up and enter life. What do I need then? Education and knowledge.

Whatever I neglect now I shall have to pay for later.

What I mean by this is that my studies represent to me my very life, the greatest part of my interests, and that is why I am so anxious about their fate.

And after all my ego stands in the first place: events and all the rest only occupy the background. My own life obscures them . . .

How interesting human nature is! Not what we learn about it in our school books, but that which is hidden deep within us and gives rise to these reflections.

I think I have come to a satisfactory conclusion. Here it is:

Man is born with a mind, which is already cast in a definite mould. Education only develops it and calls out new traits. It seems to me that man at birth does not represent a lump of clay, which can be shaped at will: for instance, either he is born intelligent or he is born stupid. Goodness can, on the other hand, be acquired. He can be made wicked or spiteful. . . . For the present, this is as far as I can get.

If I wrote down everything that is in my mind, I should write on and on. . . .

January 31

. . . It began yesterday. After dinner, when I had finished writing, a letter was received from G. containing the news that Mummie is allowed to go back to Saratoff. I was enchanted, but Father said there was no object in my going. At the moment I did not seem to mind, but could not understand why I should have felt as if something has snapped inside and completely spoilt my temper. I took refuge in that other world where there are no philosophical considerations, where one only *feels*. This mood persisted until the walk I took today; when I am like that I am quite a different person from my usual self.

Two Nellys live in me. Sometimes I would like to know which is the real one. When I am in that other world, "that" Nelly seems the real one; when I am back again in my ordinary everyday one it is "this." In fact they complete each other and make up the real me.

February 18

. . . A passionate joy comes over me when I look into the distance; there, beyond the houses, the towns, the people, all is radiant, all is full of sunshine. . . . Then it dawns upon me that my life will be different from that of theirs . . . bright, interesting. . . .

Then I see young girls, such as I shall become in three or four years' time. They live, like every one else from day to day, waiting for something. They live drab, dull lives. . . . Probably they too had visions of a bright, happy future, and gazed into the golden distance. . . . But now . . . where is that golden distance? Did they not reach it? *Can* one never reach it? Does it exist really, or only in our dreams?

For, surely, I am not the only dreamer. Are they not dreamers too? Shall I live on as they do, following the pattern woven by routine on the canvas of life? Waiting for some one?

There will be nothing. . . . No, no, not that! I am frightened. Give me my golden horizon. Let me live a full life, with all the strength of my soul.

February 23

How much I wanted to write yesterday! How I longed for my diary! But I could not write. Today there is no one at home and therefore I can put my time to good use. When I am excited or sad nothing soothes me like my diary. If I am very happy my joy calms down, subsides whilst I write. My diary has become indispensable to me.

March 3

. . . How strange it is that in the huge machine of life, past, present and future, there should be a fourteen-year-old girl who is sitting and writing all kinds of stupid things about her small soul, which to her seems something immense, and that she occupies herself so seriously with something which is really small and of no consequence. . . . But to her it seems all-important and she wholly surrenders herself to it. How strange is this abstraction; how strange the isolation of *my* little life in comparison with that other which is so immeasurably big.

March 5

. . . I have decided to fight against this feeling of apathy which takes possession of me at such moments of depression. I do not want to allow them. But in order to attain this result, I must not permit my private life to be affected by general conditions.

How shall I do this? I shall drive away my thoughts as soon as they touch upon dangerous ground. I . . . I shall *deceive myself.* Yes, one must confess that in the end it will be only self-deception. But what matter. It will hurt no one, and for me it will be better, it will do me good.

One must tell oneself that things are not so bad as they seem. This is what I want to do and I hope that I shall be able to accomplish it. I shall not surrender to this inner voice which faint-heartedly whispers to me that our life is inextricably tied up with this epoch, and moreover united in such a way that it can never be adjusted; that therefore everything is at an end and that nothing will come out of it. No, I do not want this. I shall obstinately tell myself that—how can I say it most tenderly?—that with *Mummie's* arrival all will be well. I shall not allow myself to be influenced by the newspapers, which bring sad news. I shall not brood over the fact that news is worse again, and that in consequence our position is all the more deplorable. In four or five years all *must* settle down—and I will leave it at that.

September 29

In the plans of my future life, which does not seem to be cast on feminine lines, there should apparently be no place for love and such-like soft, tender and sentimental things, but it is not so at all.

I have written more than once that in my nature there lives a tendency towards that "other" world. And with all my longing for social work, and public activity, it hurts me to part from the beauty of life and the thought of love.

But what would happen if I never experienced love? For that can happen: not every one is fated to experience it. Yes . . . what if I never love? . . . Even now, when I am thinking of it, I feel disturbed. It hurts me. . . . Not to know what it is. . . . That wonderful splendid flame of life. . . . Love. . . . Can it be that this beautiful thing to which I feel drawn so unresistingly will not be accessible to me, and that only the grey workaday world will be mine? Oh, I am afraid of this, terribly afraid. . . .

One day when I was walking with Mother, she said, "When you marry." "But perhaps I shall not marry," I suggested shyly. "That may be," answered Mother calmly. It seemed to me as if something had been torn asunder in my heart, and it felt very bitter. Would the day come when I should have to kill all my aspirations towards love and limit my interests to books and public service? Oh, not that! Not that! . . .

Of course, it is ridiculous for me, a fifteen-year-old girl, to try and unravel these questions, but once they come into my head I shall speak about them.

October 1

. . . In my dreams, however strange it may sound, I dream at the same time of children and of an independent life, which should be both comfortable and beautiful. The question of woman's fate interests me tremendously. This interest lives in me somehow fundamentally; it is called forth neither by writing nor conversation, but has taken root in me of its own accord.

Is it necessary to add that I believe with all my heart and mind that women have absolutely equal rights with men, because I consider them in no wise their intellectual inferior?

This year I have added to the books on social subjects, some that are concerned with the feminist question, and I shall read them with great enjoyment.

Of course, comparatively speaking, women have not asserted themselves up to now as capable individuals. There are many empty coquettes as well as spiritual nonentities among them, but, all the same, it is of note that now in all professions women appear who work on a level with men.

Are there also no empty-headed men? Oh many! Do not men themselves encourage the defects of women by considering them only as amusing playthings? I speak, of course, in general. There are exceptions but, taken on an average, they are in the minority.

Does the education of woman prepare her for the serious tasks of life? The evil of this education is rooted far back in the centuries. Give women scope and opportunity, and they will be no worse than men.

I notice that these thoughts remind me of a book I once read, but all the same it seems to me that they come straight out of my soul.

Well! The one does no harm to the other.

Yes, woman must have all the rights, and in time she can earn them fully. At present we have still many women who are satisfied with their empty lives, but if we raise the standard, and improve the social conditions of life, which are connected with her, woman will also rise. Even now there are many among them who would be capable of leading a conscious existence successfully. Give them that possibility. When people criticize a woman in my presence, I never feel at ease, and I realize that they are wrong, but I have not the courage to dispute with them; I lack arguments and only mentally say to myself, "Wait!"

October 14

. . . I shall arrange it, so as not to depend on love, let alone wait for it as so many girls do. I shall live. If love comes I shall take it; and if not, I shall regret it, wildly regret it, but I *shall* live all the same.

I see in my imagination a small flat, furnished with exquisite comfort. . . . Beauty everywhere, softness, cosiness. And I am the mistress of it—a woman and a personality at the same time. I live an interesting life: writers, artists, painters forgather at my house, a really interesting circle, a close, friendly community. I know no picture more attractive than this. I am free, independent. In these surroundings, in which there is even no place for it, I shall not regret love. Life is full without it. It is only the dawn of love which I should miss

. . . those moments, the memory of which beautifies all the life of man.

. . . There is something else that is strange. I see children in my imagination and think with joy about them. The husband is a figure that has never appeared in my fancies, quite a stranger in fact; I have never once thought about him.

On one side I see my little home—on the other I think with delight of my children.

October 20

I love to stand at the edge of an abyss, at the very edge, so that a single movement, and . . . today, stepping close to the brink of a precipice, although not so deep as I should have wished, the thought came into my mind that some day I should die thus, crashing headlong into the chasm.

My walk today has evoked this premonition. . . . But I feel it more now, after the walk, than during it. . . .

October 25

. . . Marriage is slavery, it prevents one from surrendering herself to that supreme happiness which the initiated call love—and so I think it is. Human personality must develop quite freely. Marriage impedes this development; even more than that, it often drives one to "moral crimes," not only because forbidden fruit is sweet, but because the new love, which could be perfectly legitimate, becomes a crime. Would man and woman be less happy if they lived together without being married, simply as "lovers"?—possibly not even in the same house, but meeting every day; in short, leading the life of a regularly married couple. If they love one another, what can hinder them from settling down together? I should like to talk this over with Aunt Aniouta . . . I must think about it.

January 9 [*1919*]

Is sexual attraction natural, or must it be suppressed? A most interesting question for study. . . . What is physical attraction? I know that the majority, if not all, will say: "It is natural." Tolstoy will remain alone in his opinion. But for me there is no proof that he is wrong.

I see life without sexual love. I do not know whether this can be, but I should incline to think that it is possible. It is simpler and more comprehensible; however, not knowing where truth is, I dare not affirm this, but want to think that it *is* the truth.

The feeling exists. And at present it expresses itself in uncouth and misshapen forms. New ones must take their place. That is what I think.

April 21

. . . I should like to read a natural explanation of what people call love. . . . It would be very interesting.

Tolstoy calls it a physical attraction of the sexes and says that in time it will disappear. The first is correct; the second, I do not know. . . .

People say that it is the best in life. They say that through its agency everything in life is transformed, everything is illuminated. They say and they write. . . .

I do not understand this fully; but even if it is an attraction between sexes, a physiological process, both books and life graft in us an unaccountable yearning for it, it exists in me apart from my will.

In any case, love must and can only be an appendix to

life, it certainly must not form its substance. Pitiful are those for whom that is the case. Thank God it is not so with me.

May 22

. . . The farther we go the stronger we feel the influence of our epoch in more senses than one. It is very positive: it has made me reflect on many important questions, like Socialism and others; it has shown me the real object of life and has widened my horizon; it has made me more "practical," more "positive," for everyday life, and has prepared me better for its different emergencies.

Between the former "Miss Nelly" and the present pupil of the carpenter Ivan Ivanitch there is a great difference, especially spiritually.

All this is good, and I am grateful to time for the way it has helped my development. But it has also done something else: all that belonged to the azure realm of dreams and visions, the world of poetry—and there was a great deal of it—has hidden itself in the depths of my soul.

May 27

Love . . . love . . . when will it come?

But one must not abandon oneself to such sorrow about something that is undefined. . . . There is no room for it in our hard-working life, which is but a preparation. Yes, one must renounce that which is too emotional. There is no need for these moods, this longing, these *attendrissements*. . . . Work is waiting for us.

These are not high-flown words, nothing conventional . . . I feel what I write and it costs me a certain effort to consent to all this. Because it represents the total sacrifice of personal happiness, and because I believe that I shall have the necessary strength to make it.

HANNAH SENESH

(1921-1944)

*H*annah Senesh was born in Hungary. Her father, a playwright and journalist, died when she was six, leaving her mother to raise Hannah and her brother George alone. With great difficulty and at three times the normal tuition, her mother enrolled Hannah at ten as one of the first Jewish students in a Protestant school. Hannah's teachers noted her brilliance and the tuition was reduced; but when she was elected to office in the school's literary society, the election was reversed because of her religion. In a diary she kept from the age of thirteen, she recorded her dreams of becoming a writer or teacher and her awareness that as a Jew her future was limited in Hungary. At seventeen she made her decision: "I don't know whether I've already mentioned that I've become a Zionist," she told her diary. "One needs something to believe in, something for which one can have whole-hearted enthusiasm. One needs to feel that one's life has meaning, that one is needed in this world."

Right after the outbreak of World War II she left her mother and brother behind and emigrated to Palestine. Her new country did not have a stifling tradition of what is appropriate work for women; but in choosing among many options the direction her life would take, Hannah echoed many of the doubts voiced by our girl-diarists who lived in more restricted cultures. Even in the freer atmosphere of a young country, the first problem to be resolved remained the same: self-discovery, the development of an authentic, independent identity. In Hannah Senesh's self-definition, love was always waiting to be expressed, not so much in terms of her sexuality but through service to others.

Her mission was thrust upon her when she joined a special group of Palestine soldiers trained by the British to help Jews escape from occupied countries. She was ready. With her unit she parachuted into Yugoslavia in March 1944, and made her way behind the lines to Hungary, where she was captured by the Nazis and imprisoned in Budapest. There she looked after children, making them dolls out of whatever was at hand, and taught the other prisoners Hebrew by drawing huge letters on cloth and holding them up to her cell window. She refused to reveal the secrets entrusted to her even when the Nazis threatened to torture her mother, housed in the same prison. She herself was cruelly tortured and on November 7, 1944, she was executed.

The following selections from her diary cover the period from the age of nineteen, when she was studying at an agricultural school in Palestine, to the eve of her departure on her mission three years later.

November 2, 1940

I dream and plan as if there was nothing happening in the world, as if there was no war, no destruction, as if thousands upon thousands were not being killed daily; as if Germany, England, Italy, and Greece were not destroying each other. Only in our little country—which is also in danger and may yet find itself in the centre of hostilities—is there an illusion of peace and quiet. And I'm sitting here, thinking of the future. And what do I think about my personal future?

One of my most beautiful plans is to be a poultry farming instructor, to travel from one farm to the other, to visit settlements, to advise and to assist, to organize, to introduce record-keeping, to develop this branch of the economy. In the evenings I would conduct brief seminars for kibbutz members, teach them the important facets of the trade. And at the same time I would get to know the people, their way of life, and would be able to travel about the country.

My other plan is to instruct (seems I only want to teach) children in some sort of school. Perhaps in the institute at Shfeya, or in a regional agricultural school. The old dream is to combine agricultural work with child guidance and teaching.

My third plan—a plan I consider only rarely—has nothing to do with agriculture or children, but with writing . . . I want to write books, or plays, or I don't know what. Sometimes I think I have talent, and that it's sinful to waste or neglect it. Sometimes I think that if I really do have talent I'll eventually write without worrying about it, that if I feel the need of self-expression, the urge to write, I'll write. The important thing is to have a command of the language. I've made considerable progress during this first year in the Land, but I must do better.

And I've yet another plan. I'd like to live on a kibbutz. This can, however, be in conjunction with other plans. I'm quite sure I would fit in, if only the possibility of working at something that really interested me existed. . . .

February 25, 1941

It's time I wrote about Alex. Even though it's more "his" affair than something we share. Several things happened last month which I didn't write about, not only because I was busy working at the incubator, but also because I find it difficult to write about matters that aren't entirely clear to me, or about which I am undecided . . .

He recently told me he loves me, and asked me to marry him. I told him that although I respect and like him, I don't feel as he does. Nonetheless, I couldn't say this with absolute certainty, and the matter was left unresolved. He comes to see me as usual, but I asked him to wait a while before demanding a definite answer.

. . . The problem I now face is whether to marry a man "just like that," to disrupt my plans, give up my independence. Naturally, it's difficult not to be impressed and flattered by the love of a man of character, a man you respect and esteem. But this is still not love, and thus there is really no reason to continue.

April 12, 1941

Why am I so lonely? Not long ago I strolled through the moshav one evening. It was a fabulous, starry night. Small lights glittered in the lanes, and in the middle of the wide road. Sounds of music, songs, conversation, and laughter came from all around; and far, far in the distance I heard the barking of dogs. The houses seemed so distant; only the stars were near.

Suddenly I was gripped by fear. Where is life leading me? Will I always go on alone in the night, looking at the sparkling stars, thinking they are close? Will I be unable to hear the songs . . . the songs and the laughter around me? Will I fail to turn off the lonely road in order to enter the little houses? What must I choose? The weak lights, filtering through the chinks in the houses, or the distant light of the stars? Worst of all, when I'm among the stars I long for the small lights, and when I find my way into one of the little houses my soul yearns for the heavenly bodies. I'm filled with discontent, hesitancy, insecurity, anxiety, lack of confidence.

Sometimes I feel I am an emissary who has been entrusted with a mission. What this mission is—is not clear to me. (After all, everyone has a mission in life.) I feel I have a duty towards others, as if I were obligated to them. At times this appears to be all sheer nonsense, and I wonder why all this particular effort . . . and why particularly me?

January 8, 1943

. . . I've had a shattering week. I was suddenly struck by the idea of going to Hungary. I feel I must be there during these days in order to help organize youth immigration, and also to get my mother out. Although I'm quite aware how absurd the idea is, it still seems both feasible and necessary to me, so I'll get to work on it and carry it through. . . .

February 22, 1943

How strangely things work out. On January 8 I wrote a few words about the sudden idea that struck me. A few days ago a man from the Kibbutz Ma-agan, a member of the Palmach, visited the kibbutz and we chatted awhile. In the course of the conversation he told me that a Palmach unit was being organized to do—exactly what I felt then I wanted to do. I was truly astounded. The *identical* idea!

My answer, of course, was that I'm absolutely ready. . . .

September 19, 1943

I arrived in the Land four years ago. Immigrant House, Haifa. Everything was new, everything beautiful, everything a world of the future. Only one figure takes me back to the past: my mother at the railway station. Four years. I never would have believed the distance between us could ever be so great, so deep. Had I known . . . Or perhaps I knew but didn't dare to admit it.

. . . And now I stand before a new assignment again, one that demands great preparation for a difficult and responsible mission. Again a sense of transition coupled with strong emotions, aspirations, tensions. And the everlasting aloneness. Now it's clearer to me than ever that this has nothing to do with outside factors. There's a certain peculiarity within me, and a lack of sociability which keeps me away from people. This is especially difficult where it concerns men.

At times I think I love, or could love, someone. But . . . There are many objective "buts" in the way, and I lack the courage to overcome them . . . I am twenty-two years old, and I don't know how to be happy.

I wear a placid mask, and at times I say to myself, What is this? Is this how my life is going to unfold? It's no longer an external matter, but something within me. I have no complaints about life, really. I'm satisfied. I can't imagine a state in which I would be more content. On the contrary. And the assignment which lies ahead draws me on. But I forget how to laugh—to really laugh, heartily, as I once could with George while wrestling on the couch until we rolled off onto the floor—laughing about nothing but the joy of living, of being young and alive. Are hardship and loneliness to blame for the lack of that particular kind of joy? Or do I bear this sorrow from the time when—at the age of seven or eight—I stood beside my father's grave and began to write poems about the hardships in life? I feel I'm just chattering. However, this is necessary too. Amid essays, speeches, and silences, it's good to converse sometimes, even if only with oneself.

. . . I long for satisfying work. In the last four years

I've done all kinds of work, not always out of conviction, always explaining to myself that it was all necessary, and never gaining any real satisfaction from it. I really wanted to be a teacher. If I had to decide today whether to emigrate to Palestine I'd do exactly as I did. . . .

In my life's chain of events nothing was accidental. Everything happened according to an inner need. I would have been miserable following a road other than the one I chose. No, perhaps this is an exaggeration. But had I chosen differently, I would not have been in harmony with myself. . . .

[Hannah wrote the following letter to her brother George to be given to him if she failed to return from her mission:]

December 25, 1943

Darling George!

Sometimes one writes letters one does not intend sending. Letters one must write without asking oneself, "I wonder whether this will ever reach its destination."

Day after tomorrow I am starting something new. Perhaps it's madness. Perhaps it's fantastic. Perhaps it's dangerous. Perhaps one in a hundred—or one in a thousand—pays with his life. Perhaps with less than his life, perhaps with more. Don't ask questions. You'll eventually know what it's about.

George, I must explain something to you. I must exonerate myself. I must prepare myself for that moment when you arrive inside the frontiers of the Land, waiting for that moment when, after six years, we will meet again, and you will ask, "Where is she?" and they'll abruptly answer, "She's not here."

I wonder, will you understand? I wonder, will you believe that it is more than a childish wish for adventure, more than youthful romanticism that attracted me? I wonder, will you feel that I could not do otherwise, that this was something I had to do?

There are events without which one's life becomes unimportant, a worthless toy; and there are times when one is commanded to do something, even at the price of one's life. . . .

SEI SHONAGON
(963-?)

*T*he *Pillow Book* of Sei Shonagon was written at the time of the Heian court in tenth-century Japan. She was twenty-seven when she entered the service of the fifteen-year-old Empress Sadako. The empress died in childbirth ten years later, and it is with those years from 990 to 1000 that *The Pillow Book* deals.

The book is partly diary, partly reflection and reminiscence, partly poetry: a personal book to hide under your pillow. Such journals were the common practice and reveal the extreme to which courtly custom and manners of love, as well as literary style, were developed. Another such diary was written by Lady Murasaki Shikibu, whose novel *The Tale of Genji* has endured for almost a thousand years. Lady Murasaki, ten years Sei Shonagon's junior, was lady-in-waiting to Empress Akiko, where Shonagon had also served. In her diary Murasaki suggests that Shonagon will lose favor and be dismissed. Shonagon's fate is unknown, but there is a legend that this wit and beauty ended her days as a lean hag selling old rags and bones and living in a dilapidated hovel.

It is chiefly through the writings of such women that the Heian period is known. But one need know nothing at all of tenth-century Japanese court life to appreciate Sei Shonagon's very exacting standards for a lover's deportment.

For secret meetings summer is best. It is true that the nights are terribly short and it begins to grow light before one has had a wink of sleep. But it is delightful to have all the shutters open, so that the cool air comes in and one can see into the garden. At last comes the time of parting, and just as the lovers are trying to finish off all the small things that remain to be said, they are suddenly startled by a loud noise just outside the window. For a moment they make certain they are betrayed; but it turns out only to be a crow that cried as it flew past.

But it is pleasant, too, on very cold nights to lie with one's lover, buried under a great pile of bed-clothes. Noises such as the tolling of a bell sound so strange. It seems as though they came up from the bottom of a deep pit. Strange, too, is the first cry of the birds, sounding so muffled and distant that one feels sure their beaks are still tucked under their wings. Then each fresh note gets shriller and nearer. . . .

It is very tiresome when a lover who is leaving one at dawn says that he must look for a fan or pocket-book that he left somewhere about the room last night. As it is still too dark to see anything, he goes fumbling about all over the place, knocking into everything and muttering to himself, "How very odd!" When at last he finds the pocket-book he crams it into his dress with a great rustling of the pages; or if it is a fan he has lost, he swishes it open and begins flapping it about, so that when he finally takes his departure, instead of experiencing the feelings of regret proper to such an occasion, one merely feels irritated at his clumsiness. . . .

It is important that a lover should know how to make his departure. To begin with, he ought not to be too ready to get up, but should require a little coaxing: "Come, it is past daybreak. You don't want to be found here . . ." and so on. One likes him, too, to behave in such a way that one is sure he is unhappy at going and would stay longer if he possibly could. He should not pull on his trousers the moment he is up, but should first of all come closer to one's ear and in a whisper finish off whatever was left half-said in the course of the night. But though he may in reality at these moments be doing nothing at all, it will not be amiss that he should appear to be buckling his belt. Then he should raise the shutters, and both lovers should go out together at the double-doors, while he tells her how much he dreads the day that is before him and longs for the approach of night. Then, after he has slipped away, she can stand gazing after him, with charming recollections of those last moments. Indeed, the success of a lover depends greatly on his method of departure. If he springs to his feet with a jerk and at once begins fussing around, tightening in the waist-band of his breeches, or adjusting the sleeves of his Court robe, hunting jacket or what not, collecting a thousand odds and ends, and thrusting them into the folds of his dress, or pulling in his over-belt—one begins to hate him.

I like to think of a bachelor—an adventurous disposition has left him single—returning at dawn from some amorous excursion. He looks a trifle sleepy; but, as soon as he is home, draws his writing-case towards him, carefully grinds himself some ink and begins to write his next-morning letter—not simply dashing off whatever comes into his head, but spreading himself to the task and taking trouble to write the characters beautifully. He should be clad in an azalea-yellow or vermilion cloak worn over a white robe. Glancing from time to time at the dewdrops that still cling to the thin white fabric of his dress, he finishes his letter, but instead of giving it to one of the ladies who are in attendance upon him at the moment, he gets up, and choosing from among his page-boys one who seems to him exactly appropriate to such a mission, calls the lad to him, and whispering something in his ear puts the letter in his hand; then sits gazing after him as he disappears into the distance. While waiting for the answer he will perhaps quietly murmur to himself this or that passage from the *Sutras*. . . .

GEORGE SAND

(1804-1876)

George Sand made her life a demonstration against the double standard. Born Amaudine Aurore Lucie Dupin, she entered a marriage of convenience at eighteen to Baron Dudevant, a lecherous bore, whom she divorced in 1836. She took her two children to Paris and raised them completely alone on income from her writing. She had open affairs with Jules Sandeau (who collaborated with her on her first few books and whose name she borrowed), Frédéric Chopin and Alfred de Musset. She became the protégée of Sainte-Beuve and a friend to such people as the painter Delacroix, the poet Heinrich Heine and the musician Franz Liszt. She wrote some eighty novels, several of which—*The Haunted Pool, The Master Bell Ringers* and *Lélia*—are considered masterpieces.

She won the admiration of England's George Eliot, who saw a "great power of God manifested in her" and "a loving, gentle humor."

George Sand suffered from the blindness of romantic love even as she defied society. This extract from her intimate journal, outpourings to Alfred de Musset written at the end of their affair, reflects emotional excesses in both herself and her lover. They had gone together to Venice, where she had become ill, and where Alfred neglected her for several amorous adventures. Then he became ill himself, of typhoid, and she nursed him with the aid of one Dr. Pietro Pagello. When she slept with Pagello, Alfred never forgave her and was ever after unresponsive to her entreaties or apologies. In a typical romantic gesture of the period, she cut off her hair and sent it to him, but he remained cool and aloof until her passion wore itself out.

———————————

Paris, November, 1834

You do not love me. You do not love me any more. I cannot blind myself to the truth. Last evening while we were together I was feeling very ill. As soon as you noticed it you went away. No doubt it was right to leave me, because you were tired last night. But to-day, not one word. You have not even sent to inquire about me. I hoped for you, waited for you, minute by minute, from eleven in the morning until midnight. What a day! Every ring of the bell made me leap to my feet. Thank God I have heart disease. If only I could die! You love me with your senses more than ever before. And I you. I have never loved anyone, I have never loved you, in this way. But I love you also with my whole being—and you do not even feel friendship for me. I wrote to you early this evening. You have not answered my note. They told my messenger you had gone out; yet you did not come to see me for even five minutes. . . . You must have returned very late. Great heavens! Where were you all evening? . . .

Will my despair ever leave me? It grows stronger day by day. The heart that used to be open to mine is now wholly closed to me. . . .

November 25, 1834

Sometimes I am tempted to go to his house and pull on his door bell until the cord breaks. Sometimes I imagine myself lying down outside his door waiting for him to come out. I would like to fall at his feet—no, not at his feet—that would be madness—but I would like to throw myself into his arms and cry out, "Why do you deny your love for me?" . . .

Alfred, you know that I love you, that I cannot love anyone but you. Kiss me, do not argue, say sweet things to me, caress me, because you do find me attractive, in spite of my short hair, in spite of the wrinkles that have come on my cheeks during these last few days. And then, when you are exhausted with emotion and feel irritation returning, treat me badly, send me away, but not with those dreadful words, *the last time.*

I will suffer as much as you wish, but let me go to you sometimes, if only once a week, for the sake of the tears, the kisses, which bring me back to life. . . .

He is wrong. Is he not wrong, my God, wrong to leave me now when my soul is purified and, for the first time, my strong will has lost its power? Is it my will that is broken? I do not know and I am content to remain ignorant. What do I care about their theories and social principles! I feel, that is all. I love. The force of my love would carry me to the ends of the earth. . . . You say, "One cannot love two men at the same time." Nevertheless that was what happened to me. It happened once, but it will not happen again. You are crazy when you say, "She will do it tomorrow because she did it yesterday!" You ought to say just the opposite. Am I stupid or insensitive? Do I not suffer from my follies and mistakes? Are lessons of no value to women like me? Am I not thirty years old and in full possession of all my powers? Yes, God in heaven, I feel that I am. I am still able to make a man happy and proud if he is willing to help me. I need a steady arm to uphold me, a heart without vanity to receive and sustain me. If I had ever found such a man I should not be where I am now. But these masterful men are liked gnarled oaks whose exterior is repellent.

And you, poet, lovely flower, your fragrance intoxicated me, poisoned me . . . When I tried to draw near, you dissolved into air before my lips could touch you. . . .

Friday

Liszt said to me today that God alone deserves to be loved. It may be true, but when one has loved a man it is very difficult to love God. It is so different. Liszt . . . added that earthly love would never get possession of him.

He is very lucky, the good little Christian!

I saw Henri [Heine] this morning. He told me that we love with the head and senses and that the heart counts for very little in love. I saw Mme. Allart at two o'clock. She told me that we must use strategem with men and pretend to be angry in order to get them back. Of them all, Sainte-Beuve alone refrained from hurting me with foolish words. I asked him the meaning of love and he answered, "It means tears; if you weep, you love."

Midnight

I cannot work. Oh loneliness . . . I can neither write nor pray. Sainte-Beuve says I need distraction. With whom? What do all these people amount to? When they have talked for an hour about things I don't care about, they disappear. They are merely shadows that come and go. I remain alone, alone forever. I want to kill myself. And who has the right to prevent me?

Oh, my poor children, how miserable your mother is!

GEORGE SAND

Saturday Midnight

. . . Madman, you are leaving me in the most beautiful mood of my life, in the phase of my love that is most real, most passionate, and most replete with suffering! . . .

And if I left Paris they would only say that I had lost my head, and you, Alfred, would, I am sure, protect me from criticism. That would be less humiliating for me than to remain here and give all those beautiful women the right to say that I disguise myself as a man in order to go to your room at night and crawl on my knees to you. Who, then, has spread this news so quickly? Surely it was not you. Would you hold me up to ridicule before those women? No. But how explain their contempt, their mocking laughter? . . .

Last night I dreamed that he was beside me, that he embraced me. I awoke swooning with joy. What a dream, my God!

Thursday morning

. . . I would be willing to live like a nun if he would show me a little affection and come to see me every day. But he would not come, or if he did, it would be in the usual contemptuous mood which is the reaction from his mood of love.

No, I must put behind me a period of time together with some data which may be referred to as a past. I must exhibit a past which will prove to him that I can love, suffer and submit.

My plan is to surround myself with men as high-minded as they are distinguished. I shall not choose powerful men, I prefer to associate with artists: Liszt, Delacroix, Berlioz, Meyerbeer. I hardly know whom else to choose. I shall be with them as a man among men.

Revelations

Of course people will gossip. They will deny the possibility of such comradeship. They will laugh at me. Alfred will hear these inuendoes and will get a wrong impression. He will cut himself off from me. Then he will take a mistress, if he has not already done so. . . . But these men who surround me will defend me. They will justify my conduct. Of course, they will. . . .

As soon as I can make some more money I shall start houskeeping again and eat at home. Then every evening I shall give a small dinner to two or three friends, as I used to do. I shall work hard. I shall go out more. I must distract myself, strengthen myself against despair.

After I have led this sane and honest life long enough to prove I can maintain it, I shall go, O my love, to ask you to shake my hand. I shall not torment you with jealousies and persecutions. I realize that when one no longer loves, one no longer loves. But I must have your friendship . . .

The capacity for passion is both cruel and divine. The sufferings of love should ennoble, not degrade. Pride is of some use here. Come, my pride, prove your worth and dignity. . . .

[The journal to de Musset filled three notebooks. Eventually, it had served its purpose, to help her restore her balance after that obsessive love. By 1837 she had regained a sense of humor about herself, and was writing another journal which she called "Daily Conversations with the Very Learned and Highly Skilled Doctor Piffoël, Professor of Botany and Psychology." The editor of her journals describes it as "conversations between George Sand's masculine and feminine selves." It is the journal of a working writer, playful, filled with random insights about love, religion, social problems and the work of other writers. It touches upon the death of her mother and her relationship with her daughter. It conveys the sense of a woman working with high energy and in full command of her power. The only reference to Alfred de Musset that it contains is in the following mention of her friend Heinrich Heine:

"Heine can say diabolically clever things. Speaking of Alfred de Musset this evening he said, 'He is a young man with a brilliant future behind him.' "]

ANAÏS NIN

A *naïs Nin was born in Paris* in 1903. Her Spanish
composer-pianist father abandoned the family when
she was eleven, and shortly after, when her mother took her
and her brothers to New York, she began an inner journey: "a
diary written to persuade my absent father to return." She left
school at fifteen, worked as an artist's model, studied dance,
underwent psychoanalysis and became herself a practicing
psychotherapist. She has moved in literary and artistic circles
in Paris and New York, has published novels, taught creative
writing and lectured extensively on the diary she continues to
use as an exploration of her mental labyrinth. The five volumes of *The Diary of Anaïs Nin*, edited for publication from
a fraction of the total manuscripts, are perhaps the most complete documentation of one woman's subjective life ever made
available to the general public.

In the following selection from Volume I, Anaïs is
twenty-eight, about to publish her first book, an appreciation
of D. H. Lawrence, and is living in France when she first
meets June, the second wife of her friend Henry Miller. Her
record of the attraction she and June felt for each other
illustrates an almost novelistic use of personal experience,
and her sense of obligation to write about the June that both
women felt Henry Miller had failed to grasp in his writing
indicates what Anaïs sees as the important function of the
Diary. She writes of her role: "What I have to say is really
distinct from the artist and art. *It is the woman who has to*

86

speak. And it is not only the woman Anaïs who has to speak, but I who have to speak for many women."

December 30, 1931

Henry came to Louveciennes with June.

As June walked towards me from the darkness of the garden into the light of the door, I saw for the first time the most beautiful woman on earth. A startlingly white face, burning dark eyes, a face so alive I felt it would consume itself before my eyes. Years ago I tried to imagine a true beauty; I created in my mind an image of just such a woman. I had never seen her until last night. Yet I knew long ago the phosphorescent color of her skin, her huntress profile, the evenness of her teeth. She is bizarre, fantastic, nervous, like someone in a high fever. Her beauty drowned me. As I sat before her, I felt I would do anything she asked of me. Henry suddenly faded. She was color and brilliance and strangeness. By the end of the evening I had extricated myself from her power. She killed my admiration by her talk. Her talk. The enormous ego, false, weak, posturing. She lacks the courage of her personality, which is sensual, heavy with experience. Her role alone preoccupies her. She invents dramas in which she always stars. I am sure she creates genuine dramas, genuine chaos and whirlpools of feelings, but I feel that her share in it is a pose. That night, in spite of my response to her, she sought to be whatever she felt I wanted her to be. She is an actress every moment. I cannot grasp the core of June. Everything Henry had said about her is true.

By the end of the evening I felt as Henry did, fascinated with her face and body which promises so much, but hating her invented self which hides the true one. This false self is composed to stir the admiration of others, inspires others to

87

words and acts about and around her. I feel she does not know what to do when confronted with these legends which are born around her face and body; she feels unequal to them.

That night she never admitted, "I did not read that book." She was obviously repeating what she had heard Henry say. They were not her words. Or she tried to speak the suave language of an English actress.

She tried to subdue her feverishness to harmonize with the serenity of the house, but she could not control her endless smoking and her restlessness. She worried about the loss of her gloves as if it were a serious flaw in her costume, as if wearing gloves were enormously important.

It was strange. I who am not always sincere was astonished and repelled by her insincerity. I recalled Henry's words: "She seems perverse to me." The extent of her falsity was terrifying, like an abyss. Fluidity. Elusiveness. Where was June? Who was June? There is a woman who stirs others' imagination, that is all. She was the essence of the theatre itself, stirring the imagination, promising such an intensity and heightening of experience, such richness, and then failing to appear in person, giving instead a smoke screen of compulsive talk about trivialities. Others are roused, others are moved to write about her, others love her as Henry does, in spite of himself. And June? What does she feel?

June. At night I dreamed of her, not magnificent and overwhelming as she is, but very small and frail, and I loved her. I loved a smallness, a vulnerability which I felt was disguised by her inordinate pride, by her volubility. It is a hurt pride. She lacks confidence, she craves admiration insatiably. She lives on the reflections of herself in the eyes of others. She does not dare to be herself. There is no June to grasp and know. She knows it. The more she is loved, the more she knows it. She knows there is a very beautiful woman who took her cue last night from my inexperience and concealed the depth of her knowledge.

Her face startlingly white as she retreated into the darkness of the garden, she posed for me as she left. I wanted to run out and kiss her fantastic beauty and say: "June, you have killed my sincerity too. I will never know again who I am, what I am, what I love, what I want. Your beauty has drowned me, the core of me. You carry away with you a part of me reflected in you. When your beauty struck me, it dissolved me. Deep down, I am not different from you. I dreamed you, I wished for your existence. You are the woman I want to be. I see in you that part of me which is you. I feel compassion for your childish pride, for your trembling unsureness, your dramatization of events, your enhancing of the loves given to you. I surrender my sincerity because if I love you it means we share the same fantasies, the same madnesses."

Henry hurts her but he keeps her body and soul together. Her love for him is her only wholeness.

June and I have paid with our souls for taking fantasies seriously, for living life as a theatre, for loving costumes and changes of selves, for wearing masks and disguises. But I know always what is real. Does June?

I wanted to see June again. When she came out of the dark again, she seemed even more beautiful to me than the first time. Also she seemed more at ease. As she went up the stairs to my bedroom to leave her coat, she stood halfway up the stairs where the light set her off against the turquoise wall. Her blonde hair piled high and carelessly on her head, pallid face, peaked eyebrows, a sly smile, with a disarming dimple. Perfidious, I felt, infinitely desirable, drawing me to her as towards death. Downstairs, Henry's laughter and lustiness were earthy, simple, and there were no secrets, no dangers in Henry. Later she sat in the high-backed chair, against the books, and her silver earrings shimmered. She talked without tenderness or softness to Henry, mocked him, was relentless. They were telling about a quarrel they had before coming, about other quarrels. And I could see then, by the anger, violence, bitterness, that they were at war. . . .

At dinner Henry and June were famished and ate quickly and talked little. Then we went together to the Grand Guignol, which June had never seen. But these extremes of comedy and horror did not move her. It was probably tame, compared with her life. She talked to me in a low voice.

"Henry does not know what he wants, likes or dislikes. I do. I can select and discard. He has no judgment. It takes him years to reach a conclusion about people." Secretly we were mocking Henry's slowness, and she was asserting the perfidious alliance of our lucidities, our quickness, our subtleties.

"When Henry described you to me," said June, "he left out all that was important. He did not see you at all!"

So we had understood each other, every detail and every nuance.

In the theatre she sat with a pale, masklike face, but impatient. "I am always impatient in theatres, at movies. I read very little. It always seems pale and watered down, compared with . . ."

"With your life?"

She had not intended to finish the phrase.

"I want firsthand knowledge of everything, not fiction, intimate experience only. Whatever takes place, even a crime I read about, I can't take an interest in, because I already knew the criminal. I may have talked with him all night at a bar. He had confessed what he intended to do. When Henry wants me to go and see an actress in a play, she was a friend of mine at school. I lived at the home of the painter who suddenly became a celebrity. I am always inside where it first happens. I loved a revolutionist, I nursed his discarded mistress who later committed suicide. I don't care for films, newspapers, 'reportages,' the radio. I only want to be involved while it is being lived. Do you understand that, Anaïs?"

"Yes, I do."

"Henry is *literary*."

I divined her life at that moment. She only believed in intimacy and proximity, in confessions born in the darkness of a bedroom, in quarrels born of alcohol, in communions born of exhausting walks through the city. She only believed in those words which came like the confessions of criminals after long exposure to hunger, to intense lights, to cross-questioning, to violent tearing away of masks.

She would not read books on travel but she sat alert in the café to catch the appearance of an Abyssinian, a Greek, an Iranian, a Hindu, who would bear direct news from home, who would be carrying photographs from his family, and who would deliver to her personally all the flavors of his country.

"Henry is always making characters. He made one out of me."

Intermission. June and I want to smoke. Henry and Joaquin do not. We create a stir as we walk out together and stand in the little cobblestone street breathing the summer air.

We face each other.

I say to her, "You're the only woman who ever answered the fantasies I had about what a woman should be."

She answered, "It's a good thing that I'm going away. You would soon be disillusioned. You would unmask me. I am powerless before a woman. I don't know how to deal with a woman."

Is she telling the truth? I feel she is not. . . .

She says, staring intently, "I thought your eyes were

blue at first. They are strange and beautiful, grey and gold, with those long black lashes. You are the most graceful woman I have ever seen. You glide when you walk."

We talked about the colors we love. She always wears black and purple. I love warm colors, red and gold.

We returned to our seats. She continues to whisper to me, indifferent to the show. "I know Henry thinks I'm mad because I want only fever. I don't want objectivity, I don't want distance. I don't want to become detached."

When she says this, I feel very close to her and I hate Henry's writing, and my own, which makes us stay aware, to register. And I want to become immersed with her.

Coming out of the theatre I take her arm. Then she slips her hand over mine, and we lock hands. The chestnut trees are shedding their pollen in wispy parachutes, and the street lamps in the fog wear thin gold halos around them like the heads of saints.

Does she find with me a rest from the tensions? Does she have this need of clarity when the labyrinth becomes too dark and too narrow?

I was infinitely moved by the touch of her hand . . .

In the café her pallor turns ashen. I see ashes under the skin of her face. Henry had said she was very ill. Disintegration. Will she die? What anxiety I feel. I want to put my arms around her. I feel her receding into death and I am willing to enter death to follow her, to embrace her. I must embrace her, I thought, she is dying before my eyes. Her tantalizing, somber beauty is dying. Her strange, manlike strength.

I am fascinated by her eyes, her mouth, her discolored mouth, badly rouged. Does she know that I feel lost in her, that I no longer understand what she is saying, feeling only the warmth of her words, their vividness? . . .

June does not reach the same sexual center of my being

as man reaches. She does not touch that. What, then, does she move in me? . . .

I am suffocated by my compassions. She is a personality expanded to the limit. I worship that courage to hurt which she has, and I am willing to be sacrificed to it. She will add me to her other admirers, she will boast about my subjection to her. She will be June plus all that I am, all that I give her. I love this magnified woman, bigger than other women.

When she talks, she has the same expression of intensity she must have while making love, that forward thrust of her whole head which gives her the appearance of a woman at the prow of a ship. The coal brown of her eyes turns to cloudy violet.

Is she drugged?. . .

The day we had lunch together, I was ready to follow her into any perversity, any destruction. I had not counted on my effect on her. I was so filled with my love for her I did not notice my effect on her.

June came to my house on Monday. I wanted an end to the mysteries, a climax to the suspense. I asked her cruelly and brutally, as Henry might have asked, "Do you love women? Have you faced your impulses towards women?"

She answered me so quietly. " . . . I have faced my feelings. I am fully aware of them. But I have never found anyone I wanted to live them out with, so far. I am not sure what it is I want to live out."

And then she turned away from my questions and said, gazing at me, "What a lovely way you have of dressing. This dress—its rose color, its old-fashioned fullness at the bottom, the little black velvet jacket, the lace collar, the lacing over the breasts. How perfect, how absolutely perfect. I like the way you cover yourself, too. There is very little nudity, only

9 3

your neck, really. I love your turquoise ring, and the coral earrings." Her hands were shaking, she was trembling. I was ashamed of my directness. I was intensely nervous. She told me that at the restaurant she had wanted to look at my bare feet in sandals but that she could not bring herself to stare. I told her I had been afraid to stare at her body, and how much I had wanted to. We talked brokenly, chaotically. She now looked at my feet in sandals and said, "They are flawless. I have never seen such flawless feet. And I love the way you walk, like an Indian woman."

Our nervousness was unbearable.

I said, "Do you like these sandals?"

"I have always loved sandals and worn them, but lately I could not afford them and I am wearing shoes someone gave me."

I said, "Come up to my room and try another pair I have, just like these."

She tried them on, sitting on my bed. They were too small for her. I saw she was wearing cotton stockings and it hurt me to see June in cotton stockings. I showed her my black cape, which she found beautiful. I made her try it on. Then I saw the beauty of her body I had not dared to look at, I saw its fullness, its heaviness; and the richness of it overwhelmed me.

I could not understand why she was so ill and so timid, so frightened. I told her that I would make her a cape like mine. Once I touched her arm. She moved it away. Had I frightened her? Could there be someone more sensitive and more afraid than I? I could not believe this. I was not afraid at that moment.

When she sat on the couch downstairs, the opening of her black, clinging dress showed the beginning of her full breasts. I was trembling. I was aware of the vagueness of our feelings and desires. She talked ramblingly, but now I knew she was talking to cover a deeper talk, talking against the things we could not express.

I came back from walking with her to the station dazed, exhausted, elated, happy, unhappy. I wanted to ask her forgiveness for my questions. They had been so unsubtle, so unlike me.

We met the next day at the American Express. She came in her tailored suit because I had said that I liked it.

She had said that she wanted nothing from me but the perfume I wore and my wine-colored handkerchief. But I reminded her she had promised she would let me buy her sandals.

First of all, I took her to the ladies' room. I opened my bag and took out a pair of sheer black stockings. "Put them on," I said, pleading and apologizing at the same time. She obeyed. Meanwhile I opened a bottle of perfume. "Put some on."

June had a hole in her sleeve.

I was happy, and June was exultant. We talked simultaneously. "I wanted to call you last night." "I wanted to send you a telegram last night." June said, "I wanted to tell you how unhappy I was on the train, regretting my awkwardness, my nervousness, my pointless talk. There was so much, so much I wanted to say."

We had the same fears of displeasing each other, of disappointing each other. She had gone to the café in the evening to meet Henry. "I felt as if drugged. I was full of thoughts of you. People's voices reached me from afar. I was elated. I could not sleep all night. What have you done to me?"

She added, "I was always poised, I could always talk well. People never overwhelmed me."

When I realized what she was revealing to me, I was

9 5

overjoyed. *I* overwhelm *her*? She loved me then? June! She sat beside me in the restaurant, small, timid, unworldly, panic-stricken, and I was moved, I was almost unbearably moved. June different, upset, changed, yielding, when she had made me so different, she had made me impulsive, strong.

She would say something and then beg forgiveness for its stupidity. I could not bear her humility. I told her, "We have both lost ourselves, but that is when one reveals most of one's true self. You've revealed your incredible sensitiveness. I am so moved. You are like me, wishing for such perfect moments, and frightened for fear of spoiling them. Neither one of us was prepared for this, and we had imagined it too long. Let's be overwhelmed, it is so lovely. I love you, June."

And not knowing what else to say, I spread between us on the seat the wine-colored handkerchief she wanted, my coral earrings, my turquoise ring. It was blood I wanted to lay at June's feet, before June's incredible humility.

Then she began to talk beautifully, not hysterically, but deeply.

We walked to the sandal shop. In the shop the ugly woman who waited on us hated us and our obvious happiness. I held June's hand firmly. I commanded: "Bring this. Bring that." I was firm, willful with the woman. When she mentioned the width of June's feet I scolded her. June could not understand the Frenchwoman, but she sensed that she was disagreeable.

We chose sandals like mine. She refused everything else, anything that was not symbolic or representative of me. Everything I wore she would wear, although she said she had never wanted to imitate anyone else ever before.

When we walked the streets, bodies close together, arm in arm, hands locked, I was in such ecstasy I could not talk. The city disappeared, and so did the people. The acute joy of our walking together through the grey streets of Paris I shall never forget, and I shall never be able to describe it. We were walking above the world, above reality, into pure, pure ecstasy.

I discovered June's purity. It was June's purity I was given to possess, what she had given to no one else. To me she gave the secret of her being, the woman whose face and body have aroused instincts around her which left her untouched, which terrified her. As I had sensed, her destructiveness is unconscious. She is imprisoned in it, and detached, and bewildered. When she met me, she revealed her innocent self. She lives in fantasies, not in the world Henry lives in.

EVELYN SCOTT
(1 8 9 3 - 1 9 6 3)

*E*velyn Scott, a young poet, ran off to Rio de Janeiro with a married man when she was twenty. The time was just before the United States entered World War I, and because she and John had neglected to obtain passports, for several years they were unable to return to the States.

She was deeply in love, but a difficult pregnancy and extreme poverty darkened the romanticism that prompted their adventure. In the portion of her diary we have excerpted, she reflects the sweet pleasures of carrying her lover's child and the way that joy is undercut by a doctor who treats her as an object and by the humiliation of being poor. The hard birth of her child foreshadows Evelyn's subsequent personal development from a naïve girl in love, defying society, to a more mature woman facing the realistic implications of that romantic defiance.

Her diary of those Rio years was published under the ironic title *Escapade*. In the thirties, Evelyn Scott became a successful (and now forgotten) popular novelist, writing to the tastes of the times. The personal intensity and searching honesty of her diary voice survive.

When I take off my clothes and stand sidewise before the cracked mirror I see that my body is no longer hollow and unfilled. It has a swelling line, a trifle grotesque, such as I have observed in the meager figures of old women.

I want to be proud of myself, and I am ashamed. When I walk out with John I wear a heavy coat. Conscious of a kind of nudity, I try to ignore the men who stare at me. I allow my coat to swing open in front. I am astonished to hear my pregnancy spoken of as if it were a casual fact.

If I could only *feel* the child! I imagine the moment of its quickening as a sudden awakening of my own being which has never before had life. I want to *live* with the child, and I am as heavy as a stone.

I hear echoing steps in the hallway that is so much of the time deserted. I understand their briskness, their decision. John is determined to bring home to me none of the anxieties of the day. He would like to admit nothing of the burden of attempting to keep books for a company that sells sewing machines. Bookkeeping! Something for which John, as a biologist, is totally unfit.

When we left home with a deliberate intention never to return, we both anticipated hardships. But I had only conceived of some sort of work which we could do together. I thought poverty was something which could be more completely shared. We first planned to go to the Amazonas and collect beetles.

John comes into the room. He makes my eyes cool with his smile. I love him. . . .

When I venture by myself into the low part of the city where we live, something objectionable always occurs. Perhaps it is because I am only twenty years old. Perhaps it is because I am shabbily dressed. I know perfectly well that I am not particularly pretty. Inwardly shrinking and cold with an obscure fear, I make it a point to look very directly at all the men who speak to me. I want to shame them by the straightforwardness of my gaze. Perhaps I am ridiculous. If I could consider sex more factually and with less mystical solemnity I might find amusement in the stupidity of these individuals who can't be so sinister after all.

When John comes home at night he is too exhausted to talk very much—even to plan about our future. He receives twenty dollars a week. Not long ago there was a mistake in his accounts and he was unable to discover it. He brought home the long sheets of paper and we worked together over them. We were certain that the error was beyond us, and that we were going to be confronted with starvation and homelessness again.

I remember growing cold and hard with despair, with resentment—not of John, but of our situation, of people at home who disapprove of what they consider our "immoral" life. I talked of hiring myself out as a servant, but John was hurt when I insisted on it. Servant girls in native homes are very badly treated. The maid who cleans our rooms lives in a kind of dark cupboard under the stairway, a place without any furnishing other than the hammock she sleeps in, and without either air or light. She works often until midnight and has to endure the contemptuous advances of all the men about. I think I was vain of my determination, but I was really glad when John discouraged me.

Sometimes, though, I would be willing to experience something painful that would relieve the monotony of existing as I do. The sun beating in on me gives my mind a dry feeling. I feel like dust.

I always detested a needle in my hand. Sewing for an hour at a time has made me vomit with distaste. Now I wish, above everything, to begin my baby dresses at once. For weeks we have been unable to lay aside enough money for such things, but I have fifty milreis—twelve dollars—and I am going to buy the material immediately.

I have felt my child quicken in me. A curious stir, a faint throb like a pulse; and my belly moved in a strange undulation. I undressed to look at myself. I was elated. All at once I had discovered a kind of hard unquestioning satisfaction in my own being. I was strong and important. A new ruthlessness seemed to be born in me, though for what end I could not conceive.

With my pregnant body it is different. My mind is filled with a kind of stillness of understanding. There is calm in my realization of myself—force that has surpassed motion. I feel integrated like a rock, but warm and breathing. I am afraid of the world—of people—but my fear surrounds me. It doesn't permeate me any longer. I believe in myself, just as I believe in things outside me through the objectivity of touch. I realized a long time ago that a belief which does not spring from a conviction in the emotions is no belief at all. When I am convinced of something, I am convinced with my whole self, as though my flesh had informed me. Now I *know*. Knowledge is the condition of my *being*.

Though I am at loss to understand the unkind assumptions of the newspapers from home that, without a single fact as to what has actually occurred, anathematize John and me in the most vulgar terms, the exposure of injustice gratifies me, and gives an almost mystical assurance to my sense of right. Yes, I want to be an outcast in order to realize fully what human beings are capable of. Now I know that fear and cruelty underlie all of society's protestations in favor of honesty and moral worth.

When I learned something of physical passion and of the violent emotion which might accompany it . . . I was compelled to feel shame for my knowledge, but I gloried in it also. I wanted to . . . construct a universe in which everything was included.

John never conceals anything from me. . .

The baby has no crib. We counted over the money we had to live on and I bought her a carriage. It is a German one, decorated with gilt like a circus chariot, with red plush curtains on the leather hood, and red chenille cords to tie them back. I have spent days and days making the baby carriage white.

Strange, I have grown so accustomed to being huge and helpless that I imagine I shall remain like this.

Doctor Januario has a small waxed mustache, large cold brown eyes with heavy lids, and he is dressed immaculately in white. He took my clothes off, felt me all over, and said I was very healthy, in very good condition. The baby is in the correct position for presentation and I can have a child without any trouble.

I felt his cold eyes all over me, ignoring me. I wanted to get away from my body that he had touched—to leave it to him. To have one's individuality completely ignored is like being pushed quite out of life. Like being blown out as one blows out a light. I began to believe myself invisible.

However, as long as John can see me I continue to exist.

I had to go into the darkness in the back of the house

and find the physician a chair. He is the first person I ever did anything for who made me feel menial.

When he finished examining me, I imagined I had lost something. I couldn't have said what. He takes away something from me.

I detest particularly his emarald watch fob and his immaculate clothing. If he were undressed he would be a great deal more naked to me than I was naked to him. He is a cold little monkey without any true pride to cover him up.

I wish that I could have my baby alone—or at least when no one but John was about. John is glad that I am so well. He tells me not to waste my emotion on Doctor Januario, but to ignore him also—to consider him a mechanism for my convenience.

When the pains began on Thursday I felt that once more there was some meaning to my body. It really belonged to me again. Every time a pain went through me it stiffened my legs so that I could scarcely move. But I was ecstatic about all this sensation. And then the pains occurred only about every hour or so and I had plenty of time to recuperate.

John has brought a servant here. He is afraid to leave me alone. I tried to conceal from him how much I was suffering because I didn't want the servant brought.

But now, on Sunday, the pains are very bad. The paroxysms are so close together that all of my energy is absorbed and my mind, which I wanted to keep clear, goes blank. I have a long, long pain inside my mind—then quiet—nothing. I feel cold inside. Blind.

On Monday morning I knew that I was caught in a mechanism of some kind that had to go on and on to the end—even if the end were death.

Revelations

Anything which is entirely beyond my control fascinates me and seems to me to have some awful and particular significance, so that, while I was frightened, I was pleased also. It is impossible to control creation. I don't mean this only in the sense of giving birth to new physical life. That which really *is* continues with the impetus which propelled its origin. I *am,* and I am going on and on to the end of myself where something else begins.

At two o'clock in the afternoon Doctor Januario called again. He looked at my body, even touched me intimately to assure himself that everything was going on all right.

But somehow I know that he has never seen me. I hate him more than ever. If nobody recognizes me, then it is a sign that I have ceased to exist. That other impersonal being who lives through pain is all that is.

Somehow my hostility makes me very acute. I know that Doctor Januario, who is accustomed only to treating the native women, is embarrassed in my presence. Because he cannot place me as a type I disconcert him and he dislikes me. We are very poor. He despises poverty. We make him uneasy.

He notices everything about me, and is examining me from the standpoint of his cold sexual curiosity. Even though we are poor he is vain of the opinions of foreigners. All of his gestures toward me are very professional, very pompous and correct. Women exist for him in two categories—those one goes to bed with, and those who are ill. He would like to despise all of them. Woman is an inferior creature. Something quite usual is occurring in regard to me, something about which he has a faint curiosity but which repels him. It also stimulates his sense of power to look on women like this. What he would like most to have explained is my relation to John and the origin of our poverty. He sees at once that John is well educated, has traveled, and has the manner of someone accustomed to authority. Doctor Januario probably thinks that John has made a fool of himself on account of me, on account of sex. And of course that is something which can't be argued. People think that in order to give up financial security one must be intoxicated.

Doctor Januario had some business to attend to, so he left me and came back at night. I could not recall how much time had passed for somehow or other pain is timeless, absolute. It has removed itself from space. It always has been and always will be for it exists independent of relations. I feel it as myself, and when it ceases I will cease.

In suffering intensely one's being cannot be reduced. And the worst of it is that I cannot even establish relations within my individuality. My body fades out and becomes one with the dark turmoil.

Only a faint point of consciousness in me continues to realize itself as separate. It sees Doctor Januario seated by the bedside, yawning, caressing his waxed mustache. Sees his instruments spread elaborately on a chair and glittering dully in the lamplight. Vague reflections are thrown back from the red-black tiling of the unceiled roof, from the blue shadows of the night.

I watch him out of the concave darkness. A breath of wind stirs the flame of the lamp and the clear fire rushes against the glass chimney, reddening it, leaving it bronzed with soot. He comes toward me and lays his hands somewhere about me, out of sight. All that is indefinite.

The absurd thing is that vanity in my own drama persists. I am determined not to make a sound. If I were here alone I would give myself that relief, but not before Doctor Januario. So much of my body has been exposed to him that I shall not reveal anything more.

John holds my hands. He tells me to make an effort to rid myself of the child. While I struggle I know it is my own being that I am trying to force out of myself. I am certain that my insides are torn out of me, disintegrating, and I wonder at my head which, as I dimly perceive, keeps alive all to itself.

It has to go on. My mind is white, still, and separate. It is conscious of itself but of nothing outside. The pressure against my spine continues. My mind continues forever, parallel to my hurt but unconnected with it. It is terrible to have such a living mind. I hate it. I want it killed, because it goes on and on so brightly and is so meaningless.

John tries to relieve me by tying a sheet around me and lifting me away from the bed in that. The pressure is just as merciless and I feel the tired ache of his arms beside.

All at once I scream. I am startled, humiliated by the unconscious sound which has come of itself out of my throat. I am on guard against the scream. I won't allow it to come up again. I ask John to apologize to the physician. I screamed without intending to. I despise women who give way in situations like this.

Doctor Januario, with a faint shrug of astonishment at my inexplicableness, acknowledges my excuse by a slight smile. I yet feel that he has never seen me, that he never will. If he and I gazed with the same eyes we should perceive different things. And I resent his perpetual suggestion of another world, a world in which nothing that I am is included. I want him to accept my reality, to come into it, or else to take himself away from me forever.

John had pled for the use of chloroform, but Doctor Januario has refused. I don't want chloroform even now. I don't want to relinquish my will utterly to the will of the physician. I must save myself from those cold shallow eyes. I cannot bear to relinquish consciousness to the hand that plays with the emerald watch fob and smothers the fastidious yawn of the full bored lips.

John said the baby was a boy. I was glad. John elevated my shoulders and I saw the baby lying there on its stomach, naked. Its conical head was lifted uncertainly and its blue eyes, fixed, without even inquiry in them, stared at me with a blind look. I had nothing but a head. There was chaos between me and the child who was stretched out near the place where I once had feet. The room seemed to me quite dark and I wondered that I could see the child so distinctly.

Doctor Januario's stony regard passed over me politely and he spoke to John in Portuguese. The heap of instruments clicked together as they fell into the bag.

When the physician had gone I relaxed in the inertia which I craved. I had become huge, passive, and undefined. I was without contours, as wide as the world. The baby wailed indistinctly. I heard the cry almost without responding to it. Nothing could touch me. I was outside time. I was rest.

I fold my eyelids against the brutal light. Little pains understood in the darkness are more beautiful in delicacy than the coarse limbs of a goddess—a goddess white as mountain fire in the sun. My little ugly ones, your eyes are lovelier than the eyes of the strong that are cognizant only of distance. There is more love in you—in me—than in the hearts of all the gods blank as the cosmos. Weak sensitive fingers, feeling things to cling by, strangle me with secrecy. But their touch is kinder than the cold palm of Deity. The strong gods are blind gods. Their sandals are of iron. The foreheads of the gods are clouds above the darkness, but I can see the night and they have never seen it.

Our windowless bedroom contained an iron bed, the makeshift dressing table on which the lamp stood, and between the wall and the baby carriage there was just room for a chair. A soiled diffused light fell over the shadows.

Dona Amalia, who lived across the street, had come in to wash the child. She begged me to preserve the navel cord and place it in a little bag around the baby's neck. She was burning dried lavender flowers in a dustpan—the invariable ritual of a native birth.

John asked me how I was. I felt well but I was certain I could never again pass through the same experience, because no human being on earth would have the strength to endure it twice. . . .

John swung up a hammock against the wall. He lay there and we talked. Every now and then, to reassure me, he got up and looked at the baby, quiet in the carriage.

Once he brought him to me. I felt the child's still eyes upon me and was astonished by the movement of his lids. His body had a faint pungent odor that enchanted and disturbed me. I wanted to hide my face against him. My senses were marvelously, voluptuously agitated.

I was pleased by the movement of his bowels, which occurred toward morning. My fastidiousness had disappeared. I enjoyed, without any restraint, everything which is designated as purely physical.

He was too young to want milk but I held his face against my breast. In all my desire for him I was conscious of a heavy sensuality, a massiveness of appreciation.

FRANCES KARLEN
SANTAMARIA

rances Karlen Santamaria was born and raised in Cleveland and attended Antioch College. She is now married to Mario Santamaria, a psychotherapist, and lives with her family in New York City.

She began to keep a diary when she was fifteen "to relieve the burden of my own adolescence."

Her son Joshua was born in 1964 when Frances Karlen and her first husband were in Greece. The diary she kept of her childbearing experience was later published as *Joshua Firstborn*. The portions we reprint describe the feelings of a nursing mother and—while attending Joshua's Jewish circumcision ceremony after their return to the United States— her reflections on the nature of parental love as a learned rather than instinctual capacity.

January 15 [1964]

Nursing Joshua gives me more pleasure each day. He fingers my clothes, grins up at me now with milk trickling down his cheek. I find pleasure, although sometimes there is also discomfort, in the sensations of feeding. The special tingling and fullness as the milk comes flooding in or is "let down," hardening and tensing the entire breast. Tension builds, and is released at the moment when the baby takes hold. It is not sexual pleasure, but the rhythm of buildup and release is not dissimilar. We are like interlocking gears. Often my milk floods in only a minute or so before he wakes and cries for it.

Sometimes the breast gets so full the milk leaks, squirting with great force in a steady stream. Occasionally, when I've wanted his attention, I have hit Arno with it at a distance of five feet.

Funny moment yesterday when I noticed a crumb on Josh's cheek and had a sudden strong desire to flick out my tongue to clean him. Catch myself at seconds with a semi-urge to lick him.

Why isn't more said about the sensuousness between mother and baby? Men paint it and seem to assume it—women don't even mention it among themselves. Either it is completely taken for granted or it isn't considered at all. It is more than a fringe benefit. His waking hours infuse my life with a steady sensuous pleasure. The growing mutual familiarity, the sensations I get each time I pick him up, the good feeling I get of his heft, his smell (which is sweet even when he's soiled because of the breast milk) and the feel of him—we merge into one another giving and taking heat, comfort, love.

Man stays closer to his mother. A woman has her mother intimately only once; man can recapture, draw strength from, and relieve physical sensations women never have again, and in turn, must give.

January 16

The night has become an entity; since Joshua's birth it seems to belong to me in a special way. Enfolded in the hours of the night, the deep intimacy with the child.

My sleep patterns have changed drastically; I used to sleep deeply, hearing nothing. Now I sleep at a different level of attention, still aware of his slight sounds. So much so, that I couldn't bear to have him in our bedroom.

Enormous sense of confidence from nursing the baby. No worry about changing the formula, or if he had enough. It is the absolutely perfect pacifier if you don't mind spending a lot of time half-dressed. If you nurse a healthy baby you know you have the right answers. So most of the time I do feel pretty sure of things, but often enough I'll ask Arno. Why is he still crying? What's the matter? We consult. Usually the answers are digestive in nature.

Arno's matter-of-factness and calmness add to my grow-ing confidence. If he were a worrier, it would be dreadful. He, too, seems to have great faith in the baby's sturdiness and sound health.

February 16

Plans for the *Briss,* the Jewish circumcision ceremony, began immediately, as Joshua was still uncircumcised. (The Greeks do not circumcise.)

It took place the next Thursday afternoon in my in-law's living room where we had been married five years before. The relatives started to come. My father and brother had flown in from Cleveland although my father was weak from pneu-monia (later I found out it was terminal cancer).

I was nervous, fearing the baby would have pain. We were not prepared for the sight of the *moyl* who arrived at three o'clock. At the circumcisions of nephews and cousins there had always been a ubiquitous little old man in a black coat and hat with a wrinkled, efficient wife to whom he spoke in Yiddish as he performed the little operation in the privacy of the bedroom. ("They say he sucks the blood," someone would inevitably whisper.) The mother, always wearing a brand-new blue nylon bathrobe kept out of sight of the proceedings until the ceremony was over and the party had begun.

Our *moyl*, a Mr. Shoulson, turned out to be a radiant young man with a fresh skin that seemed unearthly smooth and white, and a handsome goatee. (He was a weekend folksinger we found out later and a frustrated would-be medical student.) His suit was fashionable and his head with the white *yarmalka* was strong and beautiful. He worked with surgical equipment at a card table in the dining room making preparations while the baby lay happily upstairs kicking in the crib with Thel, his godmother, bending over him. He was dressed up for the occasion (*sacrifice*, I kept thinking) in a blue shirt and striped blue-and-white pants, and white booties with pom-poms she had brought that day. He was the size and weight of a six-month baby and he laughed delightedly and unsuspectingly in his deep, husky voice.

Nervous, I had a drink. When our *moyl*, the folksinger, was ready, the godfather proudly carried Joshua downstairs. He looked around at the crowd of great-uncles and aunts and grandparents with sweetness and open-eyed curiosity. Shoulson smiled and talked to him, commenting he'd never performed the operation on any but an eight-day-old child.

The baby was passed from the arms of his godfather to his father while prayers were said in Hebrew and English. Then he was placed on the crossed arms of both his grandfathers while the *moyl* prayed. Finally, he was put on the little board on the table. His arms were tied up over his head in a receiving blanket. His sturdy legs were put into wide leather bands on the board. Arno seemed excited but felt, I think, calmer than I.

The crowd gathered round the table. We took off his

striped shorts and diaper. I felt giddy and terribly worried. Mother came into the room and left quickly, refusing to watch. When the icy anesthetic was sprayed on him, Josh began to cry. He tried to wave his arms but they were pinned and he screamed with fright and surprise. There was nothing for me to do but go to him. "Give him his bottle," said the *moyl*. "It will take his mind off it."

"But he won't drink a bottle." I filled one quickly though and tried to put it to his lips and, as he had for the past month, Joshua refused anything but the breast. I leaned over him, our faces inches apart and spoke to him. He stared up at me from the board and screamed and sobbed. I could feel the *moyl* working, cutting the foreskin, stared at my baby, spoke steadily, held him, our eyes locked—his frightened and angry as though I were betraying him. And so we were, for what seemed an endless time.

I did not even know my father had stepped forward to hold his legs, and when the foreskin came away and the tiny organ was revealed, red and raw, my father, holding the small legs, buckled and asked my brother for a whisky. I did not hear. I spoke to Arno who stood by, and felt the crowd, heard laughter and whispers and realized dimly that the ordeal was probably not so terrible as it seemed, and yet my son cried and held me reproachfully with his eyes for the first time, and time did not move for me.

Finally it was done. The dressing was put on and I stepped back as the *moyl* released his arms and legs, and picked him up, arranging the diaper, the blue and white pants. The crying ceased. Shoulson held him in his arms and made a joke or two. Then he continued with the ceremony. He prayed in Hebrew in half-chant, half-song. Then in English. His robe was white and the front embroidered in heavy silver thread. Brown-bearded, white-capped, shining in silver and silk, he held my baby and prayed.

"And prolong the life of this infant—Amen."

I heard the rich syllables of the Hebrew name for the first time: Yehoshua ben Chuna. Joshua, son of Arno. We said Amen. Wine was poured. "Why is everyone crying?" I asked.

Arno and his brother embraced and I took Joshua upstairs to nurse him. Later the *moyl* told us that there had been a complication—the baby had been born, he said, "with a great redundancy of foreskin." I flushed with a kind of blank pride as though told one had acquitted oneself with a flourish, made an especially fine arabesque.

He cried on and off for the rest of the evening. Arno fixed his aspirin, and, since he was crying, to my distress, at the sight of me (he associated my face with his afternoon ordeal), his father put him to sleep, carrying him back and forth in the darkened room, and then tried to convince me I had not betrayed my son.

As I waited outside the room I realized how much we have changed in the past three months; how much I have learned about loving. I had expected that, like a little girl mocking love to her doll, my love would at once envelop my baby; instead I had to learn it, grow into it. Love doesn't come from the child's cooing and smiling, his cuteness or beauty. We are rewarded by these things at odd moments. Love comes gradually with our worry, relief, and care—with what we have invested of ourselves. We must learn the loving of a first child step by step, as we learn to sustain love in marriage. The loving of a first baby is like an acquired gift, or skill. The second child, I imagine, comes into that love ready-made.

These days, surrounded by his family, Arno seems different with the baby, as though other people, acknowledging the relationship between him and his child (that great, binding link, again) help him, too, to feel it, make it real. The extended family works to make a family of us; the symbolically linked hands and crossed arms of godfather, father, grandfather at the briss, the sense of generations of males, gives my husband a place to stand with his son.

And so, through one little crisis, one painful shot and a sore vaccination, many nights of crying and hurried consultation, and now the tiny wounded cock, we begin to be parents, and Joshua is truly, profoundly, ours.

CHARLOTTE PAINTER

*T*his extract from my latest book, Confession from the *Malaga Madhouse*, is offered as an example of a mother's record of communication between herself and her child. I hope that it also suggests that along with the child's development, a parallel process occurs in the parent.

These entries are from a diary that was rewritten and combined with a somewhat later diary, in a method I have attempted to describe in the Afterword to this book.

C.P.

I am on a trip with my six-year-old Tommy. We are looking for some way to live in a world gone mad. We have left America the beautiful. But not because we know a better place.

Before we left, I walked along the beach with Mae, talking of Where To Go. Northern California beach—bitterly cold. The perpetual morning fog hasn't lifted. Patrician-faced Mae, marooned on the beach by marriage-wreck with her two kids. She wears a heavy ski sweater from a supply of woolens that go back to her Eastern college days. Where to Go, Where to Go? Mae has money enough to live anywhere; it's a matter of choosing. Oh affluence! An impoverished writer has the

same problem. Mae is about to decide to move to the Peninsula just so that her two children, now of school age, will be
able to go to what she thinks is the best school in the world. I
shake my head. The Peninsula—suburbs, freeways, shopping
centers, solitary monotony.

We shiver and look at the bleak ocean.

All I want really is a warm beach, I say wistfully,
imagining the typewriter set up on the terrace, a cool glass of
somethingorother. A regular TV ad. Hemingway-hangover.

Mae cannot contain her scorn.

That is the silliest thing I ever heard of! she cries.

My son and I arrive in a catholic-capitalistic-commu-
nistic-monarchial dictatorship, and look at castles and empty
armor. In Mexico the natives accused your father, Tommy, of
being a protestant-communist-gringo capitalist. This reminds
me of him, but now I don't think so much any more of him,
six years dead. Except when you ask about him. Which is
often. Examples of manhood being rare.

He looks and looks, my six-year-old, in a biological
reflex. Plumber, are you an example of manhood? Milkman,
were you in a war?

Searching in the fantasy of history, he comes running in
from the "warm" beach for me to help him adjust a suit of
armor. It is made of a cardboard box with holes in the sides
which he has painted with watercolors. Under the watercolors, red print: *chocolat, virgin y los Reyes*. He hasn't cut
the holes big enough so that when he puts his arms through
them his sleeves slide up.

Hurry! The Spanish Armada is coming. To defeat the
Vikings!

I sit with my somethingorother beside the typing machine and think of my charcoal woman.

Revelations

She is a drawing by a Spanish poet I've had for a decade. The poet had made a gift of it to my lover, who was pained by it. *Con razon*, as the Spanish say. No wonder! He passed it on to me. A close-up of a Spanish woman with her child. The woman's is a peasant face, long and bleak, great sorrowing eyes. At first glance the child's face looks cheerfully round, well nourished. But draw closer and you see the art with which the poet has made charcoal tears. The child is crying. That's all, the harsh and subtle lines of their faces. I like it. It suits me. It brings shudders from my friends. How can you live with that dreadful picture, Charlotte? My husband covered her over with a felt mounting for some of his archaeological findings, fertility figurines from Mexico. After he died I took them off and looked long into the woman's face. She's been hanging around ever since. My son asked me to take her down from the wall where we last lived.

I hate that lady, Mommy. She's like some witch. She's not on the bright side.

I took her down. She is stored away now that we are in her country.

But she is still hanging around. I kept her and her child before me as I wrote my last novel. She was its heroine, a pilgrim on a lonely journey to her god. Her heaviness was my own. Her merciless need. She got into me like a spell, and even with the book behind me she lingers. But no women in Spain trudge along the dusty roadsides in black skirts. The roads are paved, the women are in factories, their daughters in minisweaters, their sons negotiating for franchises with Kimberly-Clark. The woman and her child—are they my fantasy? A fixation? A joke?

The drawing has nothing to do with my son anyway. Light and full of jokes, summerhearted. Something by Chagall would suit your room. Let's float into his skies.

The woman is stored away. I can leave her. There are other madonnas.

Let's look for something to make us gay . . .

Ibizá. Sidewalk cafe in Ibizá. The sun shone for a moment and I quickly snapped a picture. There he is in a black beret and his brown corduroy jumpsuit with its matching jacket, forever set as smiling in the fleeting sunshine of Ibizá's winter. *Café continental.*

In the rain we visited a Moorish house, sat on white slabs cushioned with color. Shelves of white, like plaster boxes, were showcases for dolls. The wife, long-haired, delicate, a doll herself. He, a tall humorist, famous painter of funny fingers and penises. The toys are fixed as in a museum, for our hosts are childless. She collects them, puppets, china faces. They are not for playing with.

How cold, to be on a rainy island in winter.

I look at the face of my son in the snapshot, and remember the dialogue at the café:

Where are we going, Mommy?

To the mainland.

What if you don't like it there either? What if we are no place by Christmas?

Worried about your presents?

No—Just, we ought to be *some*place.

We will be. I'm not that unreliable.

What's unreliable?

Inconsistent.

You mean unhappy?

I sigh. Words for the unspeakable. My own reluctance to get in touch with this longing for love.

He names the big pillow he sleeps with Someone. To remind him of his Grandfather stretched beside him waiting for him to go to sleep. Or he'll pretend it's me or his Grandmother. Someone.

In the morning . . . Look, Someone fell out of bed. Poor Someone. Hugging it up to him.

And one night . . . Do you want Someone, Mommy? Here, have Little Someone. His cradle pillow, six years old. He tosses it to me. I pull it between my breasts. Downy soft.

Oh baby, baby.

Tommy (recurrent question): Do you think this is a dream we're in right now? I keep thinking I'm asleep on Grandma's bed, not traveling around.

Grandma's high four poster bed. Naps in the sultry afternoon, with gauzy white curtains criss-crossing one another, letting in the southern breeze . . . An anachronism. Grandma's bed at night, and Grandpa beside him scratching his back until he goes to sleep. While Mommy, the one who vanishes, is off on some assignment, some trip, some wild goose chase . . . If you could only settle down, says Grandma, wondering what she could have done so wrong to give her only child such awful luck. You've been running away ever since I can remember, always looking for something else.

Is this a dream we're in right now?

The boy wakes up in his bed beside the not-so-warm beach, the sea rolling toward the shore, the call of the fishermen beyond the garden as they haul in their nets. The boy runs out the patio door, with his plastic pail, to bring back what the fishermen have given him for the cats. *Chanquetes,* today, Mom, baby *calamares!* A scrap of net, to make a chainmail costume with!

It is a dream, son. Or a journal. Fictionalized . . . If a thing is absolutely true, how can it not also be a lie? An absolute must contain its opposite.

Tommy: Did I talk in my sleep last night?

Not that I heard.

Well, I had such a dream! I heard my voice saying—something, saying, the waves are gold, the sand is silver, and the fishermen's net is ice, and all the fish are flying high above the sea. It was my own voice, mine!

THEOLOGY

Tommy: Some people don't believe in God.

Mom: That's a fact.

Tom: (eating soup): That's what I wish.

Mom (eating soup): What?

Tom: That there wasn't any. Then I couldn't be—controlled. I could fly all over. Throw candles, spill the soup. Throw things out the window.

I see. But who is it that gets upset if you spill the soup? You.

Then maybe I'm the one controlling you.

No, you'd be the same! Throwing candles, spilling, flying. We could do what we want.

God to you is a big controller of everything. Even mothers.

It's like gravity. God invented gravity, you know.

I am encouraged to laugh. I laugh so much I spill the soup. Tommy is encouraged to see me spill the soup. He flies to bed without urging. He is almost asleep, then says: But I believe in God anyway. Do you?

Yes, I say bitterly.

Tommy says, This is the way our life is, just like this, what we're doing. We're walking along the street, and then all of a sudden something bad happens, or something else, and then something good happens, and it goes along like that . . . We just go along walking down the street.

Revelations

The street is also Nowhere. In between. You can't do anything there. Except hold out your rice bowl . . .

Tommy: Why don't we go back to America? We could have a Christmas tree.

We'll have one here, you know. Let's go out to the beach. Once we had a beautiful Christmas tree in California made of driftwood. You were two then.

Okay. Let's get one here.

We find instead a bamboo root, three feet high. Very gnarled and sea-washed. Heavy. The beach is covered with them. They've made their way down streams, washed by rain into the sea, then swept by tides to the shore. Inside the house, tentacles of our root spread upward. We lean it against the table and admire its form.

Tommy takes out his watercolors, draws eyes and noses on the bamboo root, mouths. He paints rocks, too, red, green, and blue, and scatters them about the bottom of the root. We have found sand-polished glass, colors of green and yellow, and these are scattered about the tree. And with colored glitter dust he makes some stars. Our Spanish friend Estebán has shown us how to do it by weaving together five flat Spanish toothpicks. We have a few swiped from restaurants. Tommy paints them, dips them in glitter, and strings them up to dangle on the bamboo root.

He says, Remember that Christmas tree Brian and I trimmed last year?

Brian. Last year's more-than babysitter. Ten thousand miles away in school. Just the mention of Brian makes us both homesick. A pause. Tommy comes and sits on my lap in the rocking chair.

I want Brian.

We rock, looking at the sea. The wind has churned up shallow mud for a quarter of a mile out as far as we can see.

Do you think Brian had to go to war?

No, he's in school this year.

Brian—allowing himself to be crawled over, hugged, kissed even. Reminding me how short the time we share with a child is. Reciting from Milne's "Now We are Six" on his last birthday.

Brian, wondering like everybody else he knows how he can stay out of the Army long enough to do—what he's not sure.

Not persuaded enough against violence to go to jail for it.

Not persuaded he can kill either. Not interested in that Army, that War, sure enough of himself only to know that he doesn't yet know the Way . . .

I wish Brian were here, Tommy says. He told me so many things.

He picks up a box of matches, a long box with a colored picture of a Spanish soldier on it: *Soldados*. Little boxes inside have pictures on them of soldiers from half a dozen countries.

We could hang these boxes on the tree, says Tommy.

But first he wants to know what they are. What countries the soldiers come from.

Were the Spanish and the American Indians ever in a war? Was there ever such a thing as the Germans and the French against the English and the Spanish? What about if the Americans and the Spanish fought a war now—who would win?

I don't know about armies, I say.

He looks disgusted. Brian would have told me, he says.

At the table, he picks up a tangerine beside his castle set. He peels it, takes the pieces apart, lines them up. Each piece becomes a soldier. He picks up some leftover toothpicks he'd been using for tree trim. They become spears. Pieces of tangerine are stabbed to death.

A knock at the door. It's Dan, from the commune, my

young friend on the bum. He tells us he has been discharged from the army because of "insufficient character development."

What does the Army mean by insufficient character development? I ask him.

I did a crazy act for them to try to get a simple discharge. They didn't believe the act, but they did believe I was unfit to serve for doing such a lowdown thing.

He laughs and says: Not a bad term, is it? Fitting. After all, I was a speed freak in the Army. Been off speed now—developing my character, you know. But not sufficiently, never sufficiently again, I hope—oh, about a year . . . I'll tell you something, Tommy. You got a tree there that has sufficient character for us all.

Tommy, busy with his war, asks: Dan, is that a real castle you live in?

Well, you could call it that. A *palacio*.

A part of his castle has fallen down and Tommy is trying to piece it together. He says: This castle doesn't snap together too easily. Those knights sure had a lot of hard work.

Most warriors do, says Dan.

Warriors? They weren't warriors building castles.

Man, that's what the castle scene is all about, war. I may not be able to name dates, ranks, and serial numbers, but I can make a fine distinction for you. The *palacio* is where the king takes the wives and children. The *castillo* is what's up front.

Says Tommy: Where the action is!

A line of peanuts advance upon the tangerines, stab them. The tangerines shell the nuts. A terrible war, atrocities, cannibalism on the part of the general directing the troops. Castle is bombed, shattered. Wild dives into the air, lunges, side gripping, thunderous fall.

And the castle collapses! Dan cries. The *palacio* is over-run. Everything a ruin . . .

Dead bodies all around! cries the general, eating them.

Dan grips his chest. The end of courtly life . . .

Tommy peels another tangerine, explaining. These wars that always go on. You know, they don't have to. If everybody played war instead of really, really doing it.

You think you'll work it out of your system?

What does that mean?

You'll get tired of war and quit.

Oh never. I *love* it. When I grow up, that's what I'll do. *Play* knights, *play* war. And I won't have to do it in a real army then. I could never get tired of this, how could I?

Ready now for a fresh attack. Forward men!

More peanuts are lined up. Bayonet the tangerines.

Tommy shouts: Attack! Every nut in the world attack!

This way, general, sir! says Dan, intercepting peanuts. Consuming them.

Who wins? Tommy asks.

Nobody, I say, losing my mind.

They look at me. Tommy shakes his head. My mother hates war, he explains . . .

The passion for destruction, glorious destruction. Must we seek grace in violence, more than any other way?

A friend speaking of my son: Why, look how he moves, with such good coordination, such—grace . . . And he is lunging toward an unseen adversary, invisible lance slicing off an invisible head, then lifting his booted foot triumphantly to place it upon the invisible corpse. . . .

A dream of Tommy's: You and I were on this street, Mommy, and two caterpillars came along and turned into a butterfly. And the butterfly was a giant bird, that picked us up and carried us along, up, up, far above the clouds, until we could look down and see the world spinning, and we rose further up between clouds and space to an enormous big castle, and the bird was singing: Son of God, Son of God, all the way up. We were so happy. And when I saw the castle, I knew that was the place where lived Mister God. And I saw Him . . .

Son of God, Son of God . . .

A little child shall lead them.

In a dream of mine he comes into a dusty shed, a barn, wearing a hood covered with snow. He has come to say that he cannot go away with me, that his grandparents want him to stay with them. I am hurt, but agree to let him go back to them. I pull back the hood to kiss him. His hair is covered with dust. Two girls nearby on their bikes are restless: I know you're in a rush, I say to them, but I must take Tommy back to his grandparents. Outside a trash truck is blocking the way of my car, and I back up, recklessly, hurrying to get around it. Tommy, waiting on the curb, is picked up by an old Spanish woman in black, who takes him and puts him aboard the trash truck, thinking stupidly that it is going to pass his grandparents' house. Instead, it makes a right turn. I follow in the car. Tommy begins to cry, reaching out of the truck toward me. I begin to scream in Spanish: *Hijo!* We are both screaming in terrible fear. I nearly run over a little girl whose parents pull her out of the way of my car, as I rush downhill chasing the truck, which goes on and on and cannot be overtaken.

For years I have carried this crazy old lady around, a victim to her weird tricks. Can I leave her here and get home free? My little son, on a trash truck, headed in the wrong direction, when you are twenty and telling about it, remember the crazy old woman who put you on a trash truck. I know you don't blame *me*. You remember the old lady, like the one in the drawing? Did she look like me? She *felt* like me? Well, that may be, but I was also turning the car around to try to take you someplace safe. But recklessly as always. The girls on the bikes, now, they're the ones who were rushing me. Who were really *me*. Going off gaily, the two of them, the Gemini twins, the schizy ones, going off to try to be free, cycling through France, in a rush to get away from that dusty barn, that manger, that cradle of life. Oh magic child in your hood, about to be devoured by wolves, about to be dumped or ground up alive as garbage, dusty child in the road, about to be run down by a frantic woman who is driving headlong into a mother's eternal and foredoomed desire—to save her child.

I don't know where in this shrunken world to take you son, to let you grow to manhood.

Must you take him anywhere, mad one? . . .

PART II *Work*

ANNA DOSTOEVSKY

(1846-1918)

hen she was an old woman Anna Dostoevsky said, "I always need an 'idea' in life. I have always been engaged in some work or other which absorbed me completely." Born into a family in comfortable circumstances, at twenty she studied shorthand in order to be independent. Feodor Dostoevsky gave her her first job: taking dictation for his novel *The Gambler*. The forty-six-year old author was recovering from the death of his first wife and a disastrous love affair with the young Polyina Suslova. Both women had been strong personalities who had frequently humiliated him and were the prototyes of his demonic female literary characters. His contradictory nature was drawn to the submissive stenographer who worshiped him and offered practical advice on his muddled financial affairs; he quickly proposed, giving Anna the life work she would seem to have been born to perform.

In 1867, a few months after their wedding, they left Russia to escape their creditors, and while Dostoevsky indulged his passion for roulette in the European gambling casinos, Anna began a diary where, she said, "I could record freely; for I knew that no one but myself could read what I had put down in shorthand."

The selection that follows tells of the miseries the young bride endured during their three months in Dresden and

Baden. The child she was pregnant with died and they continued to roam Europe until 1871, when in a mood of deep despair over the ruin of his talent, Dostoevsky was encouraged by Anna to try his luck once again at the tables. She had no hope that he would win but knew that after satisfying his craving for risk he "would return home calmed, and that then, realizing the futility of his hopes of winning at the tables, he would sit down with renewed strength to his novel." After losing, he promised her once again never to gamble; miraculously it would seem the cycle was broken, and it was indeed his last game.

When they returned to Russia, his life abroad with her had gentled his erratic spirit, and Anna had aged. "From a timid, shy girl I had become a woman of resolute character, who could not longer be frightened by the struggle with troubles." A less complicated personality than Sophie Tolstoy, she was able to submerge herself in her husband's needs and be important to his work. When his death ended their fourteen-year marriage, she devoted herself to the service of his works and memory. Her last years were spent transcribing her early diaries, which she used in preparing her *Reminiscences*, published after her death.

Dresden, 1st May, 1867

. . . We read in the evenings and are silent for hours; at moments I glance at him or he at me with a pleasant smile, ever with joy. I am very happy. . . .

Tuesday, 16th May

Today we woke up rather late. We have no watch now (Fedya* pawned it at Homburg), and therefore we do not know the time. . . .

* Dostoevsky

Anna Dostoevsky

Saturday, 3rd June, 1867

. . . For the first time now abroad, and for the second time in my life, I walked arm-in-arm with Fedya. He proposed it, and I agreed with joy. I was delighted to walk arm-in-arm with him, although I had to take gigantic steps; for Fedya is taller than I, and his step is longer. . . .

Wednesday, 7th June, 1867

. . . Fedya began drinking tea. As he had an epileptic fit last night, he was hard to please, and the tea seemed distasteful to him. He asked me to let him pour out the tea himself, and I replied: "Please do." He did not like my reply, got angry and shouted. It hurt me; but I said nothing, blushed scarlet and went into the next room. Five minutes had not passed before Fedya came into the room quite gay, and said that he apologised. . . . Fedya has been telling me all day that I am "good," that I am a "saint," that I am free from sin . . . My dearest Fedya! I am not worthy of his praises. . . .

Friday, 23rd June, 1867

. . . On returning home Fedya decided to put away his winnings in a leather bag and not to touch them, unless all our capital went. . . .

Baden, Sunday, 25th June, 1867

. . . I asked him quite indifferently: "Have you lost?" "Yes, I have," he replied, in despair, and began again to accuse himself. He said pathetically that he reproached himself for his weakness for gambling, that he loved me, that I was his beautiful wife, and that he was not worthy of me. Then he asked me to give him some more money. . . .

Baden, Monday 26th June, 1867

. . . I certainly could not withstand his argument, and gave him the five louis. "You are behaving very nicely so far," said Fedya, "but when you are older, when you have become 'Mme. Anna Dostoevsky,' you won't allow me to behave in the way I am doing now. You will say that previously you were foolish. You will say: 'If my husband wanted to make a fool of himself I should not have allowed him to do so. A wife ought to stop her husband behaving like that.' " He said that the way I acted was much the best; for I was winning him by my kindness and meekness. . . .

Baden, Wednesday, 28th June, 1867

. . . I generally value Fedya's least attention to me. For instance, when I go to bed I say to him: "Bye-bye, Fedya," and he comes to me to say good-night, and each time I am unspeakably glad and happy. . . .

Monday, 3rd July, 1867

. . . he came back with his pockets bulging with various things. At first he handed me the cheese, oranges and lemon; then he took out of his overcoat pocket a jar the contents of which I could not make out. And it turned out to be my favorite, my dream—preserved mushrooms! Oh, what a good husband! What a dear husband to get for his wife Russian mushrooms in Baden! It is something that must not be forgotten. . . .

ANNA DOSTOEVSKY

Saturday, 8th July

Fedya went off to the tables, taking with him eighty francs, but he came back and said that he had lost all, and asked me for the last louis we had left. . . .

Friday, 14th July, 1867

. . . What if he lost our last few francs now, when we have nothing even to pawn! At last he came back. When I went to bed, he came to me and gave me a friendly good night, and we made it up. I am cross with myself. Why do I pick such empty quarrels? I have such a wonderful husband and I always irritate him.

Tuesday, 18th July, 1867

Today the weather is dull and I feel so weary. During the last few days, I have been thinking of my coming child, Misha. I am dreaming all the time about the child. Fedya said yesterday that he would go to the tables and win thirty thousand francs, so as to be able to go back to Russia, for he longs to see several persons. I, too, should like to see several persons, but the idea of going back so soon frightens me. It seems to me that Fedya will cease loving me when we go back . . . I am afraid that another woman will occupy the place in his heart which I occupy now. It seems to me that he has never loved, that he has only imagined that he has loved, that there has been no real love on his part. I even think that he is incapable of love; he is too much occupied with other thoughts and ideas to become strongly attached to anyone earthly.

Revelations

Sunday, 6th August, 1867

. . . Fedya suddenly said to me that yesterday I had been insensitive. I was indeed pained to hear it, particularly because I always thought that Fedya was a man who understood my sensitiveness. Christ! What a number of times I could have made things unpleasant for him, if I had wished it. . . .

Friday, 11th August, 1867

At eleven o'clock Fedya went off to the tables. After having packed his and my trunk in the early morning, I sat down to write a letter to my mother. When I had finished the letter Fedya returned and said that he had not only lost the forty francs which I had given him, but that he had also pawned his ring at Moppert's and had lost that money as well . . . I wanted to reproach him; but he fell on his knees before me, asking me to forgive him, saying that he was a scoundrel, that there was no punishment too severe for him, but that all the same I must forgive him. However much I was grieved by the loss of the money, yet I had to give him twenty francs to redeem the ring. But when he began counting our money, we found that we should have to pawn my earrings to have enough to take us to Geneva . . . The twenty francs I gave him seemed to cheer him up immensely. He said he would never forget the fact, that when we had no money at all, I gave him twenty francs and told him he might go to the tables and lose them; that he would never forget my goodness. Fedya went to Moppert's and got an advance of one hundred and twenty francs on the ear-rings, to be redeemed in two months' time. From there he went off to the tables. I asked him for the love of God not to stay there long; for our train was due to start in a very short time. In about twenty minutes

136

he returned home saying he had lost. I asked him not to trouble, but to help me to fasten the trunks . . . He went out to get a cab. We had still forty minutes in which to catch the train. He returned bringing with him a loaf and a half a pound of ham, and we began eating very quickly. I never ate so quickly before, and Fedya kept on hurrying me. We were both terribly exhausted. The sweat poured down our faces. We drove up to the station, bought our tickets for Geneva, and got into the train. . . .

SOPHIE TOLSTOY

(1844-1919)

*S**ophie Bers was only eighteen* when she married Leo Tolstoy. He was almost twice her age, had led a youth of soldiering, drinking, womanizing, was given to fits of unaccountable moodiness, and was the greatest literary genius of their time. She adored him; but within two months of their marriage she began to confide to her diary her misery, her inability to reconcile herself to his past, her jealousies and her failure to understand him. For the rest of her life she wrote furiously in an effort to decipher the progressive deterioration of the relationship that had begun with such high elation on both their parts.

She often tried to write about him objectively. If she couldn't be his literary companion, she wanted to be his biographer, the custodian of his diaries and papers—anything that would bring her closer to grasping the elusive power of his genius. The thirteen children she bore him exhausted her physically; her unused intellectual energies found thwarted expression in quarrels and self-pity. Her diary frequently laments his lust and expresses a yearning for a closer psychic intimacy.

When Tolstoy turned from fiction to social and philosophical causes, Sophie understood him even less. His communal primitive Christian creed mystified her and drew from her a response of deeper conformity to her rigid upbringing.

Her passion to understand him eventually unbalanced her mind. Yet throughout her diary, she saw herself in objective flashes and portrayed her ordeal with the gifts of a natural writer.

October 8, 1862

A diary once again. It makes me sad to go back to the old habits which I gave up when I got married. I used to take to writing whenever I felt depressed, and I am probably doing it now for the same reason. I have been feeling frightened ever since yesterday when he told me he did not believe in my love. . . .

What is he doing to me? Gradually I shall retreat into myself and shall poison his life. And yet I feel so sorry for him at those times when he doesn't believe in me; his eyes fill with tears and he has such a meek, wistful look. At such moments I could strangle him with love, and yet the thought pursues me: "He doesn't believe in me, he doesn't believe in me." And today I suddenly felt that we would gradually drift apart and each live our own lives, that I would create my own sad world for myself, and he a world full of work and doubt. And this relationship struck me as vulgar. I have stopped believing in his love. When he kisses me, I think to myself: "Well, I'm not the first woman." And it begins to hurt me that this love of mine, my first and last, should not be enough for him. . . .

November 13

. . . I can't find any occupation for myself. He is lucky to be so clever and talented. But I'm neither the one nor the other. One can't live on love alone; and I am so stupid that I can do nothing but think of him. He is unwell, and I begin to believe that he will die, and that is enough to make me miserable . . . When he is away or working, I always think of him, listening for his footsteps; and when he is here I keep watching his face. It is probably due to my pregnancy that I am in this abnormal state, which, to a certain extent, affects him too. It isn't hard to find work, but before doing anything one has to create some enthusiasm for breeding hens, tinkling the piano, and reading a lot of silly books and a very few good ones, or pickling cucumbers and what not. All this will come in time, when I forget my lazy old life and get used to the country. I don't want to get into the common rut and be bored; but I shan't be. I wish my husband had a greater influence over me. It's strange that I should love him so much yet feel his influence so little. . . .

In a few years I shall have created a woman's world for myself, which I shall love even more, for it will contain my husband and my children, whom one loves even more than one's parents and brothers. But I haven't reached that stage yet. I am still wavering between the past and the future. My husband loves me too much to put me on a sound footing just yet; it is difficult, anyway, and I will have to work it all out for myself; besides, he feels that I have already changed. With a little effort I can again become what I was before, although no longer a maiden, but a woman, and when this happens, both he and I will be satisfied. . . .

November 23

He disgusts me with his People. I feel he ought to choose between me, i.e. the representative of the family, and his beloved People. This is egoism, I know. But let it be. I have given my life to him, I live *through* him, and I expect him to do the same. Otherwise the place grows too depressing;

SOPHIE TOLSTOY

I ran away today because everybody and everything repelled me—Auntie and the students . . . and the walls and the whole life here, so that I laughed for joy when I ran quietly away from the house. L. did not disgust me, but suddenly I felt that he and I were miles apart, i.e. that his People could never absorb all my attention, while I couldn't take up all his attention, as he does mine. It's quite clear. If I am no good to him, if I am merely a doll, a *wife,* and not a *human being—* then it is all useless and I don't want to carry on this existence. Of course I am idle, but I am not idle by nature; I simply haven't yet discovered what I can do here . . . I know he is brilliant, poetic, and intelligent, full of *power,* but it annoys me that he should look at everything from a gloomy angle. I sometimes want to break loose from his somewhat sombre influence, to ignore it—but I can't. His influence is depressing because I begin to think in his way, to see things with his eyes, and I am afraid of losing my own self and yet not becoming like him.

Moscow, January 17, 1863

. . . the real source of all my troubles and bad moods is my egoism and my idea that his whole life, his thoughts, and his love must belong to me. It's the rule with me: no sooner do I begin to get fond of something than I pull myself up by reminding myself that I love nothing and no one except Lyova. And yet one ought to have something else to love as well, just as Lyova loves his *work,* so that I could turn to it whenever he is cold to me. Such moments are bound to come more and more frequently; but in reality it has been like this all the time. I can see it quite clearly now, for I have nothing else to occupy my mind; he, of course, is too busy to notice all the details of our relationship.

November 13

. . . He says he would like to live in Moscow. I've been expecting it. It makes me jealous to see how he can find his ideal in the first pretty woman he meets. Such a passion is terrible, blind, and incurable. I have never lived up to his ideal, and never will. I feel abandoned during the day, in the evening, at night—all the time. I am a source of satisfaction to him, a nurse, a piece of furniture, *a woman*—nothing more. I try to suppress all human feelings in myself. While the machine works and warms the milk and knits a blanket and walks up and down without thinking, life is still bearable. He has stopped loving me. Why was I not able to keep his love? But how could I? It is Fate. There was a moment—I admit it—a moment of sorrow when nothing in the world mattered any more, except the love I had lost. His writing meant nothing to me then—what did all those conversations matter between Countess So-and-so and Princess So-and-so; but afterwards I despised myself for the thought. My existence is so deadly dull, while his is so full and rich, with his work and genius and immortal fame. . . .

February 25, 1865

I am so often left alone with my thoughts that the desire to write my diary is quite natural. I sometimes feel depressed, but now it seems wonderful to be able to think everything over for myself, without having to say anything about it to other people. . . . Yesterday Lyova said that he was feeling very young; and I understood him perfectly. Now I am well once again, and not pregnant; it terrifies me to think how often I have been in that condition. He said that youth meant the capacity to say: "I can accomplish everything." As for me, I both *can* and *want* to do everything, but after a while I begin to realize there is nothing to want, and that I can't do anything beyond eating, drinking, sleeping, nursing the children, and caring for them and my husband. After all, this *is* happiness, yet why do I grow sad and weep, as I did yesterday? I am writing with a feeling of pleasant excitement, for I know that no one, not even Lyova, will read this . . . He has gone out; he doesn't spend much time with me these days.

When I am *young* I prefer not to be with him; for I fear to be stupid and irritable. Dunyasha said the other day: "The count has grown old." I wonder if it is true. He is never gay now, and I often seem to get on his nerves; his writing takes up much of his time, but gives him no pleasure. I wonder if he has lost forever his capacity to be happy and joyful? He is talking of spending next winter in Moscow. He will probably be happier in Moscow, and I shall pretend that I also want to be there. I have never admitted to him that unconsciously, in order to rise in his estimation, one can be a hypocrite even with one's own husband. I did not tell him that, for I am petty and vain, and even envious of people. But I shall be ashamed in Moscow not to have a carriage and pair, with a footman in livery, and fine dresses and a fine house, and everything in general. Lyova is extraordinary—he simply doesn't care about such things. It's a result of his wisdom and his virtue.

September 12

. . . I have always been told that a woman must love her husband and be honourable and be a good wife and mother. They write such things in ABC books, and it is all nonsense. The thing to do is *not* to love, to be clever and sly, and to hide all one's bad points—as if anyone in the world had no faults! And the main thing is *not* to love. See what I have done by loving him so deeply! It is so painful and humiliating;

but he thinks that it is merely silly. "You say one thing and always do another." But what is the good of arguing in this superior manner, when I have nothing in me but this humiliating love and a bad temper; and these two things have been the cause of all my misfortunes, for my temper has always interfered with my love. I want nothing but his love and sympathy, and he won't give it me; and all my pride is trampled in the mud; I am nothing but a miserable crushed worm, whom no one wants, whom no one loves, a useless creature with morning sickness, and a big belly, two rotten teeth, and a bad temper, a battered sense of dignity, and a love which nobody wants and which nearly drives me insane.

July 31, 1868

It makes me laugh to read over this diary. It's so full of contradictions, and one would think I was such an unhappy woman. Yet is there a happier woman than I? It would be hard to find a happier or more friendly marriage than ours. Sometimes, when I am alone in the room, I just laugh with joy, and making the sign of the cross, say to myself, "May God let this last many, many years." . . .

February 14, 1870

As I was reading Pushkin's life the other day, it occurred to me that I might render a service to posterity by recording not so much Lyova's everyday life, as his mental activities, so far as I was able to watch them. I had often thought of it before, but I had had very little time for it.

This is a good time to begin. *War and Peace* is completed, and nothing else very important has yet been begun. He spent all last summer reading and studying philosophy. . . .

Sophie Tolstoy

[This entry continues with some objectivity, and she managed to write about twenty entries during the course of the next few years about Tolstoy's activities, including an account of his famous quarrel with Turgenev. However, her subjectivity frequently took her to her more personal diary. As she had observed earlier, his influence upon her was remarkably small.]

February 27, 1877

As I was reading over Lyova's diaries today, I came to the conclusion that I will not be able to write the "material for his biography," as I originally intended. His mental life is so complicated, and his diaries excite me so much, that my thoughts grow confused and I stop seeing things clearly and reasonably. It's a pity to give up the idea. But what I can do is to record our present life and all the facts and conversations relating to his literary work; I think I could do this conscientiously and with much interest. . . .

The other day, when I asked him to tell me something about his past, he said: "Please don't ask me such things; it makes me too excited, and I am too old to live my life all over again by recalling it to memory."

October 25, 1886

Everyone, Lev Nikolaevich, as well as the children, who follow him like a flock of sheep—has come to think of me as a *scourge*. After throwing on me the whole responsibility of the children and their education, household duties, money matters, and all the other material things, which they all make much greater use of than I ever do, they come along, and, with a cold, officious, and pious expression, tell me to give a horse to a peasant, or some money, or some flour, or this, that, and the next thing.

I have nothing to do with the farming, and I have neither the time nor the knowledge to find out whether horses are required at one particular moment for a particular purpose, and all these requests, when I don't know what they are about, irritate and confuse me.

How often I have wanted to drop it all and to be done with this life. God! I am so tired of all this life and the struggle and suffering! How deep is the unconscious hatred of even one's nearest people, and how great their selfishness.

June 18, 1887

Many people blame me for not writing my diary and memoirs, since Fate has put me in touch with such a famous man. But it is so hard to break away from my *personal* attitude towards him, to be quite impartial, and, most of all, to find any time to do it; I am so terribly busy, and it's been the same all my life. I thought I would be free enough this summer to copy and sort out some of Lev Nikolaevich's manuscripts. But I've been here a whole month now, and have had to spend all this time copying "On Life and Death," on which he has worked for such a long time.

No sooner am I finished copying it than he changes it all, and I have to copy it all over again. His patience and determination are endless. . . .

August 25

I spent all day looking through Lyova's manuscripts, and sorting them out. I want to take them to the Rumiantsev Museum to be preserved. Some of them are in a dreadful muddle, and, I am sure, will never be deciphered or completed. I also want to take his letters, diaries, portraits, and everything else relating to him. I am acting in a *sensible* way, but for some reason it makes me sad. Does my desire to put everything in order mean that I shall soon die?

November 20, 1890

. . . I read his diaries on the quiet, and tried to see what I could bring into his life which would unite us again. But his diaries only deepened my despair; he evidently discovered that I had been reading them, for he hid them away. However, he didn't say anything to me.

In the old days it gave me joy to copy out what he wrote. Now he keeps giving it to his daughters and carefully hides it from me. He makes me frantic with his way of systematically excluding me from his personal life, and it is unbearably painful. . . .

December 17

. . . He would like to destroy his old diaries and to appear before his children and the public only in his patriarchal robes. His vanity is immense!

December 31

I am so used to living not my own life, but the life of Lyova and the children, that I feel I have wasted my day if I haven't done something for them. I have again begun to copy Lyova's diaries. It is sad that my emotional dependence on the man I love should have killed so much of my energy and ability; there was certainly once a great deal of energy in me. . . .

RUTH BENEDICT
(1 8 8 7 - 1 9 4 8)

he noted anthropologist Ruth Benedict was born
Ruth Fulton in New York City. Her father died before she was two, and her mother supported her and her
sister by working as a teacher and a librarian. Babyhood measles left her partially deaf and in later childhood she was
troubled by tantrums, "outside invasions" of her person, until
one night her mother, in an almost medieval rite of exorcism,
came to her with Bible and candle, invoked the aid of Jehovah
and made Ruth promise never to have another uncontrollable
episode of temper. The tantrums disappeared only to be suc-
ceeded by depressions; she felt that both were "manifestations
of the same kink. . . . protests against alienation from my
Delectable Mountains," an imaginary kingdom where she was
detached from the world of the living and learned "that if I
didn't talk to anybody about the things that mattered to me
no one could ever take them away."

After college and a tour of Europe, she taught in a
girls' school in Pasadena and began a journal which she kept
only intermittently and frequently revised over a long period
of years. The selections that follow deal principally with the
two years before she made her decision to marry Stanley
Benedict, a medical researcher with a promising career, and
with the seven childless years of marriage that followed, during

which her belief that a great love was woman's true vocation was winnowed to the harder truth that marriage, at least without children, could not hold fully the attention of her complicated mind.

During those years she occupied herself with social work, wrote poetry under the pseudonym "Anne Singleton" and worked on and off on a biographical study of three strong women of the past, Mary Wollstonecraft, Margaret Fuller and Olive Schreiner, all of whom held unconventional views on marriage. At the age of thirty-two she strayed into anthropology almost by accident when she attended some classes at the New School for Social Research. Two years later she had her Ph.D. from Columbia and was embarked on a distinguished career that made important contributions to the understanding of the nature of human culture in relation to the formation of human personality in different societies. Her best-known writings include *Patterns of Culture, Race, Science and Politics* and *The Chrysanthemum and the Sword.*

According to her friend and colleague Margaret Mead, the happiest time of Ruth's marriage was when she and Stanley came to terms about her poetry. But it was a temporary state; Mead comments: "the things she said in her verse were uncongenial to him." The idea of her having a career was even less congenial to him and eventually her professional commitments led them to separate.

In Ruth Benedict's journal there is a pervading sadness that she lived in a culture that made it difficult for love and useful work to coincide. Her own detached temperament gave her a vision of a more spiritual society in which love and work would be kept in proper perspective, eternity being the sky of such a world rather than a roof of cultural impositions on human personality.

Revelations

October, 1912.

The faithfulness of this old notebook is touching. It has travelled across half of Europe and all of America without once learning the object of its existence. It was given to me to write my home letters in while I was abroad so that they could be neatly preserved for posterity between suitable covers. The idea shocked my modesty—also my sense of proportion—and the notebook shared the scorn I heaped on the purpose it was intended for.

. . . I want it now for a very different purpose.

I want it now for my very own; I want it to help me to shake myself to rights during the next few months. I've just come through a year in which I have not dared to think; I seemed to keep my grip only by setting my teeth and playing up to the mask I had chosen. I have not dared to be honest, not even with myself. I could only try to live through day after day, day after day, and not dishonor them overmuch. In spite of myself, bitterness at having lived at all obsessed me; it seemed cruel that I had been born, cruel that, as my family taught me, I must go on living *forever*. Life was a labyrinth of petty turns and there was no Ariadne who held the clue.

I tried, oh very hard, to believe that our own characters are the justification of it all . . . But the boredom had gone too deep; I had no flicker of interest in my character. What was my character anyway? My real *me* was a creature I dared not look upon—it was terrorized by loneliness, frozen by a sense of futility, obsessed by a longing to *stop*. No one had ever heard of that Me. If they had, they would have thought it an interesting pose. The mask was tightly adjusted. . . .

So much of the trouble is because I am a woman. To me it seems a very terrible thing to be a woman. There is one crown which perhaps is worth it all—a great love, a quiet home, and children. We all know that is all that is worth while, and yet we must peg away, showing off our wares on the market if we have money, or manufacturing careers for ourselves if we haven't. We have not the motive to prepare ourselves for a "life-work" of teaching, of social work—we know that we would lay it down with hallelujah in the height of our success, to make a home for the right man.

And all the time in the background of our consciousness rings the warning that perhaps the right man will never come. A great love is given to very few. Perhaps this make-shift time filler of a job *is* our life work after all.

It is all so cruelly wasteful. There are so few ways in which we can compete with men—surely not in teaching or in social work. If we are not to have the chance to fulfil our one potentiality—the power of loving—why were we not born men? At least we could have had an occupation then. . . .

They laugh at home about my "course in old maids" this winter. It really isn't a joke at all. It's quite tragically serious. There were three at school. They retold all their twenty-year old conversations with men—conversations that of course *might* have developed into love affairs *if* they'd allowed the liberty—so that you might be led to realize they were not old maids by necessity. —All except Miss Van W——. No one had ever even let her suspect that he "was interested in her." It was she who was really tragic. She kept her cook books in the bottom of her trunk and took them out and fingered them lovingly. Her primary children adored her, and yet she had no charms of person or manner. She had one gift—she could love. But in her barren thirty-six years even that passionate necessity had grown so thick-coated with mannerisms, so padlocked with reticence that there were few to whom she discovered it. She was so tragically alone. . . . As we walked the streets of lighted bungalows at night, she would drink them in one after another, and as we neared the school, she sighed once, "There are so many homes! There ought to be enough to go around."

I shall never forget one of her confidences. We had been talking over our lives, and with a little catch in her breath and a downward flutter of her eyes, she asked hesitatingly, "Have I ever told you of Mr. Dodge? I had meant to, some-day. He had a ranch near Claremont—a good ranch. And he wanted a wife. He tried to get my best friend, Miss Allen. He would have taken anyone. But I—I never encouraged him."

It was as if she had said: "Behold, I too am brave; I too will not stop short of the ideal." It was so pitiful—so terrible. The horror of the revelation struck deep.

Then there are the girls I know in Pasadena. They are most of them ten years older than I. They are no longer young; they will probably never marry. They are fighting the ennui of a life without a purpose. Some of them are studying shorthand, some are taking music lessons, one just embroiders. They are doing their best—to trump up a reason for living. And within a year they'll find that there is no virtue even in a pay envelope to make life seem worth living.

The trouble is not that we are never happy—it is that happiness is so episodical. A morning in the library, an afternoon with someone I really care about, a day in the mountains, a good-night-time with the babies [her sister's children] can almost frighten me with happiness. But then it is gone and I cannot see what holds it all together. What is worth while? What is the purpose? What do I *want?* . . .

What is it that holds these episodes together? Much as I have rebelled against it, I cannot hit on any answer but the old one of self development. Perhaps my trouble comes from thinking of the end as my *present* self, not as a possible and very different future self. It is hard never to fall into the way of thinking that now you are ready to use your hard-won experience. Of course you mean to go on learning, but from a certain vantage point of attainment; it is always very hard for me to feel that year after year is just added *preparation*—and for what? The great instinctive answer is for Motherhood—yes, I think I could accept that with heart and soul—so much do our instincts help us out in our problems—but no girl dares count on Motherhood. Ethically, if Motherhood is worth while, it ought to be also worthy to have a hand in the growth of a child or a woman. The difference is just a question of instinct.

November, 1912.

I have been reading Walt Whitman, and Jeffries' *Story of My Heart*. They are alike in their superb enthusiasm for life—for actual personal living. To Jeffries nothing, literally nothing, is of worth except as it feeds his "soul-life, his psyche," and as a fantastic appendage, his fevered, exotic dream of the soul-life of future generations. Whitman is far sturdier and more healthful; but it is their common ground that impresses me: their unwavering, ringing belief that the *Me* within them is of untold worth and importance. I read in wonder and admiration—in painful humility. Does this sense of personal worth, this enthusiasm for one's own personality, belong only to the great expressive souls? or to a mature period of life I have not yet attained? or may I perhaps be shut from it by eternal law because I am a woman and lonely? It seems to me the one priceless gift of this life:—of all blessings on earth I would choose to have a man-child who possessed it. . . .

August 20.

How shall I say it? That I have attained to the zest for life? That I have looked in the face of God and had five days of magnificent comprehension? . . . It happened when Stanley came down last week. He had been here one week in July—a glorious week of tramping and rowing and reading, of lying on the hilltops and dreaming over the valleys. But I let him go again.

And last week he came down for two days on his way to Europe. And Oh I was so glad to see him! I think I knew it that night. But he did not see it. We went down to the Collins' Woods in the boat, and still he did not see. It was afternoon when I told him—I had hoped he would see for himself. But it had happened, and I'd rather be with him than anywhere else in God's universe.

He had been lying on the ground. He sat up and moved toward me, and said with a tenderness and awe I had never heard before, "Oh, Ruth, is it true?" And then he put his arms around me, and rested his head against me. In the long minute we sat there, he asked in the same hushed voice, "Ruth, will you marry me?" And I answered him, "Yes Stanley." After that we did not speak. Later it was I who told him first that I loved him. —And so the whole world changed. Is it not awesome—wonderful beyond expression? Every day I have grown surer, happier. Nothing in all my life would be worth setting over against our Sunday afternoon drive through Lyon Brook or our last afternoon together on the towpath.

We turn in our sleep and groan because we are parasites—we women—because we produce nothing, say nothing, find our whole world in the love of a man. —For shame! We are become the veriest Philistines—in this matter of woman's sphere. I suppose it is too soon to expect us to achieve perspective on the problem of woman's rights—but surely there is no other problem of human existence where we would be childish enough to believe in the finality of our little mathematical calculations of "done" or "not done." But here in the one supremely complicated relation of man and woman which involves the perpetual interchange of all that is most difficult to be reckoned—here we thrust in "the world's coarse thumb and finger," here we say "to the eyes of the public shalt thou justify thy existence." —Oh no! do we care whether Beatrice formed clubs, or wrote a sonnet? In the quiet self-fulfilling love of Wordsworth's home, do we ask that Mary Wordsworth should have achieved individual self-expression? In general,—a woman has one supreme power—to love. If we are to arrive at any blythness in facing life, we must have faith to believe that it is in exercising this gift, in living it out to its fullest that she achieves herself, that she "justifies her existence."

November, 1914.

I have hardly written here for a year and more. Last winter I had Stanley to write to, my work to do, my small busyness of preparation to fill my time. This year I have Stanley to talk to, to play with, to passionately love, but no longer to write to. With all my duties of housekeeping and cooking and clothes providing and visiting, I have such abundant leisure as I never dreamed of except in my year abroad. . . .

I have so much, so much—life seems so incomparably rich these days. I have been happy, happy this summer, as I did not think it was given to be unless one were very young or very blind. We have had love and companionship. . . .

—The winter is before me to accomplish anything I wish. I have difficulty only in concentrating on something . . . my pet scheme is to steep myself in the lives of restless and highly enslaved women of past generations and write a series of biographical papers from the standpoint of the "new woman." My conclusion so far as I see it now is that there is nothing "new" about the whole thing except the phraseology and the more independent economic standing of recent times —that the restlessness and groping are inherent in the nature of women and this generation can outdo the others long since past only in the frankness with which it acts upon these. . . .

December 23, 1916.

. . . The particular problem of this winter is how I may cut through the . . . entanglements of our order of life and make good in my writing. I would like to simplify our living . . . cut away the incubus of a house and coal fires and course dinners. . . . But that would trouble Stanley's work— perhaps less than I think—but for that reason it isn't fair to begin with that. . . . I'd like to get my "women" done. I felt then that they'd never "get across" till I'd acquired a better sense of an audience. That's what "Mary"* lacks. But I deliberately decided to write her to please myself, with no aim but to satisfy my own requirements. . . . I'm going back to write Margaret Fuller for an audience—to write my "introduction"—to attempt Olive Schreiner. On the practical side, I must get a publisher back of me, and that may mean rewriting "Mary" before I'm willing to send her out. It's a big job—and begory I'll do it!

New Women of Three Centuries

Christmas, 1916.

I've pledged my word to a "business" in life now. Last night Stanley and I talked. We hurt each other badly, for words are clumsy things, and he is inexorable. But, at any

* Mary Wollstonecraft

rate, he does not baby me, and honesty helps even when it is cruel.

I said that for the sake of our love—our friendship, rather—I must pay my way in a job of my own. I would not, would not drift into the boredom, the pitiableness of lives like ———— or ————. He said that, whatever the job, it would not hold me; nothing ever had, social work or teaching. Children might for a year or two, no more. As for the question of success in such a thing having any value in our relations with each other, it was nonsense; it only meant that I'd discovered now that marriage in its turn did not hold me. If I'd found we lacked friendship now, there was no solution possible— neither of us could change our personalities. He had no faith in the future.

I told him he should see. My past list of jobs proved nothing: until I loved him nothing had ever seemed to me worth the effort of attaining. I could lay hold of no motive. Now I understood; I cared and cared deeply, and for what I wanted I was willing to pay high. I should prove that I could do better than to drift into a meaningless routine. I should prove that I was no rolling stone. I should prove too that whatever I could achieve in my own life was something added to our relationship with each other. . . .

January, 1917.

. . . I long to speak out the intense inspiration that comes to me from the lives of strong women. They have made of their lives a great adventure; they have proved that out of much bewilderment of soul, steadfast aims may . . .

The Great Affirmation of any honest mind implies also the power of rejection—In actual experience the greater, the more pivotal the Affirmation, the more devastating the rejection. Take Ellen Key. With her whole soul she affirms what our dirty-minded Puritan-bred society discounts in any private conversation: monogamy. She believes greatly and sincerely that (without the need of threat and punishment) without the double handcuffs of the marriage ceremony, without the threat of the vulgarity of the divorce court, men and women are capable of giving themselves to one another simply, completely, permanently, are capable of seeing in that permanency the dignity and beauty of their love. It is an affirmation of the attainability of a spiritual act our most spiritual leaders hesitate to make; yet they stand appalled before the negation it implies.

Undated

I have always used the world of make-believe with a certain desperation. It has never been much an affair of daydreams—a useful pair of spectacles, rather, to color in some endurable fashion an unendurable mood. I remember the keen excitement of finding that I could create the perfect illusion that I was (doing this thing) for the *last time*. Tomorrow I would be dead; surely I could go thru' it *once* more even with a dash of zest. Days, weeks, almost years I wore those spectacles. They are inimitable for producing an illusion of vivacity and even gusto in the most melancholic.

. . . My spectacles now have nothing of the grim about them, but they're wonderfully effective. It's very simple: this is my daughter's life that's posing as mine. It's my daughter's love life which shall be perfect; it's my daughter's abilities which shall find scope; it's my daughter's insight that shall be true and valid; it is she who owes it to speak out her beliefs. It is she who shall not miss the big things of life. . . . —The efficacy of such spectacles I suppose no man could understand—how many women could, I wonder? Practically a great many women act all thru' their adult life in an un-make-believe version of the same underlying notion: the passionate belief in the superior worth-whileness of our children. It is stored up in us as a great battery charged by the accumulated instincts of uncounted generations. When there are no children, unless the instinct is somehow employed, the battery either becomes an explosive danger or at best the current rapidly falls off, with its consequent loss of power.

May, 1917.

How far awry my plans have gone this year! I was to make good in writing—I've not touched it. I thought I had done with the meddling of social work—I've spent my whole year at it. In a sense I'm satisfied with the job. I've called an organization into being that's doing good work, and needed work; we've got Day Nurseries in sight. A dozen other women are working well who otherwise wouldn't have had a niche to work in . . . The other day when I was getting up an open meeting and spending the day at the telephone, I wept because I came across a jumbled untouched verse manuscript. Yet I suppose I'd reverse the cause of tears if I were to pin my next decade to writing alone. And yet oh, I long to prove myself by writing! The best seems to die in me when I give it up. It is the self I love—not this efficient, philanthropic self. . . .

[Written when Ruth Benedict was thirty-three, on the verge of discovering her career in anthropology:]

October, 1920

There is good in me, and Oh! there is great good in Stanley. And we've both of us a decent measure of self-control. Why must we go on hurting each other so cruelly? I feel about it as I might if we were two children I've never had. I think I've no more resentment than if he *were* my child—and I wonder sometimes if I'm not just as powerless to right things as if I were the mother. For it isn't a question of greater self-control—the more I control myself to his requirements, the greater violence I shall do my own—kill them in the end. I know so well what he needs: —he's taken me once for all—the intimacy is proved, established; all he asks is to keep an even tenor. And, knowing this, for years I can keep away from subjects which disrupt the quiet—my own ambitions; my sense of futility; children—chiefly children. But I'm made on the exactly antithetical scheme—it is my necessary breath of life to understand and expression is the only justification of life that I can feel without prodding. The greatest relief I know is to have put something in words, no matter if it's as stabbing as this is to me; and even to have him say cruel things to me is better than an utter silence about his viewpoint, year in and year out. —And so it's insoluble—a wanton cruelty to him no less than to me. So we grow more and more strangers to the other—united only by gusts of feelings that grow to seem more and more emptiness in our lives, not part and parcel of them; and by an intolerable pity for each other as human beings cruelly tortured.

[Fourteen years later, after she had separated from Stanley and was established in her profession:]

June 9, 1934.

What is this need I have so strongly and which comes over me only the more overwhelmingly after I've been faithful for a while to my jobs and duties? It's nothing that I can recognize in the other people I see much of; their needs could all be met by certain adjustments in the external world or in their own thinking. They set up various kinds of relationships with work and things and people—love relationships or experiences of a will to power—and it's in these relationships that their life flowers or goes to waste. I can't get hold of either attitude really; work even when I'm satisfied with it is never my child I love nor my servant I've brought to heel. It's always busy work I do with my left hand, and part of me watches grudging the waste of a lifetime. It is always distraction—and from what? It's hard to say. From contemplation and detachment, from an impersonal candor that knows work and people in their proper proportions—that sees existence under the form of eternity, maybe. I wish I had lived in a generation that cultivated the spiritual life; perhaps then I wouldn't have felt so frustrated. Perhaps, though, in having this life traditionally channelled for me, I'd have been content with the fortuitous degree that was provided, that seems intolerable to me, for the great reward that my temperament has ever given me is detachment and unconcern. That can't by definition come in the course of traditional participation, even in a cult of spiritual life. As it seems to me now there is no way to achieve these rewards if one has signed on a dotted line. And if one has not, the way is painful and erratic. Perhaps one day the right environment will be hit upon and a culture will arise that by its very nature fosters spiritual life that is nevertheless detached and adventurous—something of the sort that Spinoza or Christ achieved in certain flashes. It's nothing that has appeared on earth yet.

What might it be like? Chiefly a great sureness, experience out of which belief and existing has passed with all the other traits of temporality, love that could recognize no private motive in its glad acceptance of whatever was unrolled before it. Work could not be alien to it, certainly not friendship, but to work or to live would not be distraction but largess of its own prodigal security. It would be so amply foundationed upon verities that are not the sport of time and chance that incidents of faithlessness, of failure, of death, would not touch its being. The many changes would all have departed and these to whom the life of the spirit was a reality could pass in and out of the temple at will, their smallest acts lit with the radiance of their knowledge. It's a dream.

UNKNOWN JAPANESE
WOMAN
(1866-1900)

*O*ne *of the most extraordinary* literary men of his time
was Lafcadio Hearn, an American journalist who
adopted Japan as his home, married a Japanese and became a
Buddhist and teacher at the Imperial University, and wrote
some dozen books interpreting Japan for the West. Early in
1900 he received the manuscript of a diary—"seventeen long
narrow sheets of soft paper, pierced with a silken string, and
covered with fine Japanese characters."

The writer had died and the diary was one of the few
possessions she left. Hearn's decision to undertake its translation seemed to spring not only from his appreciation of its
touching qualities but from a love of certain qualities con-
spicuous in Japanese women of his time.

Writing in 1902, he said, "I doubt if anyone not really
familiar with the life of Japan can fully understand this simple
history." And he goes on to outline circumstances that we in
the West have since become more acquainted with, that the
wife of a poor man must cook outside in freezing weather,
that the woman and her husband lived in a tiny house with
only a few mats. He explains the old Japanese custom of
arranging marriages, and that a woman of twenty-nine would

be eager to accept a poor man rather than none at all. And he tells us of the infant mortality rate and the unlikelihood of survival among young adults in poverty.

He writes, "To me the chief significance of this humble confession of struggle and failure is not in the utterance of anything exceptional, but in the expression of something as common to Japanese life as blue air and sunshine. The brave resolve of the woman to win affection by docility and by faultless performance of duty, her gratitude for every small kindness, her childlike piety, her supreme unselfishness, her Buddhist interpretation of suffering as the penalty for some fault committed in a previous life, her attempts to write poetry when her heart was breaking—all this indeed, I find touching, and more than touching. But I do not find it exceptional. The traits revealed are typical—typical of the moral nature of the woman of the people. Perhaps there are not many Japanese women of the same humble class who could express their personal joy and pain in a record at once so artless and pathetic; but there are millions of such women inheriting—from ages and ages of unquestioning faith—a like conception of life as duty, and an equal capacity of unselfish attachment."

And yet reading the diary today, we find a universality that cuts across cultural attitudes and conditioning. Is this woman's inner life so peculiar to her short span of time? She expresses a tenderness with her husband that is no less desirable to every woman for being rare. And there is in her grief a quality that brings us again to the old notion of "character." She assumes responsibility for death with the same willingness with which she assumed the life-giving process.

Perhaps it was easier for Lafcadio Hearn to ignore the repressiveness of the Japanese society he lived in than it is for us today. And his admiration of Japanese culture bore with it a definite rejection of the trappings of western society. But trappings do not make the "moral nature of the woman of the people," nor does the habit of repressing her in an abject social status. We imagine that the source of character may not be in social or political process at all, but that its mysterious inner origin even the Freudian years have not managed to explain.

We have made some adaptations in Hearn's translation for modern readers where he has offered two, sometimes three, translations; and where he has supplied original Japanese text for the poetry, we have retained only the translations.

A Woman's Diary

1895

[The first few diary entries outline the arrangements made by a matchmaker whereby the young woman of twenty-nine becomes the betrothed of Namiki-Shi, a widower. Together with her mother she visits his house, and despite her shyness, which kept her from looking at the man, she immediately gave her consent to a wedding day. When her father objected that it was too soon, that the "signs" were unfavorable, she showed her determination.]

I said:

"But I have already promised; and I cannot now ask to have the day changed . . . As for the matter of the [signs] being unlucky, even though I should have to die on that account, I would not complain; for I should die in my own husband's house. . . . And tomorrow," I added, "I shall be too busy to call on Goto [her brother-in-law]: so I must go there now."

I went to Goto's; but, when I saw him, I felt afraid to say exactly what I had come to say. I suggested it only by telling him:

"Tomorrow I have to go to a strange house."

Goto immediately asked:

"As an honorable bride?"

After hesitating, I answered at last:

"Yes."

"What kind of a person?" Goto asked.

I answered:

"If I had felt myself able to look at him long enough to form any opinion, I would not have put mother to the trouble of going with me."

"Elder Sister!" he exclaimed. "Then what was the use of going to see him at all? . . . But," he added, in a more pleasant tone, "let me wish you luck."

"Anyhow," I said, "to-morrow it will be."

And I returned home.

Now the appointed day having come . . . I had so much to do that I did not know how I should ever be able to get ready. And as it had been raining for several days, the roadway was very bad, which made matters worse for me—though, luckily, no rain fell on that day. I had to buy some little things; and I could not well ask mother to do anything for me—much as I wished for her help—because her feet had become very weak by reason of her great age. So I got up very early and went out alone, and did the best I could; nevertheless, it was two o'clock in the afternoon before I got everything ready.

Then I had to go to the hair-dresser's to have my hair dressed, and to go to the bath-house—all of which took time. And when I came back to dress, I found that no message had yet been received from Namiki-Shi; and I began to feel a little anxious. Just after we had finished supper, the message came. I had scarcely time to say good-bye to all: then I went out—leaving my home behind forever—and walked with mother to the house of Okada-Shi [the matchmaker, and a family friend].

There I had to part even from mother; and the wife of Okada-Shi taking charge of me, I accompanied her to the house of Namiki-Shi. . . .

The wedding ceremony . . . having been performed without any difficulty, and the time of the honorable leave-taking having come more quickly than I had expected, the guests all returned home.

Afterward, at the hour of meals, I felt very much distressed. . . .

Two or three days later, the father of my husband's former wife visited me, and said:

"Namiki-Shi is really a good man—a moral, steady man, but as he is also very particular about small matters and inclined to find fault, you had better always be careful to try to please him."

Now as I had been carefully watching my husband's ways from the beginning, I knew that he was really a very strict man, and I resolved so to conduct myself in all matters as never to cross his will.

The fifth day of the tenth month was the day for our first visit to my parents' house, and for the first time we went out together, calling at Goto's on the way. After we left Goto's the weather suddenly became bad, and it began to rain. Then we borrowed a paper parasol, which we used as an umbrella, and though I was very uneasy lest any of my former neighbors should see us walking thus together we luckily reached my parents' house, and made our visit of duty, without any trouble at all. While we were in the house, the rain fortunately stopped. . . .

During this last month of the year I made new spring robes for my husband and myself; then I learned for the first time how pleasant such work was, and I felt very happy . . .

Revelations

[After an outing to visit a Shinto shrine with her husband, and dining out with him in a restaurant, she wrote the following poem for her diary, freely translated by Hearn:]

> Having been taken across the Imado-Ferry, I strangely met at the temple of Mimeguri-Inair with a person whom I had never seen before. Because of this meeting our relation is now even more the relation of husband and wife. And my first anxious doubt, having passed away, my mind has become clear as the Sumida River. Indeed we are now like a pair of Miyako-birds (always together); and I even think that I deserve to be envied . . . More than the pleasure of viewing a whole shore in blossom is the pleasure I now desire—always to dwell with this person, dearer to me than any flower, until we enter the White-Haired Temple. That we may so remain, I supplicate the Gods!

On the second day of the fifth month we visited the gardens at Okubo to see the azaleas in blossom.

So far we have never had any words between us nor any disagreement; and I have ceased to feel bashful when we go out visiting or sight-seeing. Now each of us seemed to think only of how to please the other; and I felt sure that nothing would ever separate us . . . May our relation always be thus happy!

On the first day of the eighth month we went to the Temple of Asakusa to pray—that day being the first anniversary of the death of my husband's former wife. Afterward we went to an eel-house, near the Azuma bridge, for dinner, and while we were there—just about the hour of noon—an earthquake took place. Being close to the river, the house rocked very much; and I was greatly frightened. Remembering that when we went to Asakusa before in the time of cherry blossoms, we had seen a big fire, this earthquake made me feel anxious; I wondered whether lightning would come next.

About two o'clock we left the eating-house and went to the Asakusa park. From there we went by street-car to Kanda; and we stopped awhile at a cool place in Kanda to rest ourselves . . .

1897

. . . Now we were very happy because of the child that was to be born. And I thought how proud and glad my parents would be at having a grandchild for the first time. . . .

On the eighth day of the sixth month, at four o'clock in the afternoon, a boy was born. Both mother and child appeared to be as well as could be wished; and the child much resembled my husband; and its eyes were large and black. . . . But I must say that it was a very small child; for, though it ought to have been born in the eighth month, it was born indeed in the sixth. . . . At seven o'clock in the evening of the same day, when the time came to give the child some medicine, we saw, by the light of the lamp, that he was looking all about, with his big eyes wide open. During that night the child slept in my mother's bosom. As we had been told that he must be kept very warm, because he was only a seven months' child, it was decided that he should be kept in the bosom by day as well as by night.

Next day . . . at half-past six o'clock in the afternoon, he suddenly died. . . .

"Brief is the time of pleasure, and quickly turns to pain; and whatsoever is born must necessarily die";—that, indeed, is a true saying about this world.

Only for one day to be called a mother! to have a child born only to see it die! . . . Surely, I thought, if a child must die within two days after birth, it were better that it should never be born.

From the twelfth to the sixth month I had been so ill!—then at last I had obtained some ease, and joy at the birth of a son; and I had received so many congratulations about my good fortune;—and, nevertheless, he was dead! . . . Indeed, I suffered great grief.

On the tenth day of the sixth month the funeral took place, at the temple called Senpukuji, in Okubo, and a small tomb was erected.

> If I could only have known! Ah this parting with the flower, for which I would so gladly have given my own life, has left my sleeves wet with the dew!

Some little time afterward, people told me that if I planted the *sotoba** upside down, another misfortune of this kind would not come to pass. I had a great many sorrowful doubts about doing such a thing; but at last, on the ninth day of the eighth month, I had the *sotoba* reversed.

1898

On the nineteenth day of the eighth month of the thirty-first year of Meiji my second child was born, almost painlessly—a girl; and we named her Hatsu.

We invited to the feast all those who had helped us at the time of the child's birth.

Mother afterwards remained with me for a couple of days; but she was then obliged to leave me, because my sister

---

* The *sotoba* is a tall wooden lath, inscribed with Buddhist texts, and planted above a grave . . .

Kō was suffering from severe pains in the chest. Fortunately my husband had his regular vacation about the same time; and he helped me all he could—even in regard to washing and other matters; but I was often greatly troubled because I had no woman with me. . . .

Up to the time of one hundred days after my daughter's birth, I was constantly anxious about her, because she often seemed to have a difficulty in breathing. But that passed off at last, and she appeared to be getting strong.

Still, we were unhappy about one matter—a deformity; Hatsu had been born with a double thumb on one hand. For a long time we could not make up our minds to take her to a hospital, in order to have an operation performed. But at last a woman living near our house told us of a very skillful surgeon . . . and we decided to go to him. My husband held the child on his lap during the operation. I could not bear to see the operation; and I waited in the next room, my heart full of pain and fear, wondering how the matter would end. But the little one did not appear to suffer any pain; and she took the breast as usual a few minutes after. So the matter ended more fortunately than I had thought possible.

At home she continued to take her milk as before, and seemed as if nothing had been done to her little body. But as she was so very young we were afraid that the operation might in some way cause her to be sick. By way of precaution, I went with her to the hospital every day for about three weeks; but she showed no sign of sickness. . . .

On the twenty-ninth day of the fourth month Hatsu appeared to be unwell: so I wanted to have her examined by a doctor.

A doctor promised to come the same morning, but he did not come, and I waited for him in vain all that day. Next day again I waited, but he did not come. Toward evening Hatsu became worse, and seemed to be suffering great pain in her breast, and I resolved to take her to a doctor early next morning. All through that night I was very uneasy about her, but at daybreak she seemed to be better. So I went out alone, taking her on my back, and walked to the office of a doctor in Akasaka. But when I asked to have the child examined, I was told that I must wait, as it was not yet the regular time for seeing patients.

While I was waiting, the child began to cry worse than ever before; she would not take the breast, and I could do nothing to soothe her, either by walking or resting, so that I was greatly troubled. At last the doctor came, and began to examine her; and in the same moment I noticed that her crying grew feebler, and that her lips were becoming paler and paler. Then, as I could not remain silent, seeing her thus, I had to ask, "How is her condition?" "She cannot live until evening," he answered. "But could you not give her medicine?" I asked. "If she could drink it," he replied.

I wanted to go back home at once, and send word to my husband and to my father's house; but the shock had been too much for me—all my strength suddenly left me. Fortunately a kind old woman came to my aid, and carried my umbrella and other things, and helped me to get into a jinrikisha, so that I was able to return home by jinrikisha. Then I sent a man to tell my husband and my father. Mita's wife came to help me; and with her assistance everything possible was done to help the child. . . . Still my husband did not come back. But all our pain and trouble was in vain.

So, on the second day of the fifth month of the thirty-second year, my child set out on her journey to the heaven of Amida—never to return to this world.

And we, her father and mother, were yet living—though we had caused her death by neglecting to have her treated by a skilled doctor! This thought made us both sorrow greatly; and we often reproached ourselves in vain.

But the day after her death the doctor said to us: "Even if that disease had been treated from the beginning by the best possible means, your child could not have lived more than a week. . . ." Then he explained to us that the child had died from a nephritis.

Thus all the hopes that we had, and all the pains that we took in caring for her, and all the pleasure of watching her grow during those nine months—all were in vain!

But we two were at last able to find some ease from our sorrow by reflecting that our relation to this child, from the time of some former life, must have been very slight and weak.

In the loneliness of that weary time, I tried to express my heart by writing some verses: . . .

Here in this house it was that I married him;—well I remember the day—five years ago. Here was born the girl-baby—the loved one whom we hoped to rear. Caring then no longer for my person (heedless of how I dressed when I went out)—thinking only of how to bring her up—I lived. How pitiless (this doom of mine)! Never had I even dreamed that such a thing could befall me: my only thoughts were as to how my Hatsu could best be reared. When she grows up, I thought, soon we shall find her a good husband, to make her life happy. So, never going out for pleasure-seeking, I studied only how to care for my little one—how to love and to cherish my husband and my Hatsu. Vain now, alas! this hoped-for joy of living only for her sake . . . Once having known the delight of the relation of mother and child, deign to think of the heart of the mother who sees her child die before her!

> Now, while husband and wife,
> each clasping the hands of the other,

make lament together,
if anyone pausing at the entrance
should listen to their sorrow,
surely the paper window
would be moistened by tears from without.

About the time of Hatsu's death, the law concerning funerals was changed for the better; and permission was given for the burning of corpses in Okubo. So I asked Namiki to have the body sent to the temple of which his family had always been parishioners—providing that there should be no legal difficulty about the matter. Accordingly the funeral took place and the ashes were interred. . . .

My sister Kō was sick in bed with a rather bad cold at the time of Hatsu's death; but she visited us very soon after the news had reached her. And she called again a few days later to tell us that she had become almost well, and that we had no more cause to feel anxious about her.

As for myself, I felt a dread of going anywhere, and I did not leave the house for a whole month. But as custom does not allow one to remain always indoors, I had to go out at last; and I made the required visit to father's and to my sister's.

Having become quite ill, I hoped that mother would be able to help me. But Kō was again sick and Yoshi [a younger sister] and mother had both to attend her constantly: so I could get no aid from father's house. There was no one to help me except some of my female neighbors, who attended me out of pure kindness, when they could spare the time. . . .

On the fourth day of the ninth month my sister Kō died of consumption.

It had been agreed beforehand that if an unexpected

matter came to pass, my younger sister Yoshi should be received in place of Kō. As Goto-Shi found it inconvenient to live altogether alone, the marriage took place on the eleventh day of the same month; and the usual congratulations were offered.

On the last day of the same month Okada-Shi suddenly died.

We found ourselves greatly troubled by the expenses that all these events caused us.

1900

On the twentieth day of the second month, at six o'clock in the morning, my third child—a boy—was born. Both mother and child were well.

We had expected a girl, but it was a boy that was born; so, when my husband came back from his work, he was greatly surprised and pleased to find that he had a boy.

But the child was not well able to take the breast: so we had to nourish him by means of a feeding-bottle.

On the seventh day after the boy's birth, we partly shaved his head. And in the evening we had the seventh-day festival—but, this time, all by ourselves.

My husband had caught a bad cold some time before; and he could not go to work next morning, as he was coughing badly. So he remained in the house.

Early in the morning the child had taken his milk as usual. But, about ten o'clock in the forenoon, he seemed to be suffering great pain in his breast; and he began to moan so strangely that we sent a man for a doctor. Unfortunately the doctor that we asked to come was out of town; and we were told that he would not come back before night. Therefore, we thought that it would be better to send at once for another doctor; and we sent for one. He said that he would come in the evening. But, about two o'clock in the afternoon, the child's sickness suddenly became worse; and a little before three o'clock—the twenty-seventh day of the second month— (Piteous to say!)—my child was dead, having lived for only eight days. . . .

I thought to myself that, even if this new misfortune did not cause my husband to feel an aversion for me, thus having to part with all my children, one after another, must be the punishment of some wrong done in the time of a former life. And, so thinking, I knew that my sleeves would never again become dry—that the rain of tears would never cease—that never again in this world would the sky grow clear for me.

And more and more I wondered whether my husband's feelings would not change for the worse, by reason of his having to meet such trouble, over and over again on my account. I felt anxious about his heart, because of what already was in my own.

Nevertheless, he only repeated the words: "From the decrees of Heaven there is no escape."

I thought that I should be better able to visit the tomb of my child if he were buried in some temple near us. So the funeral took place in Okubo; and the ashes were buried there. . . .

> All the delight having perished,
> hopeless I remain:
> It was only a dream of Spring!

I wonder whether it was because of the sorrow that I suffered—my face and limbs became slightly swollen during the week after my boy's death.

It was nothing very serious, after all, and it soon went away. . . . Now the period of twenty-one days, the period of danger is past. . . .

[Here the diary ended. Hearn tells us that she herself died within two weeks after her child.]

DOROTHY WORDSWORTH

(1 7 7 1 - 1 8 5 5)

*D*orothy Wordsworth's parents died when she was young, and she was raised separately from her poet brother William by a succession of relatives. Their childhood dream of living together was realized when they settled at Dove Cottage near Grasmere in England's Lake District. A frugal existence but the happiest time of Dorothy's life: she kept not only house but a journal "to please William." Modest in intent, the journal was the resource for many of the finest of Wordsworth's poems. She was a born descriptive writer of nature and the life of the beggars and peddlers she observed on their long walks. Apart from her devotion to her brother, she might never have written at all. "I would detest," she said once, "to set myself up as an author."

We have printed extracts from her journal which surround William's marriage to Mary Hutchinson. It was a difficult period for Dorothy. She knew that William needed the fulfillment of marriage and she approved of his choice: Mary Hutchinson and her sister Sara were devoted friends. We must read between the lines the accommodation of feelings she experienced in making herself ready to welcome an intruder into what had been for her a complete existence at Dove Cottage. The journal had never been an outlet for Dorothy's deepest feelings or a place for analysis of the nature of her intensely close relationship with her brother. William never emerges as a character; she quotes not a line of his speech; he is rather a presence about whom her life revolves.

William was too busy to write to his fiancée. With a sense of duty free of self-pity, Dorothy essentially wrote his love letters for him, saw him off on his unexpected visits to Mary, and waited impatiently for the letter that announced their firm intention to marry. There seems to have been no question that Dorothy would live with the newlyweds.

After the marriage, despite her resolutions to continue, Dorothy wrote infrequently in the journal; in January of 1804 the entries stop abruptly. She seems to have adjusted to her new position; she loved William and Mary's children as her own and her daily companionship with Mary may have provided a substitute for journal keeping. From all evidence, the two women lived in total harmony, content with their loving work of serving genius.

Dorothy's health eventually failed and her mind was affected, probably by what would now be diagnosed as arteriosclerosis. Her strong self-discipline and exercise of personal character gave way during the last twenty years of her life to a childish querulousness. She survived her brother by five years, nursed by Mary, whose letters—another story—always referred to her sister-in-law as "Dear Dorothy."

———————————

Sunday 31st [January 1802]

William had slept very ill—he was tired and had a bad headache. We walked round the two lakes. Grasmere was very soft and Rydale was extremely beautiful from the pasture side. Nab Scar was just topped by a cloud which cutting it off as high as it could be cut off made the mountain look uncommonly lofty. We sate down a long time in different places. I always love to walk that way because it is the way I first came to Rydale and Grasmere, and because our dear Coleridge did also. When I came with Wm 6½ years ago it was just at sunset. There was a rich yellow light on the waters and the Islands were reflected there. Today it was grave and soft but not perfectly calm. William says it was much such a day as when Coleridge came with him. The sun shone out before we reached Grasmere. We sate by the roadside at the foot of the Lake close to Mary's dear name which she had cut herself upon the stone. William . . . cut at it with his knife to make it plainer. We amused ourselves for a long time in watching the Breezes some as if they came from the bottom of the lake spread in a circle, brushing along the surface of the water, and growing more delicate, as it were thinner and of a *paler* colour till they died away. Others spread out like a peacock's tail, and some went right forward this way and that in all directions. The lake was still where these breezes were not, but they made it all alive. I found a strawberry blossom in a rock. The little slender flower had more courage than the green leaves, for *they* were but half expanded and half grown, but the blossom was spread full out. I uprooted it rashly, and I felt as if I had been committing an outrage, so I planted it again. It will have but a stormy life of it, but let it live if it can . . . I brought a handkerchief full of mosses, which I placed on the chimneypiece . . . Mr. Simpson drank tea with us. We payed our rent to Benson. William's head bad after Mr S. was gone. I petted him on the carpet and began a letter to Sara.

Sunday 14th February.

A fine morning. The sun shines but it has been a hard frost in the night. There are some little snowdrops that are afraid to pop their white heads quite out, and a few blossoms of Hepatica that are half starved. William left me at work altering some passages of the Pedlar, and went into the orchard. The fine day pushed him on to resolve and . . . he said he would go to Penrith,* so Molly was dispatched for the horse. I worked hard, got the backs pasted the writing finished, and all quite trim. I . . . put up some letters for Mary H., and off he went in his blue Spenser and a pair of *new* pantaloons fresh from London . . . Before sunset I put on my shawl and walked out. The snow-covered mountains were spotted with rich sunlight, a palish buffish colour. The roads were very dirty, for though it was a keen frost the sun had melted the snow and water upon them . . . when I came in view of Rydale I cast a long look upon the mountains beyond. They were very white but I concluded that Wm would have a very safe passage over Kirkstone, and I was quite easy about him. . . .

I got tea when I reached home and read German till about 9 o'clock . . . Went to bed at about 12 o'clock. I slept in Wm's bed, and I slept badly, for my thoughts were full of William.

Tuesday 16th.

A fine morning but I had persuaded myself not to expect William, I believe because I was afraid of being disappointed. I ironed all day. He came in just at Tea time, had only seen Mary H. for a couple of hours between Emont Bridge and Hartshorn tree . . . He had had a difficult journey over Kirkstone, and came home by Threlkeld—his mouth and breath were very cold when he kissed me. We spent a sweet evening. He was better—had altered the pedlar. We went to bed pretty soon and we slept better than we expected and had no bad dreams. . . .

* i.e., to see Mary Hutchinson.

Revelations

I was so unlucky as to propose to rewrite The Pedlar. Wm got to work and was worn to death. We did not walk. I wrote in the afternoon.

Thursday [*4th*].

. . . Since he has left me (at ½ past 11) it is now two I have been putting the Drawers into order, laid by his clothes which we had thrown here and there and everywhere, filed two months' newspapers and got my dinner 2 boiled eggs and 2 apple tarts . . . I transplanted some snowdrops—The Bees are busy—Wm has a nice bright day. It was hard frost in the night. The Robins are singing sweetly. Now for my walk. I *will* be busy, I *will* look well and be well when he comes back to me. O the Darling! Here is one of his bitten apples! I can hardly find in my heart to throw it into the fire. I must wash myself, then off—I walked round the two Lakes crossed the stepping stones at Rydale Foot. Sate down where we always sit. I was full of thoughts about my darling. Blessings on him. . . .

Sunday Morning [*7th*].

A very fine clear frost. I stitched up the Pedlar—wrote out Ruth—read it with the alterations. Then wrote Mary H. Read a little German—got my dinner. Mrs Lloyd called at the door; and in came William. I did not expect him till tomorrow. How glad I was. After we had talked about an hour I gave him his dinner a Beef Steak, we sate talking and happy. . . .

DOROTHY WORDSWORTH

Saturday Morning [*13th*].

It was as cold as ever it had been all winter very hard frost. I baked pies Bread, and seed-cake . . . William finished Alice Fell, and then he wrote the Poem of the Beggar woman taken from a Woman whom I had seen in May—(now nearly 2 years ago) . . . I sate with him at Intervals all the morning, took down his stanzas etc. After dinner we walked to Rydale, for letters—it was terribly cold we had 2 or 3 brisk hail showers. The hail stones looked clean and pretty upon the dry clean Road . . . After tea I read to William that account* of the little Boys belonging to the tall woman and an unlucky thing it was for he could not escape from those very words, and so he could not write the poem. He left it unfinished and went tired to Bed. In our walk from Rydale he had got warmed with the subject and had half cast the Poem.

Wednesday [17th].

William went up into the orchard and finished the Poem . . . I went and sate with W. and walked backwards and forwards in the orchard till dinner time—he read me his poem. I broiled Beefsteaks. After dinner we made a pillow of my shoulder, I read to him and my Beloved slept—I afterwards got him the pillows and he was lying with his head on the table when Miss Simpson came in. She stayed tea. . . .

Thursday [18th].

. . . As we came along Ambleside vale in the twilight—it was a grave evening—there was something in the air that compelled me to serious thought. The hills were large, closed

* From her journal.

in by the sky. It was nearly dark when I parted from the Lloyds that is, night was come on and the moon was overcast. But as I climbed Moss the moon came out from behind a mountain mass of Black clouds—O the unutterable darkness of the sky and the earth below the moon! and the glorious brightness of the moon itself! There was a vivid sparkling streak of light at this end of Rydale water but the rest was very dark and Loughrigg fell and Silver How were white and bright as if they were covered with hoar frost. The moon retired again and appeared and disappeared several times before I reached home. Once there was no moonlight to be seen but upon the Island house and the promontory of the Island where it stands, 'That needs must be a holy place'* etc. etc. I had many very exquisite feelings and when I saw this lowly Building in the waters among the Dark and lofty hills, with that bright soft light upon it, it made me more than half a poet. I was tired when I reached home. I could not sit down to reading and tried to write verses but alas! . . .

Tuesday [23rd].

. . . He is now reading Ben Jonson I am going to read German it is about 10 o'clock, a quiet night. The fire flutters and the watch ticks I hear nothing else save the Breathing of my Beloved and he now and then pushes his book forward and turns over a leaf. . . .

Wednesday 7th [April].

Wm's birthday. Wm went to Middleham.† I walked six miles with him. . . .

* This line is untraced. It could perhaps be from an early version of *Kubla Khan*.
† To see Mary Hutchinson.

Monday 12th.

. . . The ground covered with snow. Walked to T. Wilkinson's and sent for letters. The Woman brought me one from Wm and Mary. It was a sharp windy night. Thomas Wilkinson came with me to Barton, and questioned me like a catechizer all the way. Every question was like the snapping of a little thread about my heart I was so full of thoughts of my half-read letter and other things. I was glad when he left me. Then I had time to look at the moon while I was thinking over my own thoughts. The moon travelled through the clouds tinging them yellow as she passed along, with two stars near her, one larger than the other. These stars grew or diminished as they passed from or went into the clouds. At this time William as I found the next day was riding by himself between Middleham and Barnard Castle having parted from Mary. I read over my letter when I got to the house. . . .

Tuesday 13th April.

I had slept ill and was not well and obliged to go to bed in the afternoon . . . After tea I went down to see the Bank and walked along the Lake side to the field . . . The air was become still the lake was of a bright slate colour, the hills darkening. The Bays shot into the low fading shores. Sheep resting all things quiet. When I returned Jane met me—*William* was come. The surprize shot through me. He looked well but he was tired and went soon to bed after a dish of Tea.

Thursday 15th.

. . . When we were in the woods beyond Gowbarrow park we saw a few daffodils close to the water side. We fancied that the lake had floated the seeds ashore and that the little colony had so sprung up. But as we went along there were more and yet more and at last under the boughs of the trees, we saw that there was a long belt of them along the shore, about the breadth of a country turnpike road. I never saw daffodils so beautiful they grew among the mossy stones about and about them, some rested their heads upon these stones as on a pillow for weariness and the rest tossed and reeled and danced and seemed as if they verily laughed with the wind that blew upon them over the lake, they looked so gay ever glancing ever changing. This wind blew directly over the lake to them. There was here and there a little knot and a few stragglers a few yards higher up but they were so few as not to disturb the simplicity and unity and life of that one busy highway. . . .

Sunday 18th.

. . . We sate up late. He met me with the conclusion of the poem of the Robin. I read it to him in Bed. We left out some lines.

Monday May 10th.

William is still at work though it is past 10 o'clock—he will be tired out I am sure. My heart fails in me . . . An affecting letter from Mary H. . . .

Sunday 23rd.

. . . William was very nervous. I was ill in the afternoon, took laudanum. . . .

Monday 31st.

. . . My tooth broke today. They will soon be gone. Let that pass I shall be beloved—I want no more.

Monday June 14th.

I was very unwell—went to bed before I drank my tea—was sick and afterwards almost asleep when Wm brought me a letter from Mary which he read to me sitting by the bedside. . . .

Tuesday 15th.

. . . a letter from M. H. . . . and one from Sara . . . William did not read them. M. H. growing fat.

Thursday 17th.

William had slept well. I took castor oil and lay in bed till 12 o'clock. William injured himself with working a little. —When I got up we sate in the orchard, a sweet mild day. Miss Hudson called. I went with her to the top of the hill. When I came home I found William at work, attempting to alter a stanza in the poem on our going for Mary which I convinced him did not need altering. . . .

Sunday 20th.

He had slept better than I could have expected but he was far from well all day; we were in the orchard a great part of the morning. After tea we walked upon our own path for a long time . . . We lay upon the sloping Turf. Earth and sky were so lovely that they melted our very hearts. The sky to the north was of a chastened yet rich yellow fading into pale blue and streaked and scattered over with steady islands of purple melting away into shades of pink. It made my heart almost feel like a vision to me. . . .

Friday June 25th.

Wm had not fallen asleep till after 3 o'clock but he slept tolerably. Miss Simpson came to colour the rooms. I began with white-washing the ceiling. I worked with them (William was very busy) till dinner time but after dinner I went to bed and fell asleep. When I rose I went just before tea into the garden. I looked up at my Swallow's nest and it was gone. It had fallen down. Poor little creatures they could not themselves be more distressed than I was. I went upstairs to look at the Ruins. They lay in a large heap upon the window ledge; these Swallows had been ten days employed in building this nest, and it seemed to be almost finished. I had watched them early in the morning, in the day many and many a time and in the evenings when it was almost dark I had seen them sitting together side by side in their unfinished nest both morning and night. When they first came about the window they used to hang against the panes, with their white Bellies and their forked tails looking like fish, but then they fluttered and sang their own little twittering song. As soon as the nest was broad enough, a sort of ledge for them they sate both mornings and evenings, but they did not pass the night there. I watched them one morning, when William was at Eusemere, for more than an hour. Every now and then there was a feeling motion in their wings, a sort of tremulousness and they sang a low song to one another.

DOROTHY WORDSWORTH

Thursday 7th.

. . . In the afternoon after we had talked a little, Wm fell asleep, I read the Winter's Tale. Then I went to bed but did not sleep. The Swallows stole in and out of their nest, and sater *whiles* quite still, *whiles* they sung low for 2 minutes or more at a time just like a muffled Robin. William was looking at the Pedlar when I got up. He arranged it, and after tea I wrote it out—280 lines. In the meantime the evening being fine he carried his coat to the Tailor's and went to George Mackareth's to engage the horse. He came in to me at about ½ past nine pressing me to go out; he had got letters which we were to read out of doors—I was rather unwilling, fearing I could not see to read the letters, but I saw well enough. One was from M. H., a very tender affecting letter . . . The moon was behind. William hurried me out in hopes that I should see her. We walked first to the top of the hill to see Rydale. It was dark and dull but our own vale was very solemn. The shape of Helm Crag was quite distinct, though black. We walked backwards and forwards on the White Moss path there was a sky-like white brightness on the lake. The Wyke Cottage Light at the foot of Silver How. Glow-worms out, but not so numerous as last night. O beautiful place! Dear Mary William. The horse is come Friday morning, so I must give over. William is eating his Broth. I must prepare to go. The Swallows I must leave them the well the garden the Roses, all. Dear creatures!! they sang last night after I was in bed—seemed to be singing to one another, just before they settled to rest for the night. Well, I must go. Farewell. ——

[The following morning Dorothy and William left behind the home they had shared at Dove Cottage to make a visit to France before William's marriage in October. Mary Hutchinson's wedding trip consisted of the return trip to Grasmere, accompanied by Dorothy.]

. . . On Monday 4th October 1802, my Brother William was married to Mary Hutchinson. I slept a good deal of the night and rose fresh and well in the morning. At a little after 8 o'clock I saw them go down the avenue towards the Church. William had parted from me upstairs. I gave him the wedding ring—with how deep a blessing! I took it from my forefinger where I had worn it the whole of the night before—he slipped it again onto my finger and blessed me fervently. When they were absent my dear little Sara prepared the breakfast. I kept myself as quiet as I could, but when I saw the two men running up the walk, coming to tell us it was over, I could stand it no longer and threw myself on the bed where I lay in stillness, neither hearing or seeing anything, till Sara came upstairs to me and said, 'They are coming'. This forced me from the bed where I lay and I moved I knew not how straight forward, faster than my strength could carry me till I met my beloved William and fell upon his bosom. He and John Hutchinson led me to the house and there I stayed to welcome my dear Mary. As soon as we had breakfasted we departed. It rained when we set off. Poor Mary was much agitated when she parted from her Brothers and Sisters and her home. . . .

We . . . arrived at Grasmere at about 6 o'clock on Wednesday Evening, the 6th of October 1802 . . . for my part I cannot describe what I felt, and our dear Mary's feelings would I dare say not be easy to speak of. We went by candle light into the garden and were astonished at the growth of the Brooms, Portugal Laurels, etc. etc. etc. The next day, Thursday, we unpacked the Boxes. On Friday 8th we baked Bread, and Mary and I walked, first upon the Hill side, and then in John's Grove, then in view of Rydale, the first walk that I had taken with my Sister.

DOROTHY WORDSWORTH

Thursday 4th [November].

I scalded my foot with coffee after having been in bed in the afternoon—I was near fainting, and then bad in my bowels. Mary waited upon me till 2 o'clock, then we went to bed and with applications of vinegar I was lulled to sleep about 4.

24th December 1802, Christmas Eve.

William is now sitting by me at ½ past 10 o'clock. I have been beside him ever since tea running the heel of a stocking, repeating some of his sonnets to him, listening to his own repeating, reading some of Milton's and the Allegro and Penseroso. It is a quiet keen frost. Mary is in the parlour below attending to the baking of cakes . . . Mary is well and I am well . . . It is today Christmas-day Saturday 25th December 1802. I am 31 years of age.—It is a dull frosty day. . . .

ALICE JAMES
(1848-1892)

lice James was born in New York City, the youngest of five children and the only daughter of a wealthy Swedenborgian philosopher. Her life would be unknown if it were not for her famous brothers, William the psychologist and Henry the novelist.

She suffered a typically grim Victorian girlhood, resisting its restrictions and the male teasing of the household by sassing back and developing a biting wit. By adolescence her need for assertion took the form of "neuralgia" attacks, fits of violent hysteria similar to descriptions of the tantrums experienced by Virginia Woolf and Ruth Benedict. She was an invalid by the age of twenty. Doctors could discover no organic cause beyond "nerves," various treatments were no help, and when she was thirty she asked her father for permission to commit suicide. Shrewdly, he granted it, asking her only "to do it in a perfectly gentle way in order not to distress her friends."

As Leon Edel comments, "Alice recognized that her inquiry had had a deeper purpose—that it had been one way of asserting her freedom. She told the elder Henry that 'now she could perceive it to be her *right* to dispose of her own body when life had become intolerable, she could never do it.' "*

* Leon Edel, "Portrait of Alice James," *The Diary of Alice James* (New York, Dodd, Mead & Co., 1964), p. 9.

ALICE JAMES

After her mother's death, Alice rallied for a time. She had a job to do; she was needed by her father and capably ran the household and nursed him through his final illness. For several months after his death she kept house for her brother Henry, with whom she had always had an affectionate relationship. It was a happy time for both, but Henry returned to England and Alice became friends with Katharine Peabody Loring, a vigorous and physically strong woman her own age who became her companion and nurse.

In 1884 the two women went to Europe, expecting to pay Henry a short visit in London; but Alice's nerves gave way almost immediately and she was never strong enough to return to America. Confined to a sickroom, with little experience of the world, her good mind and playful wit finally found outlet in 1889 when she began a journal in which she recorded her observations on English manners and politics and the scraps of gossip Henry brought her for amusement. When she was finally diagnosed as having an organic illness—then untreatable breast cancer—the journal became a courageous and remarkable document of the human spirit facing death. She didn't fear death itself, welcoming release from her long struggle between mind and body; but the process of dying was fearsome, one she felt an obligation to record honestly and well, revising passages by dictation until a few hours before her death at the age of forty-four.

Henry didn't know that Alice kept a journal, and when Katharine Loring presented him with a privately printed copy, he was shocked at the sight of his own gossip, often exaggerated, in print; he destroyed his copy. But later he felt that the quality of her writing brought further honor to the family name. He understood part of her story when he wrote, "in our family group girls seem scarcely to have had a chance," concluding that Alice's "tragic health was, in a manner, the only solution for her of the practical problem of life." But she possessed a personal integrity that transcends the hapless victim of circumstance. Before her death she wrote her brother William that he greatly exaggerated the tragic element "in my commonplace little journey."

> You must remember that a woman, by nature needs much less to feed upon than a man, a few emotions and she is satisfied: so when I am gone, pray don't think of me simply as a creature who might have been something else, had neurotic science been born. Notwithstanding the poverty of my outside experience, I have always had a significance for myself, and every chance to stumble along my straight and narrow little path, and to worship at the feet of my Deity, and what more can a human soul ask for?*

May 31st, 1889.

I think that if I get into the habit of writing a bit about what happens, or rather doesn't happen, I may lose a little of the sense of loneliness and desolation which abides with me. My circumstances allowing of nothing but the ejaculation of one-syllabled reflections, a written monologue by that most interesting being, *myself*, may have its yet to be discovered consolations. I shall at least have it all my own way and it may bring relief as an outlet to that geyser of emotions, sensations, speculations and reflections which ferments perpetually within my poor old carcass for its sins; so here goes, my first Journal!

* *Ibid.*, p. 15.

ALICE JAMES

June 4, 1889.

. . . I went out yesterday for the third time this year. They dragged the chair thro' a gate into a meadow and I lay in the sun whilst they picked me flowerets, with a cuckoo in the distance, circling swallows over head, broad sweeps of gentle wind slowly rustling thro' the trees near by; need I say I was happy? Someone who wants these rooms asked Miss Clarke if she had "got rid of the fidgetty old lady in the drawing room." It is so comic to hear oneself called old, even at 90 I suppose! What one reads, or rather all that comes to us is surely only of interest and value in proportion as we find ourselves therein, form given to what was vague, what slumbered stirred to life.

June 16, 1889.

. . . I have seen so little that my memory is packed with little bits which have not been wiped out by great ones, so that it all seems like a reminiscence and as I go along the childish impressions of light and colour come crowding back into my mind and with them the expectant, which then palpitated within me, lives for a ghostly moment.

July 12th

. . . It's amusing to see how, even on my microscopic field, minute events are perpetually taking place illustrative of the broadest facts of human nature. Yesterday Nurse and I had a good laugh but I must allow that decidedly she "had" me. I was thinking of something that interested me very much and my mind was suddenly flooded by one of those luminous waves that sweep out of consciousness all but the living sense and overpower one with joy in the rich, throbbing complexity of life, when suddenly I looked up at Nurse, who was dressing me, and saw her primitive, rudimentary expression (so common here) as of no inherited quarrel with her destiny of putting petticoats over my head; the poverty and deadness of it contrasted to the tide of speculation that was coursing thro' my brain made me exclaim, "Oh! Nurse, don't you wish you were inside of me!"—her look of dismay and vehement disclaimer—"Inside of you, Miss, when you have just had a sick headache for five days!"—gave a greater blow to my vanity, than that much battered article has ever received. The headache had gone off in the night and I had clean forgotten it—when the little wretch confronted me with it at this sublime moment when I was feeling the potency of a Bismarck, and left me powerless before the immutable law that however great we may seem to our own consciousness no human being would exchange his for ours, and before the fact that *my* glorious role was to stand for *Sick headache* to mankind! What a grotesque I am to be sure! Lying in this room, with the resistance of a thistle-down, having illusory moments of throbbing with the pulse of the Race, the Mystery to be solved at the next breath and the fountain of all Happiness within me—the sense of vitality, in short, simply proportionate to the excess of weakness!—To sit by and watch these absurdities is amusing in its way and reminds me of how I used to *listen* to my "company manners" in the days when I had 'em, and how ridiculous they sounded.

Ah! Those strange people who have the courage to be unhappy! *Are* they unhappy, by-the-way?

December 11, 1889.

How sick one gets of being "good," how much I should respect myself if I could burst out and make every one wretched for 24 hours; embody selfishness . . . If it were only voluntary and one made a conscious choice, it might enrich the soul a bit, but when it has become simply automatic thro' a sense of the expedient—of the grotesque futility of the perverse—it's degrading! And then the dolts praise one for being "amiable!" just as if one didn't avoid ruffling one's feathers as one avoids plum-pudding or any other indigestible compound!

December 12, 1889.

One day when my shawls were falling off to the left, my cushions falling out to the right and the duvet off my knees, one of those crises of misery in short, which are all in the day's work for an invalid Kath. exclaimed, "What an awful pity it is that you can't say *damn.*" I agreed with her from my heart. It is an immense loss to have all robust and sustaining expletives refined away from one! At such moments of trial refinement is a feeble reed to lean upon. I wonder, whether, if I had any education, I should have been more, or less, of a fool than I am. It would have deprived me surely of those exquisite moments of mental flatulence which every now and then inflate the cerebral vacuum with a delicious sense of latent possibilities—of stretching oneself to cosmic limits, and who would ever give up the reality of dreams for relative knowledge?

March 25, 1890.

Henry came on the 10th, and spent the day, Henry the patient, I should call him. Five years ago in November, I crossed the water and suspended myself like an old woman of the sea round his neck where to all appearances I shall remain for all time. I have given him endless care and anxiety but notwithstanding this and the fantastic nature of my troubles I have never seen an impatient look upon his face or heard an unsympathetic or misunderstanding sound cross his lips. He comes at my slightest sign and hangs on to whatever organ may be in eruption and gives me calm and solace by assuring me that my nerves are his nerves and my stomach his stomach—this last a pitch of brotherly devotion never before approached by the race. . . .

I was so pleased to come a little while ago across the following in a letter of William's to Wilkie in February, '66, after his return from Brazil:* "Harry, I think much improved, he is a noble fellow—so true, delicate and honorable." All of which is as true in 1890 as then. I was of course much gratified to find this further on, "—and Alice has got to be quite a nice girl"—hasn't it the true fraternal condescension in its ring! I am afraid that I have fallen from such altitudes since at various moments. . . .

June 16, 1890.

What a sense of superiority it gives one to escape reading some book which every one else is reading . . . so far I have not succumbed to Marie Bashkirtseff's *Journal.* I imagine her the perverse of the perverse and what so dreary to read of, or what part so easy to act as we walk across our little stage lighted up by our little self-conscious foot-lights? Every hour I live I become an intenser devotee to *common-sense!*

September 12, 1890.

Twas no go! I went under on Saturday, August 2nd and administered an electric shock to Harry which brought him . . . to immure himself, without a murmur, in my squalid

* Wilkie was the third son in the James family.

indigestions . . . There seems a faint hope that I may fizzle out, but the Monster *Rebound,* which holds me in its remorseless clutch, I am sure will gather itself up for many another spurt. Dr. Baldwin from Florence has been staying with Harry—I didn't see him but H. and K. both extracted the consoling answer to "Can she die?" that "They sometimes do." This is most cheering to all parties—the only drawback being that it will probably be in my sleep so that I shall not be one of the audience, dreadful fraud! a creature who has been denied all dramatic episodes might be allowed, I think, to assist at her extinction. . . .

September 27, 1890.

. . . these doctors tell you that you will die, or *recover!* But you *don't* recover. I have been at these alterations since I was nineteen and I am neither dead nor recovered—as I am now forty-two there has surely been time for either process. I suppose one has a greater sense of intellectual degradation after an interview with a doctor than from any human experience. . . .

October 26, 1890.

William uses an excellent expression when he says in his paper on the "Hidden Self" that the nervous victim "abandons" certain portions of his consciousness . . . I have passed thro' an infinite succession of conscious abandonments and in looking back now I see how it began in my childhood, altho' I wasn't conscious of the necessity until '67 or '68 when I broke down first, acutely, and had violent turns of hysteria. As I lay prostrate after the storm with my mind luminous and active and susceptible of the clearest, strongest impressions, I saw so distinctly that it was a fight simply between my body

and my will, a battle in which the former was to be triumphant to the end . . . As I used to sit immovable reading in
the library with waves of violent inclination suddenly invad-
ing my muscles taking some one of their myriad forms such as
throwing myself out of the window, or knocking off the head
of the benignant pater as he sat with his silver locks, writing
at his table, it used to seem to me that the only difference
between me and the insane was that I had not only all the
horrors and suffering of insanity but the duties of doctor,
nurse, and strait-jacket imposed upon me, too . . . When all
one's moral and natural stock in trade is a temperament forbidding the abandonment of an inch or the relaxation of a
muscle, 'tis a never-ending fight. . . .

May 31st, 1891.

To him who waits, all things come! My aspirations may
have been eccentric, but I cannot complain now, that they
have not been brilliantly fulfilled. Ever since I have been ill, I
have longed and longed for some palpable disease, no matter
how conventionally dreadful a label it might have, but I was
always driven back to stagger alone under the monstrous mass
of subjective sensations, which that sympathetic being "the
medical man" had no higher inspiration than to assure me I
was personally responsible for, washing his hands of me with
a graceful complacency under my very nose. Dr. Torry was
the only man who ever treated me like a rational being, who
did not assume, because I was a victim to so many pains, that
I was, of necessity, an arrested mental development too.

Notwithstanding all the happiness and comfort here, I
have been going downhill at a steady trot; so they sent for Sir
Andrew Clark four days ago; and the blessed being has
endowed me not only with cardiac complications, but says
that a lump that I have had in one of my breasts for three

months, which has given me a great deal of pain, is a tumour, that nothing can be done for me but to alleviate pain, that it is only a question of time, etc. This with a delicate embroidery of "the most distressing case of nervous hyperaesthesia" added to a spinal neurosis that has taken me off my legs for seven years; with attacks of rheumatic gout in my stomach for the last twenty, ought to satisfy the most inflated pathologic vanity. It is decidedly indecent to catalogue oneself in this way, but I put it down in a scientific spirit, to show that though I have no productive worth, I have a certain value as an indestructible quantity.

June 1st, 1891.

Having it to look forward to for a while seems to double the value of the event, for one becomes suddenly picturesque to oneself, and one's wavering little individuality stands out with a cameo effect and one has the tenderest indulgence for all the little *stretchings out* which crowd in upon the memory. The grief is all for K. and H., who will *see* it all, whilst I shall only *feel* it, but they are taking it of course like archangels, and care for me with infinite tenderness and patience. Poor dear William with his exaggerated sympathy for suffering isn't to know anything about it until it is all over.

June 5th, 1891.

. . . It seems that Sir A. C. said that although I might die in a week or so, I might also live some months. This is a strain, as Katharine says I have looked "prepared" for a week, and I am sure I shall not be able to keep that up for some months. . . .

Revelations

June 16, 1891.

 . . . I see a new volume of Anatole France out, which will never be read by me! For a long time past, I have only read what reads with the eyelashes, anything that stirs interest or reflection letting loose the fountain of tears. Sir A. Clarke asked K., when she saw him after his pronunciamento, if I did anything; she said I went on just as usual, and did whatever little thing I could in the way of reading or dictating. "That's right, don't induce her to give up anything; even if she is to die next week, why shouldn't she go on just as usual?" I suppose he imagined that we had entered into an elaborate system of "preparation." What a job it would be for any who undertook it though!

 . . . Within the last year Henry has published *The Tragic Muse,* brought out *The American,* and written a play . . . and his admirable comedy; combined with William's *Psychology,* not a bad show for one family! especially if I get myself dead, the hardest job of all. . . .

June 17, 1891.

We were quite grateful for the Englishry of this: K. saw the other day a very smart lady in a victoria driving in the crowd at the canonical hour, down Piccadilly to the Park, and so far carrying out to perfection the lesson of the day, but with that homely burst of nature to which the most encrusted here are subject, she was satisfying the cravings of the stomach by eating, with the utmost complacency, in the eye of man, a huge, stodgy penny bun. The perfection in all her appointments in the way of carriage, etc—with the absence of subtlety in her palate as shown by the placid consumption of the bun, and complete indifference, at this very visible moment, at exhibiting her features distorted by the ugly process

202

of masticating such an adhesive substance, had an incongruity very characteristic of the soil. They seem in matters of taste to have no sense of gradations. H. is always saying this, but it jumped at my eye from the first, and is therefore an original if not unique utterance. H., by the way, has embedded in his pages many pearls fallen from my lips, which he steals in the most unblushing way, saying, simply, that he knew they had been said by the family, so it did not matter. . . .

September 3, 1891.

It is very gratifying at this mortuary moment to learn how many people have been "struck and *impressed*"! But I can't help thinking how cheered and sustained I should have been had they only been inspired to bare their indented bosoms in the earlier stages of the weary journey.

These long pauses don't point to any mental aridity, my "roomy forehead" is as full as ever of germinating thoughts, but alas the machinery is more and more out of kilter. I am sorry for you all, for I feel as if I hadn't even yet given my message. I would there were more bursts of enthusiasm, less of the carping tone, through this, but I fear it comes by nature. . . .

December 11, 1891.

. . . The difficulty about all this dying is that you can't tell a fellow anything about it, so where does the fun come in?

January 6, 1892.

. . . Dr. Tuckey asked me the other day whether I had ever written for the press. I vehemently disclaimed the imputation. How sad it is that the purely innocuous should always be supposed to have the trail of the family serpent upon them. The domestic muse isn't considered very original. . . .

February 2, 1892.

This long slow dying is no doubt instructive, but it is disappointingly free from excitements: "naturalness" being carried to its supreme expression. One sloughs off the activities one by one, and never knows they're gone, until one suddenly finds that the months have slipped away and the sofa will never more be laid upon, the morning paper read, or the loss of the new book regretted; one revolves with equal content within the narrowing circle until the vanishing point is reached, I suppose.

Vanity, however, maintains its undisputed sway, and I take satisfaction in feeling as much myself as ever, perhaps simply a more concentrated essence in this curtailment. . . .

March 4, 1892.

I am being ground slowly on the grim grindstone of physical pain, and on two nights I had almost asked for K.'s lethal dose, but one steps hesitatingly along such unaccustomed ways and endures from second to second; and I feel sure that it can't be possible but what the bewildered little hammer that keeps me going will very shortly see the decency of ending his distracted career; however this may be, physical pain however great ends in itself and falls away like dry husks from the mind, whilst moral discords and nervous horrors sear the soul. These last, Katharine has completely under the control of her rhythmic hand, so I go no longer in dread. Oh the wonderful moment when I felt myself floated for the first time into the deep sea of divine *cessation,* and saw all the dear

ALICE JAMES

old mysteries and miracles vanish into vapour! That first
experience doesn't repeat itself, fortunately, for it might become a seduction. . . .

[Final entry by Katharine P. Loring]

All through Saturday the 5th and even in the night,
Alice was making sentences. One of the last things she said to
me was to make a correction in the sentence of March 4th
"moral discords and nervous horrors."

This dictation of March 4th was rushing about in her
brain all day, and although she was very weak and it tired her
much to dictate, she could not get her head quiet until she
had it written: then she was relieved. . . .

SYLVIA ASHTON-WARNER

*S*ylvia Ashton-Warner has become famed as a teacher
through her books *Spinster* and *Teacher,* which are
based upon diaries kept when she taught Maori children in
her native New Zealand. In *Teacher,* first published in this
country in 1963, she describes an organic method of teaching
with a Key Vocabulary, in which the child learns through
mastery of words that are important to his own life, such as
"fear," "mother," "ghost." Summarily, her method is a means
of letting the child's energy "teach itself," and its demand upon
the teacher is one of continuous communication.

Myself is based on an early diary in which she was beginning to develop as a teacher and a writer. In her early thirties,
she was working out means of dealing with many of the practical and emotional problems of a woman determined to work
and love on her own terms. In this excerpt, she writes of her
love for her husband (K), and of the love she feels for both a
man and a woman outside her marriage, and of the critical
impact of love upon work.

In a letter she wrote years after the diary of *Myself* was
written, she gives us a perspective upon love as essential to
work.

"I couldn't breathe without love in the air. I'd choke.
I ceased to exist when not in love. The radiance within blotted
out so that nothing would happen inside, nothing exploded

into action. I can quite truthfully say that I never lifted a hand unless *for* someone; never took up a brush or pen, a sheet of music or a spade, never pursued a thought without the motivation of trying to make someone love me."

From Myself

February, 1941

This is evening with the children in bed and K back at school. I must get back to study soon. I've forgotten all I learned at training college about how to teach. All I can remember about teaching is how I myself was taught when young. That strict traditional way: spare the rod and spoil the child. . . . And how we'd line up for reading and sums and get the strap if we got any wrong. The singsong tables in the morning and the strap for every spelling word wrong. All good at the time, I think, because we thought it was all right—and no one allowed to speak. But we didn't learn that at college. I've got to relearn what I was supposed to have learned. This very evening I mean to write a letter to the Country Library Service to get some books to study.

And not only for that reason. I don't mean to go down under marriage and babies as glamorous girls do, never to be heard of again. Down at heel, straggly hair and nothing important to say. I can't see why I need to. I can't see why marriage should wipe out my personality, why I should let it, I mean. Somehow . . . I don't know how what with home, school and family . . . I mean to recover and keep the things I did when single; I mean some time to be what I had meant to be—in the first place a worthwhile person, not just for myself but for those who love me. I mean to so organize my loaded time that I'll retain some for myself to paint, do music, read and even learn to write. I'm not one of these people who were born for nothing.

I'm dreadfully tired. Now I'll go to bed and hope for a good night's sleep without Dannie waking, without a nightmare about the Coast, without anxiety about the war which might take K . . . without worrying about forgetting how to teach, if I ever knew, without bleakly counting my bead-dreams that I dreamed when I was single about how I would live my life: a glamorous mysterious vivid life in the capitals of the world with those of my own kind—artists, musicians and writers. And lovers demanding a look from me, and friends thinking me wonderful. Paris, Rome, New York . . . roaming, roaming, fascinated. Getting on and off ships and trains and planes, the last word in fashion. Without remembering those dreams and seeing them against what I am now: a forgotten girl on the top of a hill drearily teaching Maoris. A forgotten girl. . . .

Sunday, March 9

Among the things about K that astound me is the way he takes his teaching seriously as though it were something other than a source of income. Up close it looks as if his work is also his *hobby*. At college we called it sheer betrayal. I don't know how he can be so *open* about it! At school he's a headmaster and not my husband. For all that, however, I did drift into a drawing lesson with his seniors while he took my little ones for wonderful games on the lawn outside, so that when he came in afterwards and saw for himself that his big ones were busy and happy he was as amazed as they were and as I was too, at what was happening beneath their fingers. Big daisies, yellow-centered, petals red-tipped, serrated with the sun and the shadow on them. In a low voice looking about, "This is what I love to see . . . activity. Do you like it?"

"Yes I do," surprised.

Approval from my headmaster. "Do you think it is good?" begged the wife.

"Of course I do," finish.

Oh, why can't he kiss me? Will I ever accustom myself to no applause . . . well, not enough, I mean? And will I ever get used to my lover-husband turning into a cold head-master?

November 12

In the middle of my yellow jaundice the new doctor is brought into the bedroom, at which I put on a magnificent show of being a bright patient, making little of my ill. He turned out to be soothing and courteous and, even more than Nurse Jean Humphrey, poised. Wonder of wonders, he has asked us *all* down to the cottage *in writing* and gives every evidence of liking to come up. He nursed me through the "yellow peril" with a thoroughness and gentleness that equalled Jean's when I had grown-up mumps and that I thought could only be found in a woman and that stirred in me the old desirous secrets on the theme of mothering. . . .

November 14

Have been raving tired for the last three weeks since the yellow j. and have been obliged to go to bed straight after tea each night. Dr. Mada has not yet got used to my staying three quarters of an hour, no more, returning about eight or before. Actually no one so far of the medical world who has lived in the cottage has been able to understand that with some people there are other things to do besides talking in the evening. I purposely avoid seeing too much of him anyway. I'm too weak emotionally to risk leaning on anyone now. My first duty to myself is to be independent, but it's far from easy at the moment, for the new occupant of the nurse's cottage is courteous and satisfying and impressively cultivated. Anyway I haven't got over Jean yet. . . .

February 16

It is a matter of note that after the years on the Coast the friendships I make harbor heartache. It seems I cannot love moderately or even singly, and I look for a mother in men and women the moment they reveal a regard. On the Coast I sought a great sea-rocking mother in the indifferent ocean who never rocked me. Moreover, being always over-avid, I demand from those I love a love equal to mine, which, being balanced people, they cannot supply. If only my neighbors across the road so far had not been a succession of medical people whose life's profession was Looking After, and if only I were not the grand look-after-ee of all time . . . the thing's fantastic. Yet when K came back from Home Guard in the evening he managed to mother me, pulling me into his bed. "You mustn't cry like that," he said.

March 10

I'm here again . . . Five-thirty in the afternoon after a day at school, with K minding the children.

During the centuries of the golden prophets, well before Christ, when the Hebrews sang psalms all day the priest at times would call a pause to give the psalmists a rest, and the word he used was "Selah." A Hebrew word. In charcoal and lipstick I wrote this word "Selah" on my door.

March 11

Today too I came here after school to Selah at half past five after preparing the evening meal. I came so joyfully the wild wet mile to get my quota of work, not to mention the necessary ration of silence, but owing to the pane of glass Saul brought still not being in I ran into a bout of the old frustration. All settled down, fire and everything, slippers on, books spread out, when a wind-chased shower plunged in wetting all my things. I can't move my table away as it is nailed to the wall and the floor, too.

So an hour went by while I collected water in the teapot from the dripping roof to make paste in a former paint tin to stick paper over the hole of the window, but the wind wouldn't have this, nor the rain either. So I finally gave up any idea of writing what I had planned coming up, wading up the road through the rain. These few lines I'm entering with a board across the gap. . . .

March 22

On Sunday evening with the children in bed . . . I talked to K about the design. "The intellect is the tool to find the truth. It's a matter of sharpening it. Since I've been studying I'm much keener-witted. That's one reason I'm learning to milk the cow. I'm going to take over your afternoon's work sometimes and you can have the time for more study. I can chop wood and feed the fowls. We'll share the time."

"I can't possibly allow you to do rough work, chop wood and do the fowls. Not when you have the desire and the ability and the opportunity to do what you do."

I was surprised to hear this.

He continued, "What I thought two months ago and what I think now are two different things. I've tried to be broader about your going away. People who can do the work you do should be allowed to do it and those who can't should hew the wood and draw the water, feed the fowls, chop the wood and milk Susie."

This distressed me.

He went on. "There's no need for you to take on my afternoon work."

"But my work loses its value unless you are happy. Everything loses its value. Your contentment comes before my work."

"I'm happy."

"No, you're not."

He looked at me with interest. I went on. "You're not getting as much time for study as I am. You're the real mother of this family; I'm just one of the children. We must share the time."

He pushed the kettle over the flames. "But your study means more to you than mine does to me."

"I question it. But in any case that's not my point. Your work means more to me than my own does to me because your work involves your contentment and that comes before my work with me."

He was interested but looked doubtful.

"It's the truth," I added. "Unless you are happy in your work mine is valueless to me."

K examined my face as though he was seeing it for the first time.

"It may not be apparent," I said, "but I love you and you come first in the world with me, before everything before anybody. You and the children. My family and home are more to me than my work. If it came to the choice it would be my work that went overboard. No doubt I've appeared to be a failure in the home but that is not indicative. Do you feel I've failed you in the home?" I called on all my courage to ask this question which could draw a devastating answer. He put out two cups and saucers. "Well, it has crossed my mind that you shouldn't have married."

Catastrophe! "But I've been a good mother! Look at me all through my babies. How I stuck to them on the Coast."

"Yes. But what I mean is that a person, any person, with your inclinations should not marry. You should have gone on with your work. Marriage has sidetracked you."

Desperately on the defensive, "I wash and dress the little boys in the morning, and Jonquil. I feed them."

"I know. What I mean is that people like you with talents and ideas should be undisturbed by marriage."

"Ah . . . but you see! I wouldn't have had these desires at all if I hadn't married. When I didn't teach and had no babies, I hardly lifted a brush. Hardly did a thing. The *need* to study, to do, to make, to think, *arises* from being married. I need to be married to work."

He poured the boiling water on the tea. "I still think that you should be allowed your work in preference to my being allowed mine. Your desire is stronger than mine."

"That's quite possible. But I'm still going to hurry up and learn to milk Susie and take over your jobs sometimes."

We had tea, ran off the dishes and went to bed. Neither of us lowered the flag, neither won, and we haven't talked about that since, but the part about his coming before my work must have registered and held for there's been a tenderness in his manner toward me like the reappearance of the sun, and that close feeling has returned. . . .

FROM TEACHER

When I teach people, I marry them. I found this out last year when I began the orchestra. To do what I wanted them to do they had to need to be like me. More than that. They

213

had to be part of me. As the season progressed the lesson began to teach itself to me. I found that for good performances we had to be one thing. One organ. And physically they had to be near to each other and to me. We had to bundle into a heap round the piano. I say "we had to," but that's not it. They *did* pile up round me at the piano, irrespective of what I tried to make them do. However, I arranged their seating to face the audience and with a view to each child being visible; nevertheless, at the end of the song, there they would all be, married all over and round me.

Rules like the best sound coming from a throat or instrument when facing the auditorium were just walked over. Although I didn't learn that thing until I heard the . . . *saw* the youth club sing a lament . . . They were too shy to face the gathering, so instinctively, they turned inward into a ring, seeing only one another. As for me, I learned this particular lesson once and for all. I know it now.

Now where was I? I was talking marriage with my orchestra. I would never have learned this through any other medium but music, I'm sure. I've never learned it all this time teaching. But now that I do know it I see it in other areas. There is quietly occurring in my infant room a grand espousal. To bring them to do what I want them to do they come near me, I draw them near me, in body and in spirit. They don't know it but I do. They become part of me, like a lover. The approach, little different. The askance observation first, the acceptance next, then the gradual or quick coming, until in the complete procuration, there glows the harmony, the peace.

And what is the birth? From the orchestra it is music, and from the infant room it is work. A long, perpetuating, never-ending, transmuting birth, beginning its labor every morning and a rest between pains every evening.

Now that I see this as espousal the prickly, difficult, obscured way clears. It's all so simple.

Tall words. Wild words. Grand words. But there is an even deeper meaning beneath it all. It's integration of my living. And integration of theirs.

All the rules of love-making apply to these spiritual and intellectual fusions. There must be only two, for instance. As soon as another allegiance pushes in, the first union breaks apart. Love interferes with fidelities. I can't teach in the true essential medium when that approaching face turns away to another interest. I have tried in the past to do this, before I knew what I know now, but the answer was grating, discord, and even hatred. When love turns away, now, I don't follow it. I sit and suffer, unprotesting, until I feel the tread of another step. . . .

Integration. That fatal, vital word continues to press upward before the inner eye. Married to the life about you. However small or however big the social horizon. For the environment at hand has little bearing on the expansion of the mind and spirit. . . .

I'm glad to know this at last, that to teach I need first to espouse. . . .

I've got so much to say that I'm going to stop trying to say it. This is the last lot of this diary. The level of it is rising over my head.

Its purpose has already been fulfilled. I was lonely, professionally. I wanted gifted, intimate understanding . . .

Before I stop I'll try to cover the very vital and organic pattern of my professional life over the last weeks. It's always when things happen that we have no time to record them. But I'll try to give the picture, the conglomeration of imagery that has been banking up before the inner eye, waiting and pushing for expression. And the order will be its own. An order of emotional importance.

Stronger than any other image in the world behind is one of Mr. Tremaine in my infant room last week saying to me softly, "I want to hear you speak." Through everything else I hear this. Right through the Ballet on Thursday evening, the evening of his visit, I heard this. True, he had brought with him Professor ———— from the chair of ———— and Dr. ———— from the chair of ———— at ———— University College to meet me, but it was this modest sentence of Mr. Tremaine's that remains the strongest thought within. The strongest sensation.

He kept from me who the visitors were. They had come to see my Maori primer books. They got me talking, Mr. Tremaine did, and these two men I lectured from the infant-room table with all the fire of conviction I had in me on the results of my recent experiments with the Key Vocabulary. . . .

"The way," I reproved Mr. Tremaine at morning tea . . . "you come out here and make me talk. You make me talk! I talk everyone down for an hour, then feel ashamed of it afterwards!"

He smiled in enjoyment. "I always find," he told us, "that if I keep quiet I learn something."

"Are you important?" I asked the visitors.

"Oh no, no!"

"Well, as long as I know. I would have passed you your tea first. Anyway Mr. Tremaine, I like your technique of dropping important people on us. If I knew they were coming I'd never be here!"

He roared at this and I wondered what for. Some secret interpretation he had. But as he shook my hand goodbye in the porch I said, "I'm attacking Maori delinquency."

"Thank you for all the work you are doing," he replied. "And I enjoyed listening to you."

That was the day I gave him my Maori Infant Reading Scheme. He stood in the cold outside, so very big and tall in his greatcoat, turning over the pages . . . "Look at this," he said tenderly. Ah, the simple rapture of fulfilment at my work being understood that cold morning. What unutterable reward for my labor.

GEORGE ELIOT
(1819-1880)

*G*eorge Eliot *was born Mary Ann* (later Marian) Evans in Warwickshire, England. From the strict religious background of her unhappy childhood and adolescence, she emerged a freethinker, and in London began to develop a career in the literary world.

The great change in her life occurred in her mid-thirties when she met and fell in love with George Henry Lewes. Lewes was the father of a growing family and the husband of an adulteress. Because he had condoned his wife's affair and given his name to another man's child, he was not permitted divorce. His liberal views made him attractive to Marian, who described him as "a man of heart and conscience wearing a mask of flippancy." They eloped without benefit of clergy to Germany, then returned to settle in Richmond, London.

Lewes was highly regarded in London as a most versatile man of letters, writing on drama, philosophy, zoology, and physiology. Quickly realizing Marian's power, he worked with her as a journalist and eventually negotiated the terms of her first novel with the publisher John Blackwood. With their encouragement, she wrote eight novels, among them *Adam Bede, Mill on the Floss* and *Middlemarch,* which place her as one of the greatest of English novelists. From the outset, she decided to write under a man's name. She and Lewes had witnessed the sharp drop in sales after the disclosure that *Jane*

Eyre was written by a woman. By the time it became generally known that she was a woman, she was already a popular success. As her career progressed, Lewes assumed more and more responsibility for making her publishing arrangements and protecting her genius from hostile criticism. This happy relationship, which facilitated her work, continued for more than twenty years until Lewes' death.

Unfortunately, George Eliot's journal was expurgated, possibly by herself, more probably by William Cross, the family friend she married two years after Lewes died. Cross was interested in preserving for posterity a rather more somber George Eliot than her friends knew. The pages dealing with her decision to live with Lewes were torn out, but we are able to extract a few that suggest the vitality of her most intimate relationship. For the range and depth of her extraordinary mind, see *The George Eliot Letters,* edited by Gordon S. Haight, Yale University Press.

From the Journal, 6 December, 1857

How I Came to Write Fiction

September 1857 made a new era in my life, for it was then I began to write Fiction. It had always been a vague dream of mine that some time or other I might write a novel, and my shadowy conception of what the novel was to be, varied, of course, from one epoch of my life to another. But I never went farther towards the actual writing of the novel than an introductory chapter describing a Staffordshire village and the life of the neighboring farm houses, and as the years passed on I lost any hope that I should ever be able to write a novel, just as I desponded about everything else in my future life. I always thought I was deficient in dramatic power, both of construction and dialogue, but I felt I should be at my ease in the descriptive parts of a novel. My "introductory chapter" was pure description though there were good materials in it for dramatic presentation. It happened to be among the papers I had with me in Germany and one evening in Berlin, something led me to read it to George. He was struck with it as a bit of concrete description, and it suggested to him the possibility of my being able to write a novel, though he distrusted—indeed disbelieved in, my possession of any dramatic power. Still, he began to think that I might as well try, some time, what I could do in fiction, and by and bye, when we came back to England and I had greater success than he had ever expected in other kinds of writing, his impression that it was worth while to see how far my mental power would go towards the production of a novel, was strengthened. He began to say very positively, "You must try and write a story," and when we were at Tenby he urged me to begin at once. I deferred it, however, after my usual fashion, with work that does not present itself as an absolute duty. But one morning as I was lying in bed, thinking what should be the subject of my first story, my thoughts merged themselves into a dreamy doze, and I imagined myself writing a story of which the title was —"The Sad Fortunes of the Reverend Amos Barton." I was soon wide awake again, and told G. He said, "O what a capital title!" and from that time I had settled in my mind that this should be my first story. George used to say, "It may be a failure—it may be that you are unable to write fiction. Or perhaps, it may be just good enough to warrant your trying again." Again, "You may write a chef-d'oeuvre at once—there's no telling." But his prevalent impression was that though I could hardly write a *poor* novel, my effort would want the highest quality of fiction—dramatic presentation. He used to say, "You have wit, description and philosophy—those go a good way towards the production of a novel. It is worth while for you to try the experiment."

We determined that if my story turned out good enough, we would send it to Blackwood, but G. thought the more probable result was, that I should have to lay it aside and try again.

But when we returned to Richmond I had to write my article on Silly Novels ("Silly Novels by Lady Novelists," Westminster Review) and my review of Contemporary Literature, so that I did not begin my story till September 22. After I had begun it, as we were walking in the Park, I mentioned to G. that I had thought of the plan of writing a series of stories containing sketches drawn from my own observation of the Clergy, and calling them "Scenes from Clerical Life" opening with "Amos Barton." He at once accepted the notion as a good one—fresh and striking; and about a week afterwards when I read him the early part of "Amos," he had no longer any doubt about my ability to carry out the plan. The scene at Cross Farm, he said, satisfied him that I had the very element he had been doubtful about—it was clear I could write good dialogue. There still remained the question whether I could command any pathos, and that was to be decided by the mode in which I treated Milly's death. One night G. went to town on purpose to leave me a quiet evening for writing it. I wrote the chapter from the news brought by the shepherd to Mrs. Hackit, to the moment when Amos is dragged from the bedside and I read it to G. when he came home. We both cried over it, and then he came up to me and kissed me saying, "I think your pathos is better than your fun."

So when the story was finished G. sent it to Blackwood, who wrote in reply, that he thought the "Clerical reminiscences would do," congratulated the author of being "worthy the honours of print and pay," but would like to see more of the series before he undertook to print. However, when G. wrote that the author was discouraged by this editorial caution, Blackwood disclaimed any distrust and agreed to print the story at once. The first appeared in the January number 1857. . . . When the story was concluded he wrote me word how Albert Smith had sent him a letter saying he had never read anything that affected him more than Milly's death, and, added Blackwood, "the men at the club seem to have mingled their tears and their tumblers together. It will be curious if you should be a member and be hearing your own praises!" There was clearly no suspicion that I was a woman. It is interesting, as an indication of the value there is in such conjectural criticism generally, to remember that when G. read the first part of "Amos" to a party . . . they were all sure I was a clergyman—a Cambridge man.

Dec. 31 (*the last night of 1857.*)

The dear old year is gone with all its *Weben* and *Streben*. Yet not gone either: for what I have suffered and enjoyed in it remains to me an everlasting possession while my soul's life remains. This time last year I was alone, as I am now, and dear George was at Vernon Hill. I was writing the introduction to "Mr. Gilfil's Love-Story." What a world of thoughts and feelings since then! My life has deepened unspeakably during the last year; I feel a greater capacity for moral and intellectual enjoyment; a more acute sense of my deficiencies in the past; a more solemn desire to be faithful to coming duties than I remember at any former period of my life. And my happiness has deepened too: the blessedness of a perfect love and union grows daily. I have had some severe suffering this year from anxiety about my sister, and what will probably be a final separation from her—there has been no other real trouble. Few women, I fear, have had such reason as I have to think the long sad years of youth were worth living for the sake of middle age. Our prospects are very bright too. I am writing my new novel. G. is full of his "Physiology of Common Life." . . . So good-by, dear 1857! May I be able to look back on 1858 with an equal consciousness of advancement in work and in heart.

January 2, 1858

George has returned this evening from a week's visit at Vernon Hill. On coming upstairs he said, "I have some very pretty news for you—something in my pocket!" I was at a loss to conjecture, and thought confusedly of possible opinions from admiring readers, when he drew the "Times" from his pocket—today's number, containing a review of the "Scenes of Clerical Life." He had happened to ask a gentleman in the railway carriage coming up to London to allow him to look at the "Times," and felt quite agitated and tremulous when his eyes alighted on the review. Finding he had time to go into town before the train started, he bought a copy there. It is a highly favorable notice, and as far as it goes, appreciatory . . .

I wonder how I shall feel about these little details ten years hence, if I am *alive*. At present I value them as grounds for hoping that my writing may succeed and so give value to my life—as indications that I can touch the hearts of my fellow men, and so sprinkle some precious grain as the result of the long years in which I have been inert and suffering. But at present fear and trembling still predominate over hope.

28 February—5 March 1858

On Sunday the 28th Mr. John Blackwood called on us, having come to London for a few days only. He talked a good deal about the "Clerical Scenes" and George Eliot, and at last asked, "Well, am I to see George Eliot this time?" G. said, "Do you wish to see him?" "As he likes—I wish it to be quite spontaneous." I left the room, and G. following me a moment, I told him he might reveal me. Blackwood was kind, came back when he found he was too late for the train, and said he would come to Richmond again. He came on the following Friday, and chatted very pleasantly—told us that Thackeray spoke highly of the "Scenes" and said *they were not written by a woman*. Mrs. Blackwood is sure they are not written by a woman. Mrs. Oliphant, the novelist, too, is confident on the same side. I gave Blackwood the M.S. of my new novel to the end of the second scene in the wood. He opened it, read the first page, and smiling said, "This will do. . . ."

[Others were not so easily fooled. Charles Dickens, an early reader and admirer, wrote immediately to Blackwood that, as the women were seen from the inside and much better drawn, the author of "Scenes" had to be a woman. In January of 1858, he wrote George Eliot that if the fictions written under that name "originated with no woman, I believe that no man ever before had the art of making himself, mentally, so like a woman, since the world began."]

VIRGINIA WOOLF

(1882-1941)

Quentin Bell's recent and very beautiful biography of Virginia Woolf has opened her personal life to many readers. Her working life is best understood through the diary she began to keep regularly in 1915, the same year she published her first novel. Like Ruth Benedict, she was a late starter; but once she had found her work—and, through her marriage to the supportive Leonard Woolf, eminently favorable circumstances for its performance—the range and variety and sheer amount of what she wrote was a remarkable testament to the self-discipline and industry that accompany a true vocation.

Anyone interested in what a writer's life is like will find the answer in her diary: the daily routine, the self-doubts, the emotional risks, the exacting personal severity, and always the voice of the potential critic hovering over the typewriter. Much has been made of Virginia Woolf's vulnerability to criticism and the terrors she experienced before the publication of every book. Because of the anguishing distractions of her periodic bouts with mental illness, favorable reviews are said to have been important to her as a certification of her sanity, especially since her writings were so concerned with the circularity of mental process, and because she was always risking new ways to express the mind's ebb and flow. But no honest writer will disavow her terrors as exaggerated; she only explored them more fully than most.

In contrast to her intermittent depressions is the buoyancy of her creative energies; while she was working in one form, onslaughts of ideas for future projects were recorded in her diary. But in 1941 the mental illness—the voices—recurred. Out of love and respect for his own work, she could not impose on Leonard another breakdown and long convalescence: she left a note of explanation on the mantel and drowned herself in the river Ouse.

In 1953 Leonard Woolf edited her diary for publication. There were twenty-six volumes of this "loosening of the ligaments" of her writing style that she practiced after tea when the real writing day was over. Despite his reservations about diary extracts giving a one-sided view of the author, he felt the book was justified because of the light it cast "upon Virginia Woolf's intentions, objects, and methods as a writer. It gives an unusual psychological picture of artistic production from within."* He selected for inclusion "practically everything which referred to her own writing," as well as extracts that show her practicing writing in different ways, those that gave her impressions of scenes and persons—"the raw material of her art"—and references to what she read. The selections that follow deal only with a few of her reflections on her writing.

Easter Sunday, April 20th [*1919*]

. . . I got out this diary and read, as one always does read one's own writing, with a kind of guilty intensity. I confess that the rough and random style of it, often so ungrammatical, and crying for a word altered, afflicted me somewhat. I am trying to tell whichever self it is that reads this hereafter

* *A Writer's Diary* (New York, Harcourt, Brace, 1954), p. ix.

that I can write very much better; and take no time over this; and forbid her to let the eye of man behold it. And now I may add my little compliment to the effect that it has a slapdash and vigour and sometimes hits an unexpected bull's eye. But what is more to the point is my belief that the habit of writing thus for my own eye is good practice. It loosens the ligaments. Never mind the misses and the stumbles. Going at such a pace as I do I must make the most direct and instant shots at my object, and thus have to lay hands on words, choose them and shoot them with no more pause than is needed to put my pen in the ink. I believe that during the past year I can trace some increase of ease in my professional writing which I attribute to my casual half hours after tea. Moreover there looms ahead of me the shadow of some kind of form which a diary might attain to. I might in the course of time learn what it is that one can make of this loose, drifting material of life; finding another use for it than the use I put it to, so much more consciously and scrupulously in fiction. What sort of diary should I like mine to be? Something loose knit and yet not slovenly, so elastic that it will embrace anything, solemn, slight or beautiful that comes into my mind. I should like it to resemble some deep old desk, or capacious hold-all, in which one flings a mass of odds and ends without looking them through. I should like to come back, after a year or two, and find that the collection had sorted itself and refined itself and coalesced, as such deposits so mysteriously do, into a mould, transparent enough to reflect the light of our life, and yet steady, tranquil compounds with the aloofness of a work of art. The main requisite, I think on rereading my old volumes, is not to play the part of censor, but to write as the mood comes or of anything whatever; since I was curious to find how I went for things put in haphazard, and found the significance to lie where I never saw it at the time. But looseness quickly becomes slovenly. A little effort is needed to face a character or an incident which needs to be recorded. Nor can one let the pen write without guidance; for fear of becoming slack and untidy . . .

Tuesday, March 9th [1920]

In spite of some tremors I think I shall go on with this diary for the present. I sometimes think that I have worked through the layer of style which suited it—suited the comfortable bright hour after tea; and the thing I've reached now is less pliable. Never mind; I fancy old Virginia, putting on her spectacles to read of March 1920 will decidedly wish me to continue. Greetings! my dear ghost; and take heed that I don't think 50 a very great age. Several good books can be written still . . .

Tuesday, May 11th

It is worth mentioning, for future reference, that the creative power which bubbles so pleasantly in beginning a new book quiets down after a time, and one goes on more steadily. Doubts creep in. Then one becomes resigned. Determination not to give in, and the sense of an impending shape keep one at it more than anything. I'm a little anxious. How am I to bring off this conception? Directly one gets to work one is like a person walking, who has seen the country stretching out before. I want to write nothing in this book [*Jacob's Room*] that I don't enjoy writing. Yet writing is always difficult.

Monday, October 25th (*First day of winter time*)

Why is life so tragic; so like a little strip of pavement over an abyss. I look down; I feel giddy; I wonder how I am ever to walk to the end. But why do I feel this: Now that I say it I don't feel it . . . Melancholy diminishes as I write. Why then don't I write it down oftener? Well, one's vanity forbids. I want to appear a success even to myself. Yet I don't get to the bottom of it. It's having no children, living away from friends, failing to write well, spending too much on food, growing old. I think too much of whys and wherefores; too much of myself. I don't like time to flap round me. Well then, work. Yes, but I soon tire of work—can't read more than a little, an hour's writing is enough for me. Out here no one comes in to waste time pleasantly. If they do, I'm cross. . . .

Friday, April 8th [1921]

And I ought to be writing *Jacob's Room!* and I can't, and instead I shall write down the reason why I can't—this diary being a kindly blankfaced old confidante. Well, you see, I'm a failure as a writer. I'm out of fashion: old: shan't do any better . . . Now the solid grain of fact is that Ralph sent my book out to *The Times* for review without date of publication in it. Thus a short notice is scrambled through to be in "on Monday at latest," put in an obscure place, rather scrappy, complimentary enough, but quite unintelligent. I mean by that they don't see that I'm after something interesting. So that makes me suspect that I'm not. . . .

Well, this question of praise and fame must be faced . . . How much difference does popularity make? . . . What depresses me is the thought that I have ceased to interest people—at the very moment when, by the help of the press, I thought I was becoming more myself. One does *not* want an established reputation, such as I think I was getting, as one of our leading female novelists. I have still, of course, to gather in all the private criticism, which is the real test. When I have weighed this I shall be able to say whether I am "interesting" or obsolete. Anyhow, I feel quite alert enough to stop, if I'm obsolete. I shan't become a machine, unless a machine for grinding articles. As I write, there rises somewhere in my head that queer and very pleasant sense of something which I want to write; my own point of view. I wonder, though, whether this feeling that I write for half a dozen instead of 1500 will pervert this—make me eccentric—no, I think not. But as I said, one must face the despicable vanity which is at the root of all this niggling and haggling. I think the only prescription for me is to have a thousand interests—if one is damaged, to be able instantly to let my energy flow into Russian, or Greek, or the press, or the garden, or people, or some activity disconnected with my own writing.

Tuesday, February 23rd [1926]

I am blown like an old flag by my novel. This one is *To the Lighthouse*. I think it is worth saying for my own interest that at last, at last, after that battle *Jacob's Room*, that agony—all agony but the end—*Mrs. Dalloway*, I am now writing as fast and freely as I have written in the whole of my life; more so—20 times more so—than any novel yet. I think this is the proof that I was on the right path; and that what fruit hangs in my soul is to be reached there. Amusingly, I now invent theories that fertility and fluency are the things: I used to plead for a kind of close, terse effort. Anyhow this goes on all the morning: and I have the devil's own work not to be flogging my brain all the afternoon. I live entirely in it, and come to the surface rather obscurely, and am often unable to think what to say when we walk round the Square, which is bad, I know. Perhaps it may be a good sign for the book though. Of course it is largely known to me: but all my books have been that. It is, I feel that I can float everything off now;

and "everything" is rather a crowd and weight and confusion in the mind.

Saturday, March 20th

But what is to become of all these diaries, I asked myself yesterday. If I died, what would Leo make of them? He would be disinclined to burn them; he could not publish them. Well, he should make up a book from them, I think; and then burn the body. I daresay there is a little book in them; if the scraps and scratchings were straightened out a little. God knows. This is dictated by a slight melancholia, which comes upon me sometimes now and makes me think I am old; I am ugly. I am repeating things. Yet, as far as I know, as a writer I am only now writing out of my mind.

Saturday, October 27th [1928]

Thank God my long toil at the women's lecture is this moment ended. I am back from speaking at Girton, in floods of rain. Starved but valiant young women—that's my impression. Intelligent, eager, poor; and destined to become schoolmistresses in shoals. I blandly told them to drink wine and have a room of their own. . . . I get such a sense of tingling and vitality from an evening's talk like that; one's angularities and obscurities are smoothed and lit. How little one counts, I think: how little anyone counts; how fast and furious and masterly life is; and how all these thousands are swimming for dear life. I felt elderly and mature. And nobody respected me. They were very eager, egotistical, or rather not much impressed by age and repute. Very little reverence or that sort of thing about. . . .

Revelations

Sunday, May 12th [1929]

Here, having just finished what I call the final revision of *Women and Fiction* [*A Room of One's Own*], so that L. can read it after tea, I stop; surfeited. And the pump, which I was so sanguine as to think ceased, begins again. About *Women and Fiction*, I am not sure—a brilliant essay?—I daresay: it has much work in it, many opinions boiled down into a kind of jelly, which I have stained red as far as I can. But I am eager to be off—to write without any boundary coming slick in one's eyes: here my public has been too close; facts; getting them malleable, easily yielding to each other.

Tuesday, May 28th

Now about this book, *The Moths*. How am I to begin it? And what is it to be? I feel no great impulse; no fever; only a great pressure of difficulty. Why write it then? Why write at all? Every morning I write a little sketch, to amuse myself. I am not saying, I might say, that these sketches have any relevance. I am not trying to tell a story. Yet perhaps it might be done in that way. A mind thinking. They might be islands of light—islands in the stream that I am trying to convey; life itself going on. The current of the moths flying strongly this way. A lamp and a flower pot in the center. The flower can always be changing. But there must be more unity between each scene than I can find at present. Autobiography it might be called. . . .

Monday, August 19th

. . . I have just set the last correction to *Women and Fiction,* or *A Room of One's Own.* I shall never read it again, I suppose. Good or bad? Has an uneasy life in it, I think: you feel the creature arching its back and galloping on, though as usual much is watery and flimsy and pitched in too high a voice.

Wednesday, October 23rd

. . . I will here sum up my impressions before publishing *A Room of One's Own*. It is a little ominous that Morgan [E. M. Forster] won't review it. It makes me suspect that there is a shrill feminine tone in it which my intimate friends will dislike. I forecast, then, that I shall get no criticism, except of the evasive jocular kind . . .; that the press will be kind and talk of its charm and sprightliness; also I shall be attacked for a feminist and hinted at for a Sapphist . . . I shall get a good many letters from young women. I am afraid it will not be taken seriously. Mrs. Woolf is so accomplished a writer that all she says makes easy reading . . . this feminine logic . . . a book to be put in the hands of girls. I doubt that I mind much. The Moths; but I think it is to be waves, is trudging along; and I have that to refer to, if I am damped by the other. It is a trifle, I shall say; so it is; but I wrote it with ardour and conviction. . . .

Saturday, February 7th [1931]

Here in the few minutes that remain, I must record, heaven be praised, the end of *The Waves*. I wrote the words O Death fifteen minutes ago, having reeled across the last ten pages with some moments of such intensity and intoxication that I seemed only to stumble after my own voice, or almost, after some sort of speaker (as when I was mad) I was almost afraid, remembering the voices that used to fly ahead. Anyhow, it is done; and I have been sitting these 15 minutes in a state of glory, and calm, and some tears. . . . How physical the sense of triumph and relief is! Whether good or bad, it's done; and as I certainly felt at the end, not merely finished, but rounded off, completed, the thing stated—how hastily, how fragmentarily I know. . . .

What interests me in the last stage was the freedom and boldness with which my imagination picked up, used and tossed aside all the images, symbols which I had prepared. I am sure that this is the right way of using them—not in set pieces, as I had tried at first, coherently, but simply as images, never making them work out; only suggest. Thus I hope to have kept the sound of the sea and the birds, dawn and garden subconsciously present, doing their work underground.

Friday, July 27th [1934]

. . . Odd how the creative power at once brings the whole universe to order. I can see the day whole, proportioned—even after a long flutter of the brain such as I've had this morning it must be a physical, moral, mental necessity, like setting the engine off. A wild windy hot day—a tearing wind in the garden; all the July apples on the grass. I'm going to indulge in a series of quick sharp contrasts: breaking my moulds as much as ever I like. Trying every kind of experiment. Now of course I can't write diary or letters or read because I am making up all the time. Perhaps Bob T. was right in his poem when he called me fortunate above all—I mean in having a mind that can express—no, I mean in having mobilised my being—learned to give it complete outcome—I mean, that I have to some extent forced myself to break every mold and find a fresh form of being, that is of expression, for everything I feel or think. So that when it is working I get the sense of being fully energised—nothing stunted. But this needs constant effort, anxiety and rush.

Here in *Here and Now* I am breaking the mold made by *The Waves*.

Wednesday, November 14th

A note: despair at the badness of the book: can't think how I ever could write such stuff—and with such excitement: that's yesterday: today I think it good again. A note, by way of advising other Virginias with other books that this is the way of the thing: up down up down—and Lord knows the truth.

Thursday, January 16th [1936]

Seldom have I been more completely miserable than I was about 6:30 last night, reading over the last part of *The Years*. Such feeble twaddle—such twilight gossip it seemed; such a show up of my own decrepitude, and at such huge length. I could only plump it down on the table and rush upstairs with burning cheeks to L. He said: "This always happens." But I felt, No, it has never been so bad as this. I make this note should I be in the same state after another book. Now, this morning, dipping in, it seems to me, on the contrary, a full, bustling live book . . .

Sunday, March 8th [1941]

. . . I mark Henry James' sentence: observe perpetually. Observe the oncome of age. Observe greed. Observe my own despondency. By that means it becomes serviceable. Or so I hope. I insist upon spending this time to the best advantage. I will go down with my colors flying. This I see verges on introspection; but doesn't quite fall in. Suppose I bought a ticket at the Museum; biked in daily and read history. Suppose I selected one dominant figure in every age and wrote round and about. Occupation is essential. And now with some pleasure I find that it's seven; and must cook dinner. Haddock and sausage meat. I think it is true that one gains a certain hold on sausage and haddock by writing them down.

KÄTHE KOLLWITZ

(1867-1945)

The talent of the German graphic artist and sculptor Käthe Kollwitz was recognized and encouraged early by her father, Karl Schmidt, a master-builder and a preacher of the Latitudinarian Community in Königsberg. As a girl, she could not be admitted to the Berlin Academy; she took private drawing lessons and later attended the Girls' Art School in Munich. She continued to develop as an artist after her marriage to Karl Kollwitz, who supported her ambitions, and after the birth of their sons Hans and Peter. Karl Kollwitz was a doctor in the working-class district of Berlin, where she lived for more than fifty years. In 1919 she became the first woman to be elected to the Berlin Academy. She served as director of the Academy's masterclasses for graphic art from 1928 until she was dismissed by the Nazis in 1932.

The strength and tragic vision of her early work concerned itself with workers. A series of etchings, *The Weavers*, inspired by Gerhart Hauptmann's play, was awarded a gold medal, which the Kaiser vetoed. "But from then on," she wrote, "at one blow I was counted among the foremost artists of the country." She began to work in sculpture as well as etching and lithography.

After the death in battle of her younger son, Peter, in 1914, the figure of death brooded over her work. The face of the women in her drawings and sculpture—protecting their children from death or relinquishing them—is often her own. In order to keep Peter close, she began to work on a sepulcher for him.

Her work with its implicit statement of "no more war" was banned by Hitler in 1936. She loved Germany but came to reject the concept of sacrifice of youth for nationalistic ideals.

When her grandson Peter fell on the Russian front in 1942, her son Hans wrote that "she bore herself proudly, did not grieve openly, scarcely wept; she tried to give us strength to bear it." For many years Hans urged her to set down an account of her life, but she replied that if anything in her life had been important, it was her work. Yet to please him, in 1922 she presented him with a handwritten account of her childhood and youth. In those notes what she says about her sexuality bears upon the strong compassion toward women revealed in her work: "Although my leaning toward the male sex was dominant, I also felt frequently drawn toward my own sex—an inclination which I could not correctly interpret until much later on. As a matter of fact I believe that bisexuality is almost a necessary factor in artistic production; at any rate, the tinge of masculinity within me helped me in my work."

The notes and her diary reveal, in Hans' words, "how she struggled with the antagonist within herself, and how essential that struggle was to her development."

Käthe Kollwitz is an appropriate figure to end our section on work, for in her life, marriage, motherhood and art fuse into a statement of love.

September 24, 1909

I looked at some Dürer drawings of hands in the print collection. Except for a very few things I am no longer so overwhelmed by Dürer. His stroke is distasteful to me, and so is his excessively subjective feeling for form.

KÄTHE KOLLWITZ

December 30, 1909

On Saturday the Secession show was opened. I went there with Hans. My things were hung well, although the etchings were separate. Nevertheless I am no longer so satisfied. There are too many good things there that seem fresher than mine. . . .

April 1910

I repeatedly dream that I again have a little baby, and I feel all the old tenderness again—or rather more than that, for all the feelings in a dream are intensified. What I have in these dreams is an inexpressibly sweet, lovely physical feeling. First it was Peter who lay asleep, and when I uncovered him it was a very small baby exuding the warm bodily fragrance of babies.

April 1910

I am gradually approaching the period in my life when work comes first. When both the boys went away for Easter, I hardly did anything but work. Worked, slept, ate and went for short walks. But above all I worked. And yet I wonder whether the "blessing" is not missing from such work. No longer diverted by other emotions, I work the way a cow grazes. . . .

April 1910

This period in my life seems to me very fine. Great piercing sorrows have not yet struck me; my darling boys are growing more independent. I can already see the time when they will break loose from me, and at the moment I look forward to it without sorrow. For then they will be mature enough for a life wholly their own, and I shall still be young enough for my own life.

May 15, 1910

How strongly I feel that this is a dividing period in their [her sons', Hans' and Peter's] lives. How soon now something very real and definite will emerge out of the boys' lovelorn enthusiasms. Sensuality is burgeoning . . . it shows up in every one of their movements, in everything, everything. It is only a matter of opening a door and then they will *understand* it too, then the veil will be gone and the struggle with the most powerful of instincts begin . . . often they will feel it their enemy, and sometimes they will almost suffocate for the joy it brings. . . . I feel at once grave, ill at ease and happy as I watch our children—our *children*—growing to meet the greatest of instincts. May it have mercy on them!

September 29, 1910

My wish is to die after Karl. I could endure living alone better than he could. I am also closer to the children. But if I should die Karl could not manage alone. If I die, Karl would find it unbearable by himself. He loves the children enough to die for them, and yet there is alienation between them . . . I know no person who can love as he can, with his whole soul. Often this love has oppressed me; I wanted to be free. But often too it has made me so terribly happy. . . . Only a year ago I thought that once Hans was out of the house—but in any case as soon as both boys were out of the house—I should like to go away for a long time. To Paris. Now I desire this much less strongly. I get working nowadays as often as I need. That is what counts.

KÄTHE KOLLWITZ

September 1, 1911

I imagine the following sculpture as utterly beautiful: a pregnant woman chiseled out of stone. Carved only down to the knees so that she looks the way Lise said she did the time she was pregnant with Maria: "As if I am rooted to the ground." The immobility, restraint, introspection. The arms and hands dangling heavily, the head lowered, all attention directed inward. And the whole thing in heavy, heavy stone. Title: *Pregnancy.*

New Year's Day, 1912

. . . No progress in my relationship with Karl. What he always speaks of, what seems to him still the sole worthwhile goal of our long living together—that we should grow together in the deepest intimacy—I still do not feel and probably never will learn to feel.

Are not the ties with the boys also growing slacker? I almost think so. For the last third of life there remains only work. It alone is always stimulating, rejuvenating, exciting and satisfying. . . .

August 27, 1914

A piece by Gabriele Reuter in the *Tag* on the tasks of women today. She spoke of the joy of sacrificing—a phrase that struck me hard. Where do all the women who have watched so carefully over the lives of their beloved ones get the heroism to send them to face the cannon? . . .

September 30, 1914

Cold, cloudy autumnal weather. The grave mood that comes over one when one knows: there is war, and one cannot hold on to any illusions any more. Nothing is real but the frightfulness of this state, which we almost grow used to. In such times it seems so stupid that the boys must go to war. The whole thing is so ghastly and insane. Occasionally there comes the foolish thought: how can they possibly take part in such madness? And at once the cold shower: they *must, must!* All is leveled by death; down with all the youth! Then one is ready to despair.

Only one state of mind makes it at all bearable: to receive the sacrifice into one's will. But how can one maintain such a state?

[Peter Kollwitz was killed on October 22, 1914.]

December 9, 1914

My boy! On your memorial I want to have your figure on top, *above* the parents. You will lie outstretched, holding out your hands in answer to the call for sacrifice: "Here I am." Your eyes—perhaps—open wide, so that you see the blue sky above you, and the clouds and birds. Your mouth smiling. And at your breast the pink I gave you.

February 15, 1915

. . . I do not want to die, even if Hans and Karl should die. I do not want to go until I have faithfully made the most of my talent and cultivated the seed that was placed in me until the last small twig has grown. This does not contradict the fact that I would have died—smilingly—for Peter, and for Hans too, were the choice offered me . . . Peter was seed for the planting which should not have been ground. He was the sowing. I am the bearer and cultivator of seed-corn. What Hans will become, the future will show. But since I am to be the cultivator, I want to serve faithfully. Since recognizing that, I am almost serene and much firmer in spirit. It is not only that I am permitted to finish my work—I am obliged to finish it. This seems to me to be the meaning of all the babble about culture. Culture arises only when the individual fulfils his cycle of obligations. . . .

August 28, 1915

. . . How Karl and I are now growing more and more intimately used to one another . . . Yes, new flowers have grown up which would not have grown without the tears shed this year. . . .

September 1915

What can the goal of humanity be said to be? For men to be happy? No, or at any rate that is only a subsidiary goal. The goal is the same as it is for the individual. The individual strives first of all for happiness . . . happiness in love, and so on. On a somewhat higher plane is the joy of self-development. Bringing all one's forces to maturity . . . The goal is to develop divinity, spirituality.

January 17, 1916

. . . Where are my children now? What is left to their mother? One boy to the right and one to the left, my right son and my left son, as they called themselves. One dead and one so far away, and I cannot help him . . . My whole life as a mother is really behind me now. I often have a terrible longing to have it back again—to have children, my boys, one to the right and one to the left; to dance with them as formerly when spring arrived and Peter came with flowers and we danced a springtide dance.

January 31, 1916

My unpleasant position on the jury. I always find myself forced to defend the cause of a woman. But because I can never really do that with conviction, since most of the work in question is mediocre (if the works are better than that the other jury members will agree), I always become involved in equivocations.

For our silver wedding anniversary

Dear Husband: When we married, we took a leap in the dark. We were not building upon a firm foundation, or at least one firmly believed in. There were grave contradictions in my own feelings. In the end I acted on this impulse: jump in—you'll manage to swim. . . .

I have never been without your love, and because of it we are now so firmly linked after twenty-five years. Karl, my dear, thank you. I have so rarely told you in words what you have been and are to me. Today I want to do so, this once . . .

From the bottom of my heart I am thankful to the fate which gave us our children and in them such inexpressible happiness.

If Hans is let live, we shall be able to see his further development, and perhaps we may expect children of his. If he too is taken, then all the sunlight that out of him lighted, warmed and made everything golden will be smothered; but we shall still hold tight to one another's hands to the end. . . .

Your Käthe

Käthe Kollwitz

Stagnation in my work.

When I feel so parched, I almost long for the sorrow again. And then when it comes back I feel it stripping me physically of all the strength I need for work.

Made a drawing: the mother letting her dead son slide into her arms. I might make a hundred such drawings and yet I do not get any closer to him. I am seeking him. As if I had to find him in the work. . . .

October 11, 1916

. . . Is it a breach of faith with you, Peter, if I can now see only madness in the war? Peter, you died believing. . . .

July 26, 1917

Work is still going very well . . . It is as if a fog had lifted. . . .

March 19, 1918

. . . If all the people who have been hurt by the war were to exclude joy from their lives, it would almost be as if they had died. Men without joy seem like corpses. . . .

. . . At the beginning it would have been wholly impossible for me to conceive of letting the boys go as parents *must* let their boys go now, without inwardly affirming it—letting them go simply to the slaughterhouse. That is what changes everything. The feeling that we were betrayed then, at the beginning. And perhaps Peter would still be living had it not been for this terrible betrayal. Peter and millions, many millions of other boys. All betrayed. . . .

Revelations

October 1, 1918

. . . Wildly contradictory feelings. Germany is losing the war . . . Will the patriotic emotion flare up once more so powerfully that a last-ditch defense will start? . . . *not another day* of war when it is clear that the war is lost.

December 26, 1919

There are days when Mother sleeps most of the time, murmuring softly in her dreams and daydreaming when she is awake. Always about children . . . It is really so sweet to see how the dreams and visions and fantasies of so old a mother always return to her children. So after all they were the strongest emotion in her life.

February 26, 1920

I want to do a drawing of a man *who sees the suffering of the world*. That can only be Jesus, I suppose. In the drawing where Death seizes the children there is also a woman in the background who sees the suffering of the world. The children being seized by death are not hers; she is too old for that. Nor is she looking; she does not stir, but she knows about the world's suffering. . . .

End of October, 1921

A lovely, happy period of work. The *Mothers* is making progress day by day. How wonderful life is at such times.

Karl had a pleasant experience recently. He lectured to a group of women and young girls. I did not wait up for him, but went to bed. Around eleven o'clock I heard young voices singing, moving past our house and then fading away. The girls had accompanied Karl home, singing.

Karl is blithe. How good it is for me when I sometimes complain about too little time, and so on—the way he unsentimentally and yet with the greatest kindness thrusts my nonsense aside.

December 1922

. . . Peter [Hans's son] on the high chair, also at the table, with his back to me. All around his head the fine white hair, shot through with light. It so reminded me of our own children. Afterwards, when I held him on my lap, he kept pointing at me and saying, "Here, Gandmother." A pause between "Gand" and "mother," and then the word "mother" slipping out quickly, carelessly.

June 1924

The first day of Whitsun, a joyous and happy day for me. I went out to spend it with the children. Magnificent weather. . . . The twins are precious. Sturdy, droll, innocent little white heads. Babbling their own language. When Ottilie sits between them to feed them and gives each in turn a spoonful of pap, the one who doesn't have her turn clenches her fists and her face turns red at having to wait, while the other opens her mouth for the spoon with the smuggest air of contentment. It is wonderful to see. Happy Ottilie, who is so thoroughly maternal. Whatever comes later on, these three years of work with the babies will always give her a kind of satiated feeling. She is a mother through and through, much as she sometimes rants against being one.

Little Peter has given me a pink.

Revelations

When I entered Mother's room today to bring her down to supper, I saw a strange scene. Like something out of a fairy tale. Mother sat at the table, under the lamp, in Grandfather's easy chair. In front of her were snapshots she was looking through. Diagonally across her shoulders sat Frau Klingelhof's big cat.

Mother used to be unable to stand cats. But now she likes to have the cat on her lap. The cat warms her hands. Sometimes it seems to me that Mother thinks the cat is a baby. When it wants to get down, Mother clasps it anxiously, as if she were afraid the baby will fall. Then her face is full of concern. She actually struggles with the cat.

In the picture Helmy Hart took of Mother, which shows only the head, Mother has a strange expression. The wisdom of great age is there. But it is not the wisdom that thinks in thoughts; rather it operates through dim feelings. These are not the "thoughts hitherto inconceivable" that Goethe had, but the summation of eighty-seven years of living, which are now unclearly felt. Mother muses. Yet even that is not quite it, for musing implies, after all, thinking. It is hard to say what the picture expresses. The features themselves do not definitely express one thing or another. Precisely because Mother no longer thinks, there is a unity about her. A very old woman who lives within herself in undifferentiated perception. Yes, that is right; but in addition: who lives within herself according to an order that is pure and harmonious. As Mother's nature always was.

It seems more and more evident to me that Mother does not recognize the cat for what it is, but thinks it is a baby. Often she wraps it up in a blanket and holds it just like a child. It is touching and sweet to see my old mother doing this.

Käthe Kollwitz

New Year's Eve, 1925

Recently I began reading my old diaries. Back to before the war. Gradually I became very depressed. The reason for that is probably that I wrote only when there were obstacles and halts to the flow of life, seldom when everything was smooth and even . . . I distinctly felt what a half-truth a diary presents . . . I put the diaries away with a feeling of relief that I am safely out of those times. Yet they were times which I always think of as the best in my life, the decade from my mid-thirties to my mid-forties. . . .

New Year's, 1932

Age remains age, that is, it pains, torments and subdues. When others see my scant achievements, they speak of a happy old age. I doubt that there is such a thing as a happy old age.

September 1938

War has been averted! Thank you, Chamberlain!

In the debate on the imminent danger of war, someone in the British Parliament said: "There is nothing in the world important enough to justify unleashing another world war." *I agree absolutely! Nothing* in the world. God knows, not Deutschland, Deutschland *über* alles!

February 3, 1940

Just a year ago Karl got so sick I thought he would not pull through. . . . Often, during the worst of it, when I no longer had any hope, I wished the end would come for him. I was all prepared for it, and when he seemed to improve I took

249

it for a temporary postponement of the inevitable end. Now I am thankful that his tolerable state of health looks as though it will last a while. Yet when the end does suddenly come, parting will again be very hard.

I am working on the small group in which the man—Karl—frees himself from me and withdraws from my arms. He lets himself sink. . . .

July 1940

Karl has died, July 19, 1940.

April 1941

Recently I dreamed that I was together with the others in a room. I knew that Karl lay in the adjoining room. Both rooms opened out into an unlit hallway. I went out of my room into the hall and saw the door to Karl's room being opened, and then I heard him say in his kind, loving voice: "Aren't you going to say good night to me?" Then he came out and leaned against the wall, and I stood before him and leaned my body against his, and we held each other's hands and asked each other again and again: "How are you? Is everything all right?" And we were so happy being able to feel one another.

December 1941

My days pass, and if anyone asks me how things are I usually answer, "Not so good," or something of the sort.

Today I thought it over and decided that I am really not badly off. Naturally I cannot say that things are good—no one could say that. For we are at war and millions of human beings are suffering from it, and I along with them. Moreover,

I am old and infirm. And yet I am often amazed at how I endure it without feeling altogether unhappy. For there are moments on most days when I feel a deep and sincere gratitude. Not only when we hear from Peter . . . but also when I sit at the open window and there is a blue sky or there are moving clouds. And also when I stretch out in bed at night, dog-tired. . . .

. . . I am afraid of dying—but being dead, oh yes, that to me is often an appealing prospect. If it were only not for the necessity of parting from the few who are dear to me here.

October 1942

Hans has been here. On Wednesday October 14. When he came into my room very silently, I understood that Peter was dead. He fell on September 22.

May 1943

[The last diary entry.]

Hans has reached the age of 51. Air-raid alarm the night of May 14. It was the loveliest of May nights. Hans and Ottilie did not go to sleep until very late. They sat in the garden and listened to a nightingale.

After work Hans came, then Ottilie and finally Lise. The four of us sat together. On his birthday table, below the grave relief, I had placed the lithograph *Death Calls*, the print of which I worked over. Then there was a drawing I had made of Karl one time when he was reading aloud to me. We were sitting around the living room table at the time. This drawing is a favorite of Hans'. And there was also the small etching, *Greeting*, which is closely connected with his birthday. . . .

Early next morning, Hans came again and brought a great bouquet of lilies from the garden. What happiness it is for me that I still have my boy whom I love so deeply and who is so fond of me.

Goethe to Lavater, 1779: "But let us stop worrying our particular religions like a dog its bone. *I have gone beyond purely sensual truth.*"

PART III *Power*

"He who, being a man, remains a woman,
will become a universal channel."
LAO-TZU

FRANCES ANNE KEMBLE
(1809-1893)

anny Kemble went to work at the age of twenty. In order to save her actor-manager father's faltering Covent Garden Theater, she appeared as Juliet and was an immediate theatrical sensation. She disliked acting, believing it eroded the personality and that the stage was a "disgusting travesty." She wanted to be a writer and had written plays and poetry since childhood. But her fame as a gifted actress spread, and she and her father left England to tour the United States, where she was courted by a wealthy Philadelphian, Pierce Butler. Against the advice of friends, who felt him her intellectual inferior, she married him. He was attractive and well-mannered and she anticipated a quiet family life and the chance to write.

The marriage was in trouble from the beginning. A fierce libertarian who in England had always aligned herself with the working classes, Fanny claimed that she discovered only after the wedding that Pierce's wealth came from slave-operated rice plantations in Georgia. She was horrified at the concept of her husband's owning the lives of others and told him so often, urging him to prepare his slaves for the responsibilities of eventual independence. She angered him further by arranging to publish a journal of her reflections on American taste and manners in which she said that marriage should be an equal partnership in which neither party should try to coerce the other. A deeply conventional man, incapable of understanding the fiery woman he thought he had bought as an adornment to his social-climbing life, Pierce tried to break Fanny's contract with the publisher. She left him, but got no farther than a Philadelphia hotel. She had given all her earnings to her father when she married. Penniless and pregnant, she returned to her husband the same night to try and make the marriage work.

Fanny had always wanted to see with her own eyes the living conditions of her husband's "dreadful possessions," which he assured her were of the best. When ill health led him to winter in the warmer climate of his Georgian plantation, he reluctantly allowed her to accompany him. Her abstract notions of the injustice of slavery were soon painfully concrete. She found herself in the uncomfortable position of a visiting deity, an intermediary between the slaves—especially the women—and their overseers.

She recorded the horrors she witnessed and her own helplessness in a journal that took the form of unmailed letters to her friend Elizabeth Sedgwick. Publication of the journal was impossible. Even if Pierce Butler had consented to documentation of his treatment of the slaves—and he was considered one of the most benevolent owners—Fanny was aware of the irony of the wife of a plantation owner renouncing the economic practice by which she was fed and clothed.

Her *Journal of a Residence on a Georgian Plantation in 1838–39* finally was published during the Civil War. In the intervening years Fanny tried to accommodate her ethical beliefs to the demands of her husband, but she was unable to keep still. In an ugly and widely publicized lawsuit, she was divorced by Pierce Butler, deprived of her daughters and left without income. Fortunate in having a profession to support her, she once again became a celebrated figure of the stage, taking the name Mrs. Fanny Kemble. She retired finally to England, where she spent her last years writing. The complete story is told in *Fanny Kemble and the Lovely Land* by Constance Wright, Dodd, Mead and Co., 1972.

January, 1839

Dear Elizabeth,

. . . I must inform you of a curious conversation which took place between my little girl and the woman who performs for us the offices of chambermaid here—of course one of Mr. Butler's slaves. What suggested it to the child, or whence indeed she gathered her information, I know not; but children are made of eyes and ears, and nothing, however minute escapes their microscopic observation. She suddenly began addressing this woman.

"Mary, some persons are free and some are not (the woman made no reply). I am a free person (of a little more than three years old). I say, I am a free person, Mary—do you know that?"

"Yes, missis."

"Some persons are free and some are not—do you know that, Mary?"

"Yes, missis, here," was the reply; "I know it is so here, in this world."

Here my child's white nurse, my dear Margery, who had hitherto been silent, interfered, saying, "Oh, then you think it will not always be so?"

"Me hope not, missis."

I am afraid, Elizabeth, this woman actually imagines that there will be no slaves in heaven; isn't that preposterous, now, when, by the account of most of the Southerners, slavery itself must be heaven, or something uncommonly like it? Oh, if you could imagine how this title "Missis" addressed to me and to my children, shocks all my feelings! Several times I have exclaimed: "For God's sake do not call me that!" and only been awakened by the stupid amazement of the poor creatures I was addressing to the perfect uselessness of my thus expostulating with them; once or twice, indeed, I have done more—I have explained to them, and they appeared to comprehend me well, that I have no ownership over them, for that I held such ownership sinful, and that, though I was the wife of the man who pretends to own them, I was, in truth, no more their mistress than they were mine. Some of them, I know, understood me, more of them did not. . . .

I forgot to tell you that in the hospital were several sick babies, whose mothers were permitted to suspend their field labor in order to nurse them. Upon addressing some remonstrances to one of these, who, besides having a sick child, was ill herself, about the horribly dirty condition of her baby, she assured me that it was impossible for them to keep their children clean; that they went out to work at daybreak, and did not get their tasks done till evening, and that then they were too tired and worn out to do anything but throw themselves down and sleep. This statement of hers I mentioned on my return from the hospital, and the overseer appeared extremely annoyed by it, and assured me repeatedly that it was not true. . . .

This morning I paid my second visit to the infirmary, and found there had been some faint attempt at sweeping and cleaning, in compliance with my entreaties. The poor woman Harriet, however, whose statement with regard to the impossibility of their attending properly to their children had been so vehemently denied by the overseer, was crying bitterly. I asked her what ailed her, when, more by signs and dumb show than words, she and old Rose informed me that Mr. O—— had flogged her that morning for having told me that the women had not time to keep their children clean. It is part of the regular duty of every overseer to visit the infirmary at least once a day, which he generally does in the morning, and Mr. O——'s visit had preceded mine but a short time only, or I might have been edified by seeing a man horsewhip a woman.

. . . I will tell you a story which has just formed an admirable illustration for my observation of all the miseries of which this accursed system of slavery is the cause, even under the best and most humane administration of its laws and usages. Pray note it, my dear friend, for you will find, in the absence of all voluntary or even conscious cruelty on the part of the master, the best possible comment on a state of things which, without the slightest desire to injure and oppress, produces such intolerable results of injury and oppression.

We have, as a sort of under nursemaid and assistant of my dear M[argery], whose white complexion, as I wrote you, occasioned such indignation to my Southern fellow travelers, and such extreme perplexity to the poor slaves on our arrival here, a much more orthodox servant for these parts, a young woman named Psyche, but commonly called Sack, not a very graceful abbreviation of the divine heathen appellation. She cannot be much over twenty, has a very pretty figure, a graceful, gentle deportment, and a face which, but for its color (she is a dingy mulatto), would be pretty, and is extremely pleasing, from the perfect sweetness of its expression; she is always serious, not to say sad and silent, and has always an air of melancholy and timidity, that has frequently struck me very much, and would have made me think some special anxiety or sorrow must occasion it, but that God knows the whole condition of these wretched people naturally produces such a deportment, and there is no necessity to seek for special or peculiar causes to account for it. Just in proportion as I have

259

found the slaves on this plantation intelligent and advanced beyond the general brutish level of the majority, I have observed this pathetic expression of countenance in them, a mixture of sadness and fear, the involuntary exhibition of the two feelings, which I suppose must be the predominant experience of their whole lives, regret and apprehension, not the less heavy, either of them, for being in some degree, vague and indefinite—a sense of incalculable past loss and injury, and a dread of incalculable future loss and injury.

I have never questioned Psyche as to her sadness, because, in the first place, as I tell you, it appears to me most natural, and is observable in all the slaves whose superior natural or acquired intelligence allows of their filling situations of trust or service about the house and family; and, though I cannot and will not refuse to hear any and every tale of suffering which these unfortunates bring to me, I am anxious to spare both myself and them the pain of vain appeals to me for redress and help, which, alas! it is too often utterly out of my power to give them. It is useless, and, indeed, worse than useless, that they should see my impotent indignation and unavailing pity, and hear expressions of compassion for them, and horror at their condition, which might only prove incentives to a hopeless resistance on their part to a system, under the hideous weight of whose oppression any individual or partial revolt must be annihilated and ground into the dust. Therefore, as I tell you, I asked Psyche no questions; but, to my great astonishment, the other day M[argery] asked me if I knew to whom Psyche belonged, as the poor woman had inquired of her with much hesitation and anguish if she could tell her who owned her and her children. She has two nice little children under six years old, whom she keeps as clean and tidy, and who are sad and as silent as herself. My astonishment at this question was, as you will readily believe, not small, and I forthwith sought out Psyche for an explanation.

She was thrown into extreme perturbation at finding that her question had been referred to me, and it was some time before I could sufficiently reassure her to be able to comprehend, in the midst of her reiterated entreaties for pardon, and hopes that she had not offended me, that she did not know herself who owned her. She was, at one time, the property of Mr. K[ing], the former overseer, of whom I have already spoken to you, and who has just been paying Mr. [Butler] a visit. He, like several of his predecessors in the management, has contrived to make a fortune upon it (though it yearly decreases in value to the owners, but this is the inevitable course of things in the Southern states), and has purchased a plantation of his own in Alabama, I believe, or one of the Southwestern states. Whether she still belonged to Mr. K[ing] or not she did not know, and entreated me, if she did, to endeavor to persuade Mr. [Butler] to buy her. Now you must know that this poor woman is the wife of one of Mr. [Butler]'s slaves, a fine, intelligent, active, excellent young man, whose whole family are among some of the very best specimens of character and capacity on the estate. I was so astonished at the (to me) extraordinary state of things revealed by poor Sack's petition, that I could only tell her that I had supposed all the Negroes on the plantation were Mr. [Butler]'s property, but that I would certainly inquire, and find out for her, if I could, to whom she belonged, and if I could, endeavor to get Mr. [Butler] to purchase her, if she really was not his.

Now, E[lizabeth], just conceive for one moment the state of mind of this woman, believing herself to belong to a man who in a few days was going down to one of those abhorred and dreaded Southwestern states, and who would then compel her, with her poor little children, to leave her husband and the only home she had ever known, and all the ties of affection, relationship, and association of her former life, to follow him thither, in all human probability never again to behold any living creature that she had seen before; and this was so completely a matter of course that it was not even thought necessary to apprise her positively of the fact, and the only thing that interposed between her and this most miserable fate was the faint hope that Mr. [Butler] *might have* purchased her and her children. But if he had, if this great deliverance had been vouchsafed to her, the knowledge of it was not thought necessary; and with this deadly dread at her heart she was living day after day, waiting upon me and seeing me, with my husband beside me, and my children in my arms in blessed security, safe from all separation but the one reserved in God's great providence for all His creatures. Do you think I wondered any more at the woebegone expression of her countenance, or do you think it was easy for me to restrain within prudent and proper limits the expression of my feelings at such a state of things? And she had gone on from day to day enduring this agony, till I suppose its own intolerable pressure and M[argery]'s sweet countenance and gentle sympathizing voice and manner had constrained her to lay down this great burden of sorrow at our feet.

I did not see Mr. [Butler] until the evening; but, in the meantime, meeting Mr. O——, the overseer, with whom, as I believe I have already told you, we are living here, I asked him about Psyche, and who was her proprietor, when, to my infinite surprise, he told me that *he* had bought her and her children from Mr. K[ing], who had offered them to him, saying that they would be rather troublesome to him than otherwise down where he was going. "And so," said Mr. O——, "as I had no objection to investing a little money that way, I bought them." With a heart much lightened, I flew to tell poor Psyche the news, so that, at any rate, she might be relieved from the dread of any immediate separation from her husband. You can imagine better than I can tell you what her sensations were; but she still renewed her prayer that I would, if possible, induce Mr. [Butler] to purchase her, and I promised to do so.

Early the next morning, while I was still dressing, I was suddenly startled by hearing voices in loud tones in Mr. [Butler]'s dressing room, which adjoins my bedroom, and the noise increasing until there was an absolute cry of despair uttered by some man. I could restrain myself no longer, but opened the door of communication and saw Joe, the young man, poor Psyche's husband, raving almost in a state of frenzy, and in a voice broken with sobs and almost inarticulate with passion, reiterating his determination never to leave this plantation, never to go to Alabama, never to leave his old father and mother, his poor wife and children, and dashing his hat, which he was wringing like a cloth in his hands, upon the ground, he declared he would kill himself if he was compelled to follow Mr. K[ing]. I glanced from the poor wretch to Mr. [Butler], who was standing, leaning against a table with his arms folded, occasionally uttering a few words of counsel to his slave to be quiet and not fret, and not make fuss about what there was no help for. I retreated immediately from the horrid scene, breathless with surprise and dismay, and stood for some time in my own room, with my heart and temples throbbing to such a degree that I could hardly support myself. As soon as I recovered myself I again sought Mr. O——, and inquired of him if he knew the cause of poor Joe's distress. He then told me that Mr. [Butler], who is highly pleased with Mr. K[ing]'s past administration of his property, wished, on his departure for his newly acquired slave plantation, to give him some token of his satisfaction, and *had made him a present* of the man Joe, who had just received the intelligence that he was to go down to Alabama with his new owner the next day, leaving father, mother, wife, and children behind. You will not wonder that the man required a little judicious soothing under such circumstances, and you will also, I hope, admire the humanity of the sale of his wife and children by the owner who was going to take him to Alabama, because *they* would be encumbrances rather than otherwise down there. If Mr. K[ing] did not do this after he knew that the man was his, then Mr. [Butler] gave him to be carried down to the South after his wife and children were sold to remain in Georgia. I do not know which was the real transaction, for I have not had the heart to ask; but you will easily imagine which of the two cases I prefer believing.

When I saw Mr. [Butler] after this most wretched story became known to me in all its details, I appealed to him, for his own soul's sake, not to commit so great a cruelty. Poor Joe's agony while remonstrating with his master was hardly greater than mine while arguing with him upon this bitter piece of inhumanity—how I cried, and how I adjured, and how all my sense of justice, and of mercy, and of pity for the poor wretch, and of wretchedness at finding myself implicated in such a state of things, broke in torrents of words from my lips and tears from my eyes! God knows such a sorrow at seeing anyone I belonged to commit such an act was indeed a new and terrible experience to me, and it seemed to me that I was imploring Mr. [Butler] to save himself more than to spare these wretches. He gave me no answer whatever, and I have since thought that the intemperate vehemence of my entreaties and expostulations perhaps deserved that he should leave me as he did without one single word of reply; and miserable enough I remained.

Toward evening, as I was sitting alone, my children having gone to bed, Mr. O—— came into the room. I had but one subject in my mind; I had not been able to eat for it. I could hardly sit still for the nervous distress which every thought of these poor people filled me with. As he sat down looking over some accounts, I said to him: "Have you seen Joe this afternoon, Mr. O——?" (I give you our conversation as it took place.)

"Yes, ma'am; he is a great deal happier than he was this morning."

"Why, how is that?" asked I, eagerly.

"Oh, he is not going to Alabama. Mr. K[ing] heard that he had kicked up a fuss about it" (being in despair at being torn from one's wife and children is called *kicking up a fuss;* this is a sample of overseer appreciation of human feelings), "and said that if the fellow wasn't willing to go with him, he did not wish to be bothered with any niggers down there who were to be troublesome, so he might stay behind."

"And does Psyche know this?"

"Yes, ma'am, I suppose so."

I drew a long breath; and whereas my needle had stumbled through the stuff I was sewing for an hour before, as if my fingers could not guide it, the regularity and rapidity of its evolutions were now quite edifying. The man was for the present safe, and I remained silently pondering his deliverance and the whole proceeding, and the conduct of everyone engaged in it, and, above all, Mr. [Butler]'s share in the transaction, and I think, for the first time, almost a sense of horrible personal responsibility and implication took hold of my mind, and I felt the weight of an unimagined guilt upon my conscience; and yet, God knows, this feeling of self-condemnation is very gratuitous on my part, since when I married Mr. [Butler] I knew nothing of these dreadful possessions of his, and even if I had I should have been much puzzled to have formed any idea of the state of things in which I now find myself plunged, together with those whose well-doing is as vital to me almost as my own.

With these agreeable reflections I went to bed. Mr. [Butler] said not a word to me upon the subject of these poor people all the next day, and in the meantime I became very impatient of this reserve on his part, because I was dying to prefer my request that he would purchase Psyche and her children, and so prevent any future separation between her and her husband, as I supposed he would not again attempt to make a present of Joe, at least to anyone who did not wish to be *bothered* with his wife and children. In the evening I was again with Mr. O—— alone in the strange, bare, wooden-walled sort of shanty which is our sitting room, and revolving in my mind the means of rescuing Psyche from her miserable suspense, a long chain of all my possessions, in the shape of bracelets, necklaces, brooches, earrings, etc., wound in glittering procession through my brain, with many hypothetical calculations of the value of each separate ornament, and the very doubtful probability of the amount of the whole being equal to the price of this poor creature and her children; and then the great power and privilege I had foregone of earning money by my own labor occurred to me, and I think, for the first time in my life, my past profession assumed an aspect that arrested my thoughts most seriously. For the last four years of my life that preceded my marriage I literally coined money, and never until this moment, I think, did I reflect on the great means of good, to myself and others, that I so gladly agreed to give up forever for a maintenance by the unpaid labor of slaves—people toiling not only unpaid, but under the bitter conditions the bare contemplation of which was then wringing my heart. You will not wonder that when, in the midst of such cogitations, I suddenly accosted Mr. O——, it was to this effect: "Mr. O——, I have a particular favor to beg of you. Promise me that you will never sell Psyche and her children without first letting me know of your intention to do so, and giving me the option of buying them."

Mr. O—— is a remarkably deliberate man, and squints, so that, when he has taken a little time in directing his eyes to you, you are still unpleasantly unaware of any result in which you are concerned; he laid down a book he was reading, and directed his head and one of his eyes toward me and answered: "Dear me, ma'am, I am very sorry—I have sold them."

My work fell down on the ground, and my mouth opened wide, but I could utter no sound, I was so dismayed and surprised; and he deliberately proceeded: "I didn't know, ma'am, you see, at all, that you entertained any idea of making an investment of that nature; for I'm sure, if I had, I would willingly have sold the woman to you; but I sold her and her children this morning to Mr. [Butler]."

My dear E[lizabeth], though [Mr. Butler] had resented my unmeasured upbraidings, you see they had not been without some good effect, and though he had, perhaps justly, punished my violent outbreak of indignation about the miserable scene I witnessed by not telling me of his humane purpose, he had bought these poor creatures, and so, I trust, secured them from any such misery in future. I jumped up and left Mr. O—— still speaking, and ran to find Mr. [Butler], to thank him for what he had done, and with that will now bid you good-by. Think, E[lizabeth], how it fares with slaves on plantations where there is no crazy Englishwoman to weep, and entreat, and implore, and upbraid for them, and no master willing to listen to such appeals.

My dearest Elizabeth, I write to you today (February 26) in great depression and distress. I have had a most painful conversation with Mr. Butler, who has declined receiving any of the people's petitions through me. Whether he is wearied with the number of these prayers and supplications, which he would escape but for me, as they probably would not venture to come so incessantly to him, and I, of course, feel bound to bring every one confided to me to him, or whether he has been annoyed at the number of pitiful and horrible stories of misery and oppression under the former rule of Mr. K[ing], which have come to my knowledge since I have been here, and the grief and indignation caused, but which cannot, by any means, always be done away with, though their expression may be silenced by his angry exclamations of: "Why do you listen to such stuff?" or "Why do you believe such trash? don't you know the niggers are all d——d liars?" etc., I do not know; but he desired me this morning to bring him no more complaints or requests of any sort, as the people had hitherto had no such advocate, and had done very well without, and I was only kept in an incessant state of excitement with all the falsehoods they "found they could make me believe." How well they have done without my advocacy, the conditions which I see with my own eyes, even more than their pitiful petitions, demonstrate; it is indeed true that the sufferings of those who come to me for redress, and, still more, the injustice done to the great majority who cannot, have filled my heart with bitterness and indignation that have overflowed my lips, till, I suppose Mr. [Butler] is weary of hearing what he has never heard before, the voice of passionate expostulation and importunate pleading against wrongs that he will not even acknowledge, and for creatures whose common humanity with his own I half think he does not believe, but I must return to the North, for my condition would be almost worse than theirs—condemned to hear and see so much wretchedness, not only without the means of alleviating it, but without permission even to represent it for alleviation; this is no place for me, since I was not born among slaves, and cannot bear to live among them.

Perhaps, after all, what he says is true: when I am gone they will fall back into the desperate uncomplaining habit of suffering, from which my coming among them, willing to hear and ready to help, has tempted them. He says that bringing their complaints to me, and the sight of my credulous commiseration, only tend to make them discontented and idle, and brings renewed chastisement upon them; and that so, instead of really befriending them, I am only preparing more suffering for them whenever I leave the place, and they can no more cry to me for help. And so I see nothing for it but to go and leave them to their fate; perhaps, too, he is afraid of the mere contagion of freedom which breathes from the very existence of those who are free; my way of speaking to the people, of treating them, or living with them, the appeals I make to their sense of truth, of duty, of self-respect, the infinite compassion and the human consideration I feel for them —all this, of course, makes my intercourse with them dangerously suggestive of relations far different from anything they have ever known; and, as Mr. O—— once almost hinted to me, my existence among slaves was an element of danger to the "institution." If I should go away, the human sympathy that I have felt for them will certainly never come near them again.

MARY BOYKIN CHESNUT

(1 8 2 3 - 1 8 8 6)

*T*his *diary was first edited* by Mary Boykin Chesnut. She began it at the outbreak of the Civil War when she was thirty-seven and kept it from day to day on whatever scraps of paper were available. After the war she sensibly decided the diary should be preserved in some orderly form and set about the monumental task of transcribing the almost 400,000 words into notebooks. Later edited by Ben Ames Williams as *Diary From Dixie,* this is a rare and sweeping chronicle of the texture of daily life in that period as well as a self-portrait of a woman of vigorous and complex character.

As a diarist, Mary had unusual qualifications. She was the daughter of a distinguished South Carolinian who had served as governor and in the House of Representatives and the Senate. At seventeen she had married Colonel James Chesnut, later a senator himself and, during the war, a brigadier general and an aide to President Jefferson Davis. Therefore she knew the Confederate leaders and the views of the high-born, as well as something of the life of the poorer whites and the slaves. The Chesnuts were childless, and she traveled about during the war, observing its toll on the people from several points of view. She had that essential quality of a good diarist of being an interesting individual herself: intelligent, outspoken, articulate, widely read. She was a good friend and devoted wife, candid about the faults of others and of herself. She understood both intellectually and emotionally the sexual connotations of slavery and its relationship to the marriage institution as misuse of power. Her vision extended beyond the personal diary to a broad view of an outer reality in which both North and South were culpable.

Before the war the Chesnuts lived at Mulberry Plantation, his parents' home near Camden, South Carolina, "the very pleasantest most easy-going life I ever saw." After the South's defeat they built Sarsfield, nearby, where they lived for almost twenty years before their deaths.

Ben Ames Williams acknowledged his debt to Mary's diary for background and characterization for his novel *House Divided*. He writes: "If only true history concerns itself not so much with what statesmen and generals *did* at a given time as with what men and women *were,* then this Diary is a masterpiece of history in the highest and fullest sense."

February 15, 1861

I came to Charleston on November 7th and then went to Florida to see my mother. On the train, just before we reached Fernandina, a woman called out: "That settles the hash!" Tanny touched me on the shoulder and said: "Lincoln's elected." "How do you know?" "The man over there has a telegram." Someone cried: "Now that the black radical Republicans have the power I suppose they will Brown us all."

I have always kept a journal, with notes and dates and a line of poetry or prose, but from today forward I will write more. . . .

Revelations

. . . Brewster says the war specks are growing in size. Nobody at the North, or in Virginia believes we are in earnest. They think we are sulking and that Jeff Davis and Stephens are getting up a very pretty little comedy. The Virginia delegates were insulted at the peace conference; Brewster said, "kicked out." He says every word the papers tell about Lincoln's vulgarity is true, and his wife and son are as bad.

March 1, 1861

. . . Brewster says Lincoln passed through Baltimore disguised, and at night, and that he was wise to do so, for just now Baltimore is dangerous ground. Senator Stephen A. Douglas told Mr. Chesnut that "Lincoln is awfully clever," and that he had found him a heavy handful.

Went to pay my respect to Mrs. Jefferson Davis. She met me with open arms. We did not allude to anything by which we are surrounded. We eschewed politics and our changed relations. I came home and went to bed after a chat with Mr. Chesnut, which after all is the best fun.

March 4, 1861

. . . I have seen a Negro woman sold upon the block at auction. I was walking. The woman on the block overtopped the crowd. I felt faint, seasick. The creature looked so like my good little Nancy. She was a bright mulatto, with a pleasant face. She was magnificently gotten up in silks and satins. She seemed delighted with it all, sometimes ogling the bidders, sometimes looking quite coy and modest; but her mouth never relaxed from its expanded grin of excitement. I dare say the poor thing knew who would buy her. My very soul sickened.

It was too dreadful. I tried to reason. "You know how women sell themselves and are sold in marriage, from queens downwards, eh? You know what the Bible says about slavery, and marriage. Poor women, poor slaves."

March 14, 1861

"Now this is positive," they say. "Fort Sumter is to be relieved, and we are to have no war." . . . If there be no war, how triumphant Mr. Chesnut will be. He is the only man who has persisted from the first that this would be a peaceful revolution. Heaven grant it may be so! . . .

I wonder if it be a sin to think slavery a curse to any land. Men and women are punished when their masters and mistresses are brutes, not when they do wrong. Under slavery, we live surrounded by prostitutes, yet an abandoned woman is sent out of any decent house. Who thinks any worse of a Negro or mulatto woman for being a thing we can't name? God forgive us, but ours is a monstrous system, a wrong and an iniquity! Like the patriarchs of old, our men live all in one house with their wives and their concubines; and the mulattoes one sees in every family partly resemble the white children. Any lady is ready to tell you who is the father of all the mulatto children in everybody's household but her own. Those, she seems to think, drop from the clouds. My disgust sometimes is boiling over . . .

I think this journal will be disadvantageous for me, for I spend my time now like a spider spinning my own entrails, instead of reading as my habit was in all spare moments.

(Charleston, South Carolina)
April 8, 1861

. . . Things are happening so fast. My husband has been made an aide-de-camp of General Beauregard. Three hours ago we were quietly packing to go home. The Convention had adjourned. Now he tells me the attack upon Fort Sumter may begin tonight. . . .

April 13, 1861

. . . How gay we were last night. Reaction after the dread of all the slaughter we thought those dreadful cannons were making such a noise in doing. Not even a battery the worse for wear.

Fort Sumter has been on fire. He has not yet silenced any of our guns, or so the aides—still with swords and red sashes by way of uniform—tell us. But the sound of those guns make regular meals impossible. None of us go to table, but tea trays pervade the corridors going everywhere. Some of the anxious hearts lie on their beds and moan in solitary misery. Mrs. Wigfall and I solace ourselves with tea in my room. These women have all a satisfying faith. "God is on our side," they cry. When we are shut in, we, Mrs. Wigfall and I, ask: "Why?" Answer: "Of course, He hates the Yankees! You'll think that well of him."

Not by one word or look can we detect any change in the demeanor of these Negro servants. Lawrence sits at our door, as sleepy and as respectful and as profoundly indifferent. So are they all. They carry it too far. You could not tell that they even hear the awful noise that is going on in the bay, though it is dinning in their ears night and day. And people talk before them as if they were chairs and tables, and they make no sign. Are they stolidly stupid, or wiser than we are, silent and strong, biding their time. . . .

May 19, 1861

Back in Montgomery . . . I drove out with Mrs. Davis. She finds playing Mrs. President of this small Confederacy slow work, after leaving friends . . . in Washington. I do not blame her. The wrench has been awful with us all. But we don't mean to be turned into pillars of salt. . . .

July 14, 1861

. . . Now every day we grow weaker and they stronger, so we had better give a telling blow at once. Already we begin to cry out for more ammunition, and already the blockade is beginning to shut it all out . . .

I did not know there was such a "bitter cry" left in me; but I wept my heart away today when my husband went off. Things do look so black . . .

July 24, 1861

. . . They brought me a Yankee soldier's portfolio from the battlefield . . . One might shed a few tears over some of the letters. Women—wives and mothers—are the same everywhere. . . .

July 27, 1861

. . . Here is one of Mr. Chesnut's anecdotes of the Manassas. He had in his pocket a small paper of morphine. He put it there to alleviate pain . . . Later in the day he saw a man lying under a tree who begged for water. He wore the Federal Uniform. As Mr. Chesnut carried him the water, he asked where he was from. The man refused to answer. "Poor fellow, you have no cause to care about all that now. You can't hurt me and God knows I would not harm you. What else do you want?" "Straighten my legs. They are doubled up under me." The legs were smashed. Mr. Chesnut gave him some morphine to let him know at least a few moments of peace.

He said to me: "This is my first battle. I hope my heart will not grow harder."

August 27, 1861

. . . I do not know when I have seen a woman without knitting in her hand. "Socks for the soldiers" is the cry. One poor man said he had dozens of socks and but one shirt. He preferred more shirts and fewer stockings . . .

I hate slavery. You say there are no more fallen women on a plantation than in London, in proportion to numbers, but what do you say to this? A magnate who runs a hideous black harem with its consequences under the same roof with his lovely white wife, and his beautiful and accomplished daughters? He holds his head as high and poses as the model of all human virtues and these poor women whom God and the laws have given him. From the height of his awful majesty, he scolds and thunders at them, as if he never did wrong in his life. Fancy such a man finding his daughter reading "Don Juan": "You with that immoral book!" And he orders her out of his sight. You see, Mrs. Stowe did not hit the sorest spot. She makes Legree a bachelor.

October 7, 1861

. . . We ought to be grateful that anyone of us is alive, but nobody is afraid of their own Negroes. I find everyone, like myself, ready to trust their own yard. I would go down on the plantation tomorrow and stay there even if there were no white person in twenty miles. My Molly and all the rest I believe would keep me as safe as I should be in the Tower of London.

MARY BOYKIN CHESNUT

October 13, 1861

. . . We went in the afternoon to the Negro church on the plantation . . . Jim Nelson . . . the stateliest darky I ever saw, tall and straight as a pine tree, with a fine face, and not so very black but a full-blooded African, was asked to lead in prayer. He became wildly excited, on his knees, facing us with his eyes shut. He clapped his hands at the end of every sentence, and his voice rose to the pitch of a shrill shriek, yet was strangely clear and musical, occasionally in a plaintive minor key that went to your heart. Sometimes it rang out like a trumpet. I wept bitterly. It was all sound, however, and emotional pathos. There was literally nothing in what he said. The words had no meaning at all. It was the devotional passion of voice and manner which was so magnetic. The Negroes sobbed and shouted and swayed backward and forward, some with aprons to their eyes, most of them clapping their hands and responding in shrill tones: "Yes, God!" "Jesus!" "Savior!" "Bless de Lord, amen," etc. It was a little too exciting for me. I would very much have liked to shout, too. . . .

. . . Suddenly, as I sat wondering what next, they broke out into one of those soul-stirring Negro camp-meeting hymns. To me this is the saddest of all earthly music, weird and depressing beyond my powers to describe.

(Mulberry Plantation, Camden, South Carolina)
November 28, 1861

"Ye who listen with credulity to the whispers of fancy"—pause, and look on this picture and that.

On the one side Mrs. Stowe, Greeley, Thoreau, Emerson . . . They live in nice New England homes, clean, sweet-smelling, shut up in libraries, writing books which ease

277

their hearts of their bitterness against us. What self-denial they do practice is to tell John Brown to come down here and cut our throats in Christ's name. Now consider what I have seen of my mother's life, my grandmother's, my mother-in-law's. These people were educated at Northern schools, they read the same books as their Northern contemporaries, the same daily papers, the same Bible. They have the same ideas of right and wrong, are high-bred, lovely, good, pious, doing their duty as they conceive it. They live in Negro villages. They do not preach and teach hate as a gospel, and the sacred duty of murder and insurrection; but they strive to ameliorate the condition of these Africans in every particular. They set them the example of a perfect life, a life of utter self-abnegation. Think of these holy New Englanders forced to have a Negro village walk through their houses whenever they see fit, dirty, slatternly, idle, ill-smelling by nature. These women I love have less chance to live their own lives in peace than if they were African missionaries. They have a swarm of blacks about them like children under their care, not as Mrs. Stowe's fancy painted them, and they hate slavery worse than Mrs. Stowe does. . . . I say we are no better than our judges in the North, and no worse. We are human beings of the nineteenth century and slavery has to go of course. All that has been gained by it goes to the North and to Negroes. The slave owners, when they are good men and women, are martyrs. I hate slavery. I even hate the harsh authority I see parents think it is their duty to exercise toward their children. . . .

November 30, 1861

. . . Yes, how I envy those saintly Yankee women, in their clean cool New England homes, writing books to make their fortunes and to shame us. The money they earn goes to them. Here every cent goes to pay the factor that supplies the plantation. . . .

When this establishment at Mulberry breaks up, the very pleasantest most easy-going life I ever saw will be gone. Mrs. Chesnut, with all her angelic mildness and sweetness, has a talent for organizing, training, making things comfortable, moving without noise and smoothly. He [her father-in-law] roars and shouts if a pebble of an obstacle is put in his way. Somehow I find her the genius of the place.

My sleeping apartment is large and airy, with windows opening on the lawn east and south. In those deep window seats, idly looking out, I spend much time. A part of the yard which was once a deer park has the appearance of the primeval forest; the forest trees have been unmolested and are now of immense size. In the spring, the air laden with perfumes, violets, jasmine, crabapple blossoms, roses. Araby the blest never was sweeter in perfume. And yet there hangs here as on every Southern landscape the saddest pall. There are browsing on the lawn, where Kentucky bluegrass flourishes, Devon cows and sheep, horses, mares and colts. It helps to enliven it. . . .

From my window high (I sit here in the library alone a great deal), I see carriages approach. Colonel Chesnut drives a pair of thoroughbreds, beauties, mahogany bays with shining coats and arching necks. It is a pleasure to see Scip drive them up. Tiptop and Princess are their names. Mrs. Chesnut has her carriage horses and a huge family coach for herself, which she never uses. The young ladies have a barouche and their own riding horses. We have a pair, for my carriage; and my husband has several saddle horses. There are always families of the children or grandchildren of the house visiting here, with carriage to cellar without intermission. As I sit here writing, I see half a dozen carriages under the shade of the trees, coachmen on their boxes, talking, laughing. Some are "hookling," they call it. They have a bone hook something like a crochet needle, and they hook themselves woolen gloves. Some are reading hymn books or pretending to do so. The small footmen are playing marbles under the trees. A pleasant, empty, easy-going life, if one's heart is at ease. But people are not like pigs; they cannot be put up and fattened. So here I pine and fret. . . .

(*Columbia, South Carolina*) *March 19, 1862*

He who runs may read. Conscription means that we are in a tight place. This war was a volunteer business. Tomorrow conscription begins—the last resort . . .

Conscription has waked the Rip Van Winkles. The streets of Columbia were never so crowded with men. To fight and to be made to fight are different things. . . .

June 9, 1862

. . . When we read of the battles in India, in Italy, in the Crimea, what did we care? It was only an interesting topic, like any other, to look for in the paper. Now, you hear of a battle with a thrill and a shudder. It has come home to us. Half the people that we know in the world are under the enemy's guns. A telegram comes to you and you leave it on your lap. You are pale with fright. You handle it, or dread to touch it, as you would a rattlesnake, or worse; for a snake could only strike you. How many, many of your friends or loved ones this scrap of paper may tell you have gone to their death.

When you meet people, sad and sorrowful is the greeting. They press your hand, and tears stand in their eyes or roll down their cheeks as they happen to have more or less self-control. They have brothers, fathers, or sons as the case may be in the battle; and this thing now seems never to stop. . . .

. . . A woman . . . heard her son was killed, but had hardly taken in the horror of it when they came to say it was all a mistake. She fell on her knees with a shout of joy. "Praise the Lord, oh my soul!" she cried in her wild delight. The swing back of the pendulum from the scene of weeping and wailing of a few moments before was very exciting. In the midst of this hubbub, the hearse drove up with the poor boy in his metallic coffin.

Does anybody wonder so many women die. Grief and constant anxiety kill nearly as many women as men die on the battlefield. (This woman) is at the point of death with brain fever; the sudden change from joy to grief was more than she could bear. . . .

(Richmond, Virginia)   November 30, 1863

Anxiety pervades. Lee is fighting Meade, Bragg falling back before Grant, Longstreet—the soldiers call him Peter the Slow—sitting down before Knoxville.

December 7, 1863

. . . Today a poor woman threw herself on her husband's coffin and kissed it. She was weeping bitterly, and so did I, in sympathy. Mr. Chesnut could see me and everyone he loved hung, drawn and quartered without moving a muscle; he could have the same gentle operation performed on himself and make no sign. When through my tears I told him so, he answered in unmoved tones: "So can any civilized man! Savages, Indians at least, are more dignified in that particular than we are. Hysterical grief never moves me. It annoys me. You think yourself a miracle of sensibility; but self-control is what you need. That is all that separates you from those you look down upon as unfeeling."

December 10, 1863

. . . My husband laid the law down last night. I felt it to be the last drop in my full cup. "No more feasting in this house! This is no time for junketing and merry-making. There is a positive want of proper feeling in the life you lead." "You said you brought me here to enjoy one winter before you took me home and turned my face to a dead wall." But he is the master of the house. To hear is to obey. . . .

January 11, 1864

General Preston told us of the impression the first dead Confederate soldiers' faces, grim in death, lying stiff and stark, made upon him at Shiloh: cold, staring open-eyed. They were all hard frozen, these dead bodies . . .

Everybody who comes in brings a little bad news, not much in itself; but the cumulative effect is depressing indeed.

January 31, 1864

Mrs. Davis gave her "Luncheon to Ladies" on Saturday. Many more persons were there than at any of those luncheons which have gone before. We had gumbo, ducks and olives, *suprême de volaille,* chickens in jelly, oysters, lettuce salad, chocolate cream, jelly cake, claret cup, champagne, etc. . . .

Today, for a pair of forlorn shoes, I gave eighty-five dollars . . . Mr. Pettigrew says: "You take your money to market in the market basket and bring home what you buy in your pocketbook."

MARY BOYKIN CHESNUT

(Mulberry Plantation, Camden, South Carolina)
May 27, 1864

. . . It is impossible to sleep here because it is so solemn and still. The moonlight shines in my window, sad and white; and the wind, the soft south wind, comes over a bank of violets, lilacs, roses, and orange blossoms with magnolia flowers thrown in . . .

I was telling them today of a woman who came to Mrs. Davis in Richmond, hoping to get her help. She wanted her husband's pardon. He was a deserter. The woman was shabbily dressed, chalk-white and with a pinched face. She spoke very good English, and there was an attempt to be dressed up apparent in her forlorn clothes; knots of ribbon, rusty artificial flowers, and draggled feathers in her old hat. Her hands hung down by her side. She was strong, and her way of telling her story was hard and cold enough. She told it simply, but over and over again, with slight variations as to words and never as to facts. She seemed afraid we would forget. The army had to pass so near her. Her poor little Susie had just died, and the boy was ailing; food was so scarce and so bad. They all had chills, and she was so miserable. The Negroes had all gone to the Yankees. There was nobody to cut wood, and it was so cold. "The army was coming so near. I wrote, and I wrote: 'If you want to see the baby alive, come! If they won't let you, come anyhow!' So you see, if he is a deserter, I did it. For they would not let him come. Only colonels and generals can get furloughs now. He only intended to stay one day, but we coaxed and begged him, and then he stayed and stayed; and he was afraid to go back afterwards. He did not mean to be a coward, nor to desert, so instead of going back to his regiment, he went on the gunboats on the river, to serve there . . . They are going to shoot him. But it was I who did it. I would not let him alone. Don't you see?"

Mrs. Davis went to the President. She was gone ever so long . . . Then Mrs. Davis came in, smiling. "Here it is, all you want." The creature stood straight up; then she fell down on the sofa, sobbing as if soul and body would come asunder. So I fled, blind with tears. . . .

June 2, 1864

. . . I paid today, for two pounds of tea, forty pounds of coffee, and sixty pounds of sugar, $800.

(Lincolnton, North Carolina)   February 16, 1865

. . . Sherman was at Orangeburg, barely a day's journey from Columbia, and he left a track as blackened as a fire in the prairies.

So my time had come too. My husband urged me to go home. He said Camden would be safe enough, that they had no spite to that old town as they have to Charleston and Columbia. Molly too. She came in, weeping and wailing, wiping her red-hot face with her cook's grimy apron. She said I ought to go among our own black people on the plantation. They would take care of me better than anyone else.

So I agreed to go. . . .

February 22, 1865

Isabella has been reading my diaries. How we laugh at my sage ratiocinations all come to naught, my famous insight into character proved utter folly. The diaries were lying on the hearth ready to be burned, but she told me to hold on, to wait awhile. . . .

MARY BOYKIN CHESNUT

February 25, 1865

. . . Yesterday, the wagon in which I was to go to Flat Rock drove up to the door, covered with a tent-like white cloth. Ellen flew to me. "Oh Missis, for the love of the Lord, don't go off in that there thing! Poke your head out of the end of that wagon and you'll be po' buckra for true. I don't min' rain, not an ole brass cent; but you gwine lef boxes and trunks here, an you lef boxes and trunks in Richmond full o' good clothes, and you lef ever so much in Columbia, and it all done burn up. For Lord sake, Missis, go home and stay dere, 'stead of keep running round 'stributing your things everywhere."

. . . I sat down and wrote to my husband, words so much worse than anything I can put in this book; and as I wrote I was blinded by tears of rage. Indeed I nearly wept myself away. In vain. Years, death, depopulation, bondage, fears; these have all been borne. . . .

March 1, 1865

. . . Ellen and I are shut up here by the rain, rain, everlasting rain. As our money is worthless, are we to starve? Heavens; how grateful I was today when Miss McLean sent me a piece of chicken. . . .

March 5, 1865

Is the sea drying up? It is going up into mist and coming down on us in this water spout, the rain. It raineth every day, and the weather represents our tearful despair on a large scale. It is also Lent; quite convenient, for we have nothing to eat, so we fast and pray and go draggling to church like drowned rats to be preached at . . .

Allan Green walked home with me . . . I forced myself to listen to Allan, and to say: "Yes, yarn is our circulating medium. It is the current coin of the realm. At a factory here, Mrs. Glover traded off a Negro woman for yarn. The woman wanted to go there as a factory hand, it suited all round." "That's nothing. Yesterday a Negro man was sold for a keg of nails."

General Chesnut said many people were light-hearted at the ruin of the great slave owners. He quoted someone: "They will have no Negroes now to lord it over! They can swell and peacock about and tyrannize now over only a small parcel of women and children, those only who are their very own family." . . .

(Chester, South Carolina) April 22, 1865

This yellow Confederate quire of paper, blotted by my journal, has been buried three days with the silver sugar dish, the teapot, milk jug, and a few spoons and forks that follow my fortunes . . . It has been a wild three days, aides galloping around with messages, Yankees hanging over us like the sword of Damocles. We sat up at Mrs. Bedon's, dressed, without once going to bed for forty-eight hours, and we were aweary.

Colonel Cadwallader Jones came up with a dispatch, sealed and secret. It was for General Chesnut. I opened it. Lincoln, Old Abe Lincoln killed, murdered! Seward wounded! Why? By whom? It is simply maddening. I sent off messenger after messenger for General Chesnut. I have not the faintest idea where he is, but I know this foul murder will bring down worse miseries on us . . .

Now look out for bands of marauders, black and white; lawless, disbanded soldiers, from both armies.

Mary Boykin Chesnut

May 2, 1865

I am writing from the roadside below Blackstock's, *en route* to Camden. Since we left Chester, solitude; nothing but tall blackened chimneys to show that any man has ever trod this road before us. This is Sherman's track! It is hard not to curse him.

I wept incessantly at first. "The roses of the gardens are already hiding the ruins," said Mr. Chesnut, trying to say something. Then I made a vow. If we are a crushed people, I will never be a whimpering, pining slave. . . .

(Camden, South Carolina) May 16, 1865

We are scattered, stunned, the remnant of heart left alive in us filled with brotherly hate. We sit and wait until the drunken tailor who rules the United States issues a proclamation and defines our anomalous position. . . .

June 4, 1865

President Davis is in a dungeon, and in chains. Men watch him day and night . . . Our turn next, maybe. Not among the Negroes does fear dwell now, nor uncertainty nor anxiety. It dwells here, haunting us, tracking us, running like an accursed discord through all the music tones of our existence.

July 26, 1865

I do not write often now, not for want of something to say but from a loathing of all I see and hear. Why dwell upon it . . .

What is the matter? Enough! I will write no more!

CAROLINA MARIA
DE JESUS

arolina Maria de Jesus was born in a small town in Brazil. Her mother, an illiterate farm worker, insisted that Carolina attend school so that she would have a better life. She hated school until the day she learned to read. She recalls: "It was a Wednesday, and when I left school I saw a paper with some writing on it. It was an announcement of a local movie house. 'Today. Pure Blood. Tom Mix.' I shouted happily—'I can read! I can read!' " For two years she was first in her class, but when her mother got a better job on another farm, Carolina's education stopped. At sixteen she went to work as a maid for white families in São Paulo. "But I was too independent and didn't like to clean up their messes. Besides I used to slip out of the house at night and make love." When she found herself pregnant, she moved to São Paulo's *favela,* a rotting stench-filled slum inhabited by uneducated blacks who could find no work. She built herself a crude shack like the others, and when her son João was born, she strapped him to her back and went out with a burlap sack to collect paper from the garbage heaps, which she sold to junkyards. On good days she made twenty-five or thirty cents, many days she made nothing.

She soon had a second son José Carlos, by a Spaniard who returned to Europe. In 1943 she bore a daughter, Vera Eunice, by a wealthy white São Paulan who from time to time gave her a bit of money. With three children to support, her life became almost unendurably hard. To keep from thinking about her troubles, she wrote. Poems, novels, and plays about rich people and royalty and nature, which gave her a fantasy world from which she could escape the ugliness surrounding her. She also kept a diary. With simple dignity and bitter humor she recorded on the blank pages of notebooks she found in trash cans the world of the *favela,* where prostitutes kept open house, men beat their women in the streets and children died of malnutrition and neglect. Disliked by neighbors for her standoffish ways, she struck out at the cause of all their misery: the politicians who, to get the slum-dwellers to vote, promised reform, then promptly forgot their promises once in office.

The power a black woman with only two years of schooling can exert if she simply tells the truth and knows her own worth and speaks up—Carolina's power was to be felt. One day a young journalist, covering the inauguration of a playground, heard a tall black woman shout to a group of men who were fighting with the children for a place on the swings: "If you continue mistreating these children, I'm going to put you in my book!" The reporter, Audalio Dantas, persuaded Carolina to give him excerpts from her diaries, and next day he ran them in the newspaper. His readers demanded more. For a year he edited the diaries. Although he cut them, he did not change Carolina's own fierce words. Finally, they were published as a book. The diary has sold more copies than any other Brazilian book in history. Today Carolina lives in a brick house in the suburbs of São Paulo. She holds the title of Honorary Member of the São Paulo Law University. She lectures and gives speeches on television.

When a state senator asked Carolina to autograph her book for him, she wrote: "I hope that you give the poor people what they want and stop putting the tax money into your own pocket. Sincerely, Carolina Maria de Jesus."

Revelations

The birthday of my daughter Vera Eunice. I wanted to buy a pair of shoes for her, but the price of food keeps us from realizing our desires. Actually we are slaves to the cost of living. I found a pair of shoes in the garbage, washed them, and patched them for her to wear. . . .

I was ill all day. I thought I had a cold. At night my chest pained me. I started to cough. I decided not to go out at night to look for paper. I searched for my son João. He was . . . near the market. A bus had knocked a boy into the sidewalk and a crowd gathered. João was in the middle of it all. I poked him a couple of times and within five minutes he was home.

I washed the children, put them to bed, then washed myself and went to bed. I waited until 11:00 for a certain someone. He didn't come. I took an aspirin and laid down again. When I awoke the sun was sliding in space. My daughter Vera Eunice said: "Go get some water, Mother!"

July 16

I got up and obeyed Vera Eunice. I went to get the water. I made coffee. I told the children that I didn't have any bread, that they would have to drink their coffee plain . . . I was feeling ill and decided to cure myself. I stuck my finger down my throat twice, vomited, and knew I was under the evil eye . . . I thought of the worrisome life that I led. Carrying paper, washing clothes for the children, staying in the streets all day long. Yet I'm always lacking things, Vera doesn't have shoes and she doesn't like to go barefoot. For at least two years I've wanted to buy a meat grinder. And a sewing machine.

I came home and made lunch for the two boys. Rice,

beans, and meat, and I'm going out to look for paper. I left the children, told them to play in the yard and not go into the street, because the terrible neighbors I have won't leave my children alone. I was feeling ill and wished I could lie down. But the poor don't rest nor are they permitted the pleasure of relaxation. I was nervous inside, cursing my luck. I collected two full sacks of paper. Afterward I went back and gathered up some scrap metal, some cans, and some kindling wood . . .

When I came home there was a crowd at my door. Children and women claiming José Carlos had thrown stones at their houses. They wanted me to punish him.

July 18

I got up at 7. Happy and content. Weariness would be here soon enough. . . .

Dona Silvia came to complain about my children. That they were badly educated. I don't look for defects in children. Neither in mine nor in others. I know that a child is not born with sense. When I speak with a child I use pleasant words. What infuriates me is that the parents come to my door to disrupt my rare moments of inner tranquillity. But when they upset me, I write. I know how to dominate my impulses. I only had two years of schooling, but I got enough to form my character. The only thing that does not exist in the favela is friendship. . . .

My kids are not kept alive by the church's bread. I take on all kinds of work to keep them. And those women have to beg or even steal. At night when they are begging I peacefully sit in my shack listening to Viennese waltzes. While their husbands break the boards of the shack, I and my children sleep peacefully. I don't envy the married women of the favelas who lead lives like Indian slaves.

I never got married and I'm not unhappy. Those who

wanted to marry me were mean and the conditions they imposed on me horrible.

July 19

. . . When those female witches invade my shack, my children throw stones at them. The women scream:

"What uneducated brats!"

I reply:

"My children are defending me. You are ignorant and can't understand that. I'm going to write a book about the favela, and I'm going to tell everything that happened here. And everything that you do to me. I want to write a book, and you with these disgusting scenes are furnishing me with the material."

Silvia asked me to take her name out of my book. . . .

July 21

I woke with the voice of Dona Maria asking me if I wanted to buy bananas or lettuce . . . Then I went to wash clothes. While the clothes were bleaching I sat on the sidewalk and wrote. A man passed by and asked me:

"What are you writing?"

"All the cheating that the favela dwellers practice. Those human wrecks."

He said:

"Write it and give it to an editor so he can make revisions."

. . . I spent the rest of the afternoon writing. At 4:30 . . . I gave the children a bath and got ready to go out. I went out to pick up paper but I felt ill. I hurried because it was cold. When I got home it was 10:30. I turned on the radio, took a bath, and heated some food. I read a little. I don't know how to sleep without reading. I like to leaf through a book. The book is man's best invention so far.

July 27

. . . Senhor Gino came to ask me to go to his shack. That I am neglecting him. I answered: no!

I am writing a book to sell. I am hoping that with this money I can buy a place and leave the favela. I don't have time to go to anybody's house. Senhor Gino insisted. He told me:

"Just knock and I'll open the door."

But my heart didn't ask me to go to his room.

May 15, 1958

. . . I classify São Paulo this way: The Governor's Palace is the living room. The mayor's office is the dining room and the city is the garden. And the favela is the back yard where they throw the garbage.

May 19

. . . What our President Senhor Juscelino has in his favor is his voice. He sings like a bird and his voice is pleasant to the ears. And now the bird is living in a golden cage called Catete Palace. Be careful, little bird, that you don't lose this cage, because cats when they are hungry think of birds in cages. The *favelados* are the cats, and they are hungry. . . .

I washed the floor because I'm expecting a visit from a future deputy and he wants me to make some speeches for him. He says he wants to know the favelas and if he is elected he's going to abolish them.

The sky was the color of indigo, and I understood that I

adore my Brazil. My glance went over to the trees . . . the leaves moved by themselves. I thought: they are applauding my gesture of love to my country. I went on looking for paper. . . .

May 20

. . . my children ran to tell me that they had found some macaroni in the garbage. As the food supply was low I cooked some of the macaroni with beans. And my son João said to me:

"Uh, huh. You told me you weren't going to eat any more things from the garbage."

It was the first time I had failed to keep my word. I said:

"I had faith in President Kubitschek."

"You had faith, and now you don't have it any more?"

"No, my son, democracy is losing its followers. In our country everything is weakening. The money is weak. Democracy is weak and the politicians are very weak. Everything that is weak dies one day."

The politicians know that I am a poetess. And that a poet will even face death when he sees his people oppressed.

June 1

. . . I haven't said anything about my dear mother. She was very good. She wanted me to study to be a teacher. It was the uncertainties of life that made it impossible for her to realize her dream. But she formed my character, taught me to like the humble and the weak. That's why I have pity on the *favelados*. I know very well that there are contemptible people here, persons with perverted souls. Last night Amelia and her companion fought. She told him that he was with her only for the money she gave him. You only had to listen to Amelia's voice to know she enjoyed the argument. She had many children. Gave them all away. She has two boys at home that she doesn't want. She neglects children and collects men.

A man enters by the door. A child is the root of the heart. . . .

June 7

. . . When I was a girl my dream was to be a man to defend Brazil, because I read the history of Brazil and became aware that war existed. I read the masculine names of the defenders of the country, then I said to my mother:

"Why don't you make me become a man?"

She replied:

"If you walk under a rainbow, you'll become a man."

When a rainbow appeared I went running in its direction. But the rainbow was always a long way off. Just as the politicians are far from the people. I got tired and sat down. Afterward I started to cry. But the people must not get tired. They must not cry. They must fight to improve Brazil so that our children don't suffer as we are suffering. I returned and told my mother:

"The rainbow ran away from me."

June 23

I stopped at the butcher to buy a half kilo of beef . . . I was confused about the differences in prices. The butcher explained to me that filet was more expensive. I thought of the bad luck of the cow, the slave of man. Those that live in the woods eat vegetation, they like salt, but man doesn't give it because it's too expensive. After death they are divided, weighed, and selected. And they die when man wants them

295

to. In life they give money to man. Their death enriches the man. Actually, the world is the way the whites want it. I'm not white, so I don't have anything to do with this disorganized world. . . .

June 24

When I returned to the favela I found Vera in the street. She tells me everything that goes on. She said the police had come to tell Paredão that his mother was dead.

She was a very good woman. Only she drank too much.

. . . Vera came to tell me there was a fight . . . It was Maria Mathias who was giving one of her hysterical spectaculars. A spectacular at the critical age. Only women and doctors will understand what I mean. . . .

July 30

I got 15 cruzeiros and went by the shoemaker to see if Vera's shoes were ready, because she complains when she has to go barefoot. They were, and she put on the shoes and began to smile. I stood watching my daughter's smile, because I myself don't know how to smile.

. . . I started thinking about the unfortunate children who, even being tiny, complain about their condition in the world. They say that Princess Margaret of England doesn't like being a Princess. Those are the breaks in life.

August 12

I left my bed at 6:30 and went to get water. There was a long line. The worst thing about it is that malice is the main subject. There was a Negress there who acted as if she'd been vaccinated by a phonograph needle. She talked about her daughter and son-in-law who were constantly fighting. And Dona Clara had to listen to it because she was the only one paying attention.

Lately it has become very difficult to get water, because the amount of people in the favela has doubled. And there is only one spigot.

September 8

Today I'm happy. I'm laughing without any reason. I'm singing. When I sing I make up the verses. I sing until I get tired of the song. Today I made this song:

> There is a voodoo curse on you
> And who did it, I know who.
> It was little Mary.
> The one you loved before.
> She said she loved you too
> But you showed her the door.

January 16, 1959

I went to the post office to take out the notebooks that returned from the United States. I came back to the favela as sad as if they had cut off one of my arms. *The Reader's Digest* returned my novels. The worst slap for those who write is the return of their works. . . .

May 6

At 9:30 the reporter appeared. I exclaimed:

"You said you would be here at 9:30 and not one minute late!"

He said that many people wanted to see him because they liked his articles. We got into a taxi. Vera was happy because she was in an automobile. We went to Arouche Square and the reporter started to photograph me. He took me to the São Paulo Academy of Letters. I sat in the doorway and put the sack of paper beside me. The janitor came and told me to get away from the door. He grabbed my sack. A sack that for me has an incalculable value, because I earn my daily bread with it. The reporter said that it was he who had told me to sit in the doorway. The janitor said that he wasn't allowed to let just anybody who wanted to sit in the front of the entrance.

We went to Seventh of April Street and the reporter bought a doll for Vera. I told the salesgirls that I had written a diary that was going to be published in O *Cruzeiro*.

June 8

When I got home and opened the door I found a note. I recognized the reporter's writing . . . The note said that the article on me would come out on the 10th, in O *Cruzeiro*. That the book was going to be published. I filled with emotion.

Senhor Manuel arrived . . .

"They earn money from your work and won't pay you. They're tricking you. You should never have given him the book."

I was not impressed with the skepticism of Senhor Manuel.

June 9

. . . I was reading stories to the children when there was a knock at the window. João said:

"Mama, there is a man here with glasses."

I went to see. It was Vera's father.

"Come in!"

"Where do you get in?"

"Go around front."

He came inside. He let his eyes wander around the shack.

He asked:

"Aren't you cold here? Doesn't it rain in?"

"It rains, but I'm used to it."

"You wrote me that the girl was ill, I came to see her. Thank you for the letters. I thank you because you promised to protect me and not reveal my name in your diary."

. . . He gave 100 cruzeiros. José Carlos thought that was very little, because he had other bills of 1,000.

June 10

. . . When João returned he said the story was out. I searched all my pockets for money. I had 13 cruzeiros. I lacked two. Senhor Luiz loaned them to me. And João went to get it. My heart was beating just like the springs in a watch. What would they write about me? When João came back with the magazine, I read it—"A Picture of the Favela in Carolina's diary."

I read the article and smiled. . . .

June 11

. . . I fed the children and sat on the bed to write. There was a knock at the door. I sent João to see who it was and shouted:

"Enter, black woman!"

"She isn't a black woman, Mama. It's a white woman and she has a copy of *O Cruzeiro* in her hands."

She came in. A very pretty blonde. She said that she had

read the article in *O Cruzeiro* and wanted to take me to the *Diário da Noite* newspaper office to get help for me.

At the newspaper I got choked with emotion. The boss Senhor Antonio was on the third floor. He gave me a magazine to read. Afterward he went to get lunch for me, steak, potatoes and a salad. I was eating what I had dreamed about! I was in a pretty room.

Reality was much prettier than a dream.

. . . I am so happy! It feels as if my dirty life is now being washed.

July 13

. . . We went to a shoe shop and I bought a pair of shoes for Vera. When Senhor Manoel, a *nortista,* tried the shoes on her, she said:

"Shoes, please don't wear out! Because later Mama has to work hard to buy another pair, and I don't like to walk barefoot."

January 1, 1960

I got up at 5 and went to get water.

MARTHA MARTIN

*I*n *the early nineteen fifties* a Macmillan editor found in her pile of unsolicited manuscripts a diary from Anchorage, Alaska, that told a remarkable and strange story of survival. Despite some suspected doctoring, the manuscript had such authentic detail that the editor wrote the author, and her hopes were confirmed—it was a real diary kept by a pregnant woman stranded alone on an Alaskan shore for several months, who delivered her own child.

Martha Martin was the pseudonym of the wife of a gold prospector. Every summer in the remote southeastern Alaskan wilds she cooked and kept camp for her husband and his partner while they searched for the vein that would make them all rich. Sometime in the nineteen twenties (no dates are offered in the diary), they were closing their camp for the winter when Martha's husband left her alone while he took their skiff on an errand to a nearby island. Martha was collecting tools on the mountainside near their mine when a sudden storm unloosed an avalanche that pinned her, unconscious, beneath rocks for days. When she came to, she made her way back to their summer cabin, which still contained some food. Here her diary begins:

> "I can hardly write, but I must. For two reasons. First I am afraid I may never live to tell my story, and second, I must do something to keep my sanity."

Revelations

Help did not arrive. Severely wounded, Martha improvised a splint for her broken arm, a cast for her broken leg. After several brave but failed attempts to leave the camp and return to civilization, the advent of winter forced her to prepare for the birth of her child without help. Every day she found resources and talents she hadn't known she possessed. The story is fascinating for its sheer adventure and her ingenuity; but its most interesting aspect is her growing delight in her Crusoe-like role of the solitary self-sufficient woman adjusting to her primitive conditions and reuniting with nature, free of man's traditional landlordship.

A brief postscript to the diary informs us that her husband Don had been similarly stranded by the storm and that they were eventually reunited. The child Donnas later died. The diary was forgotten for years until a woman writer encouraged Martha to submit it for publication. A script doctor slapped on an overlay of women's magazine style, but once most of the diary was reclaimed, Martha Martin emerged as a natural writer, unaware of her experience as literary metaphor perhaps, but still expressing a universal if deeply hidden desire for autonomy.

———————

I killed a sea otter today. I actually did kill a sea otter. I killed him with the ax, dragged him home, and skinned him. I took his liver out, and ate part of it. I'm going to eat the rest of it, and his heart, too. His liver was quite large, bigger than a deer's, and it had more lobes to it. It was very good liver, and I enjoyed it.

Most of today was devoted to the sea otter; getting the hide off was a real task. It's a lovely skin, the softest, silkiest, thickest fur I have ever seen. I am going to make a robe for my baby out of the beautiful fur. My darling child may be born in a lowly cabin, but she shall be wrapped in one of the earth's most costly furs.

It was such a splendid piece of luck. Lucky in more ways than one. The otter might have killed me, although I have never heard of such a thing.

This morning I went to the woods to gather a load of limbs. As I was coming home with them, I saw the tide was nearly out, and I thought I'd walk over to the bar and take a look at the boat . . . I was going along, swinging the ax in my left hand, managing the crutch with the right hand, . . . not thinking of anything in particular, when right beside me I heard a bark. It was like a dog bark; not a bow-wow bark, more of a yip. I looked around and saw a huge creature reared up on its haunches. I saw its white teeth.

Without thinking, I swung the ax at the side of its head, saw it hit, felt the jar in my arm, heard the thud. As I swung the ax, I turned and tried to run. I was so terrified the thing would nab me from behind that I could hardly move. I glanced over my shoulder to see how close it was. It hadn't budged from where it dropped . . .

I got down on my knees and examined it from one end to the other. First off, I noticed the lovely fur. I took off my glove and ran my fingers through the nice silky coat. I decided right then I would have the skin. I saw it as a baby blanket . . .

It is very much against the law to kill a sea otter. Right now I don't care a rap for law. I'd like to have a picture of a game warden who could arrest me now. I am safe enough from the law, and I think I always will be. Under the circumstances I doubt if any judge would send me to jail for what I have done . . .

I dragged my kill home, and was a long time doing so. I'll bet the creature weighed a hundred pounds. I worked and worked, rested, pulled, and dragged, rested some more, and by and by I reached the cabin with my prize . . .

I decided to skin it exactly the way the men do a deer. I have watched them many times, but I never helped or paid much attention. I didn't know very much about skinning a fur-bearing animal when I went to work on that creature. How I wished I had an Indian squaw to instruct and help me . . .

The head was a mess, so I just cut the skin at the neck line and let the head fur go. I chopped off the feet and threw them in the stove. After I got the legs and sides skinned, I turned the otter on his belly and worked the skin off his back down to the tail. I had more trouble with that tail than I did with all the rest of the animal, I wanted it for a neckpiece, and I tried to get the bony tail out without slitting the skin. It can't be done . . .

My hands got awful cold examining the innards, rather smelly, too. I had let the fire go down, and there wasn't enough hot water for me to scrub properly. I made up the fire, washed a little, and then sat down to rest and gloat over my wonderful sea-otter fur . . .

I woke up in the night, and felt rested, so I got up, lit the carbide lamp, and sat here writing all about my sea otter.

I had planned to work on my otter skin today, but when I looked out this morning I saw Old Nick was flaunting a plume [a sign that a cold wind was coming up] . . . I put all my energy into gathering wood and left the skin alone . . .

Goodness, I have lots of work to do before I am ready for my little darling. I must get the fur finished for her. I am determined my child shall have a priceless gift . . .

I've begun scraping off the fat from my otter skin, and it's about half done. I have learned a few things about scraping skins: they scrape better when they are stretched tight over the end of a block of wood, and the fat comes off easier when it is cold. Another thing, when a skin looks scraped, it still has lots of fat on it. I know I'll have to go over the whole hide at least twice . . .

At last I have finished scraping the otter skin. It is all very nicely done, and not one single hole did I cut in it . . . I am going to scrub it well in lots of warm soapy water . . .
Goodness me, I have more chores than a farmer . . .

Hurray! My otter skin is nailed to the door. It's the biggest thing—much bigger than I thought it was. It nearly covers the whole door . . .
The wind still howls, swirls, and rages. It's awful cold, maybe ten below. All the peaks look like volcanoes with their great trailing plumes . . . I brought in some more wood today, but I didn't stay out long. It was too cold and windy . . .
While I was out in the cold, my breasts ached. They drew up and the nipples stuck out firm, and they ached. When I came in I examined them, and found they were swelling and have water in them, not milk, but clear water. Soon my child will be here, and I am not yet ready to receive her. So much to do and so little time . . .

I have decided to burn the floor. I'll cut the part I have already taken up, now, and save the rest for reserve. There are seven sills, all logs ten to twelve inches through, under the floor, which is nailed to them. If I can dig around them, saw them in two, pry them out, and cut them into blocks, they'll make a lot of fine wood. They are yellow cedar, and so is the puncheon . . .
The otter skin is a disappointment. It's as hard as a board, and I'm just sick about it. I might make it into a Robinson Crusoe umbrella, but it can never become an infant's robe in its present stiff state. I remember reading or hearing that the Eskimoes chew skins to make them soft. It

would take a lot of chewing to make this big skin soft. I just can't chew it, and I won't even try.

The fur is lovely, and it smells clean. I put my face in it, and it's the softest thing I've ever touched. I do wish the skin wasn't so stiff. There must be some way I can fix it. Baby must have one present.

If we were home she would have many gifts—a ring, a silver cup with her name on it, a necklace, a silver spoon, a baby book, dresses with lace and ribbons, fine soft knitted things. Even in this northland she would have gifts if anyone knew we were here . . .

I believe I have found a way to soften the otter skin. I doubled over a corner of it, and it didn't break as I thought it might, so I folded it some more. No breaks. I kept on folding and creasing it, and now it is no longer board-like; but it's still a very long way from being as soft as I want it to be.

I washed a few clothes today. I want clean things for the coming of my child. Surely she will be here soon. I am getting things ready to receive her, and I have done a lot of sewing. Tomorrow I will bathe and make myself presentable for a newborn child . . .

I made a birth cloth today from one of Don's union suits. It is all wool and should serve nicely to wrap a newborn child in . . .

I plan to use string raveled from a flour sack to tie the cord. I boiled a piece to make sure it is clean . . .

I've worked again on the fur, and I'm pleased with the result. I used a different system—pulled it back and forth around the bunk pole. I admire the fur more and more, and I want so much to get it soft enough to use for my baby . . .

The milk case is pretty well filled with baby things. Don's shaving soap is in one of the pockets. Shaving soap should be good for baby. It seems right to bathe my child with her father's shaving soap . . .

Only a few more days now until I will have a child in my arms.

I have been working and working at the otter skin, and I am making progress . . . A dozen times a day I pick it up, rub a part of it between my hands, brush it, hold it to my face, hold it at arm's length to admire it . . .

The wind has died away. It is very much warmer, and a haze covers the sky. I went wood gathering and was delighted with my outing. I saw twenty-six deer, and I brought some boughs for the ones who will pay me a friendly call . . . Two ravens came to eat the otter. I wonder how they knew it was there . . . Maybe they smelled it. My thrush never comes back, and I liked it so much. Those mean old jays—I really shouldn't feed them a crumb . . .

I baked bread, lots of it, far more than I need for myself. The deers are fond of bread, and I thought I'd have an extra amount on hand. Five of them came today to bum a handout, and I didn't disappoint them. I think all of them have been here several times before, but I can be sure of only one— Sammy with the mark on his throat. He is the tamest of the lot, and knows me. He even eats out of my hand . . .

I pounded up my cast and put it on the floor with the gravel. It was quite hard, much harder than I thought. If I had fallen, the cast would have given my arm good protection. Now that my arm is well, I haven't worn the cast for weeks. I don't use my crutch any more, either, but I'm not disposing of it yet . . .

I always think of the child as a girl. What if it's a boy? Oh, it couldn't be . . .

Revelations

This awful deep snow and hard cold is going to kill off much of our wild life. Poor creatures, what a pity they can't all be like bears and sleep the winter through. But then, what would I do without my friendly bums to come around and ask for bread and lick their chops at me?

Since the baby came down to live in the lower part of my abdomen, I have been constipated, and I don't like it. I think it's the cause of my swollen ankles. I had absolutely nothing here to correct it, so I looked around to see what the wilderness might provide, and hit on the idea of eating seaweed. Certainly it can be called roughage . . . I went along the beach and gathered a mess . . . I picked it over well, washed it thoroughly, and ate quite a lot—ate it raw. It wasn't too awful, but I certainly don't like the stuff. It was very effective, almost more effective than I desired it to be. I was busy all day with the honey bucket . . .

The otter skin is getting to be as soft as I want it to be. I have invented another way to soften it. I made a small mallet and gently pound the folded fur over a block of wood . . .

The fur is finished, and it's exactly as I wished it to be. I am very proud of it. So soft and warm—such a lovely thing. I shall wrap my baby in it when she goes for her outings, and we will walk pridefully along the beach . . .

Snow seals every crack, so I only burn a little wood when there is no wind, and open the door for air.

I have bathed and washed my head. My hair has grown about three inches and is as curly as can be.* I like short hair

* Martha had treated her scalp wounds with bacon grease, but mice nibbled at the grease while she slept and she cut her hair to the roots.

because it's so easy to wash and dry. I think I may keep it short and never again be bothered with hairpins . . .

My body is heavy, and my movements are slow and not too definite. I am becoming clumsy and awkward. I don't like it. Maybe I should sit down and just twiddle my thumbs until Baby comes. I do hope she comes before I use up all this water and burn all my wood . . .

I brought a few branches and put a bouquet of cedar and hemlock boughs on my windowsill and placed the finest of Don's ore specimens on either side of it. The window has a nice look, as though a man and a woman lived here . . .

There was a little show of blood, and when I saw it I remembered my mother saying it was a sure sign that the child would be born soon . . .

I have never seen a child born. I always felt inadequate to help and was too modest to want to be a spectator. I have never seen anything born—not even a cat . . . I am no longer afraid, yet I do wish someone were with me to help me take care of the child . . .

[Martha's child was born after two days of labor, during which she cooked, cared for herself and wrote recollections of life with her husband to try "to order my thoughts, be calm, and not bother my head about all I don't know." Again, she found herself able to cope alone, to deliver the child, to rest, to tie the cord, cut it, and then deliver the afterbirth. And the next day she went on with her narrative.]

My darling little girl-child, after such a long and troublesome waiting I now have you in my arms. I am alone no more. I have my baby.

I went outside for a short walk on the beach today. It's the first time I've been out since the baby came. The tide was nearly low, and there were dozens of deer on the beach, maybe forty or fifty, maybe as many as a hundred . . . Poor things, they are starving . . . I just can't let all the deer starve. I can cut a little brush, maybe enough to keep some of them alive . . .

Several of them followed me back to the cabin and begged for food. I fed them a little, and promised more. I promised to bake lots of bread and make a feast . . . It will be the christening feast for the baptism of Donnas. I'll invite the deer to come share our joy and gladness and our food . . .

Yesterday was lovely. A beautiful late winter day with a bright sun and a warm southerly breeze. It was a perfect christening day . . . When the deer saw me go for a little walk and heard me call to them, they came, and all went well.

Donnas was dressed in all her finery and wrapped in the otter robe, only her little face showing deep down in the fur . . .

"Donnas Martin, I baptize thee in the name of the Father, and of the Son, and of the Holy Ghost. Amen."

I dipped the tips of my fingers in the water and signed my child with the sign of the cross. Then I threw more bread morsels to our guests, whose attention had begun to wander . . .

I held my baby close, wrapped well in her fur robe, loved her and talked to her. It's wondrous good to talk. It's been so long since I've talked to anyone . . . I told her all about us.

"I'm the queen," I told her, "and you are the little princess. The cabin is our palace. None are here to dare dispute our word."

I told her the deer are our helpers and our friends, our subjects and our comfort, and they will give us food and clothing according to our needs. I told her of the birds, the little ptarmigan, the geese, ducks, grouse, and the kindly owl; the prankish ravens and the lordly eagle. Told her of the fishes, the clams, and the mussels. Told her of the mink and the otter, and the great brown bear with his funny, furry cub. Told her of the forest and of the things it will give us; of roots, stems, leaves, and berries, and the fun of gathering them; of the majestic mountain uprising behind us with a vein of gold-bearing ore coming straight from its heart. Told her that all these things were ours to have and to rule over and care for. . . .

This afternoon I went out and cut brush for the deer. I left baby alone in the cabin, explaining that it was my duty as reigning queen to provide for my subjects. I told her famine was now on our land and I must go cut brush . . .

When deer are hungry, they behave differently than when well fed. When a deer is feeling good, he will look up for his food, at least some of the time; but when he is weak with hunger he looks down all the time. There's lots of browse within reach if they would only stretch their necks to get it, but they act stupid, and don't seem to know anything about the food within their reach. Perhaps they are too weak to stretch up: maybe they get dizzy looking up . . .

Half an hour before dark seven gray arctic geese came in and settled on the beach almost in front of the cabin. They are either sick or exhausted, or maybe they're tame geese. I went out to look at them, being careful not to frighten them away. I was ready to duck back into the cabin at the first sign of alarm. They didn't seem alarmed, and I went quite close to them. I then gave them food, and they paid no attention to me. Why should wild geese act so? Has something happened to me since my baby came?

This is the last piece of usable paper. But that doesn't matter, for I no longer have such need to write. I have no problems to ponder through . . . I am not lonely any more; I have my baby for company . . .

Soon someone will come and find us here . . .

Maybe the Indians will come to their fish camp . . .

The Indians have come, good, good Indians. Shy, fat, smelly, friendly, kindhearted Indians.

Early this morning Donnas and I were out on the beach, she getting the benefit of the warm spring sun, and I putting the finishing touches on the bottom of my overturned dinghy. I looked up from my work and saw two Indian canoes near the far side of the Arm.

I rushed to the cabin, grabbed my gun, and fired call shots. I shouted and waved. The canoes turned and started toward my shore.

Hurriedly I made up the fire and set coffee water to boil. I brought out my baby's best clothes and got her into them in a jiffy. I ran outside and waved, saw I had time, rushed back and prettied myself up.

The cabin was already clean, and there were fresh blueberry blossoms on the windowsill and on the table. I shook out the otter skin to fluff the fur, wrapped Donnas in it, and went to the water's edge. There we awaited our guests.

Both canoes grounded at about the same time, and right in front of me. For a little while we just looked at each other. I was all trembly, and it was hard to behave with dignity. After what seemed a rather long time, I did manage to say, "Good morning."

"Hello." A breathing space, then another "Hello."

"I'm glad to see you." That came a little easier.

"You bet," was the reply, and following a pause, "By golly."

There was a consultation in Siwash.

"Not dead?"

"No, not dead."

So the conversation went on until I had told my story. No one made a move to get out of the canoes, and it occurred to me they might be waiting politely for an invitation. I hastened to extend one, ending with, "And come see my baby." I held her out toward them.

They piled out, nineteen of them. They didn't seem to see the baby, or me either. All eyes were on the otter skin. There was much Siwash talk, then the spokesman fingered the fur. "Against law. You go jail."

They all laughed.

"Where you get otter?"

I pointed to the spot on the beach where I had killed the animal, then I acted out the part. That seemed to loosen my tongue, and I talked a streak. The Indians laughed and laughed. They came and fingered the fur, stroked it, looked at the underside.

Then an old squaw said, "Pret-ty good." Splendid words of praise . . .

I knew these poor people needed all the fish they could catch, and I hated to ask them to take time out to do anything for me, yet I thought I had been here long enough, so I asked to be taken to Big Sleeve.

"You bet," was the quick answer. But the west wind was blowing, and it would increase until sundown. It would be better to go in the morning . . .

I was glad for a little more time in my cabin. I almost didn't want to leave at all, I was so mixed up. . . .

Selma Lagerlöf

(1858-1940)

*T*he *first woman* to win the Nobel Prize for Literature, Sweden's Selma Lagerlöf very early discovered in herself unusual gifts. The diary she kept during her fourteenth year foreshadows not only her literary concerns but also evolutionary possibilities in the human psyche. The diary was remarkable not for its apparent events (she was merely spending a few months visiting humdrum relatives in Stockholm while undergoing treatment for lameness) but for its subsurface events.

Often Selma was in communication with a mythic creature called Marit of Sotbraten, an imp who thrived on the suffering of children. Selma recounted in disturbing detail an experience of simultaneity, in which she lived out at the same time two events of her life separated by many years. The most dramatic episode of the diary, which is excerpted here, involved the family household cook, a woman of a macabre turn of mind, who arranged to take Selma and two cousins to visit the Carolinian Institute, a medical school, which she had promised them was more interesting than the National Museum. Selma's reaction to this visit, as well as other psychic events, had a positive effect upon her imagination. Living before the phrase "altered states of consciousness" had been created, at fourteen she felt some pressure to deny her vision, but in later years her fiction was rooted in legend which often spanned the supernatural. In the saga *Gosta Berlings* and in *Jerusalem* she created for her readers access to the miraculous. Her children's classic, *The Wonderful Adventures of Nils*, has been translated throughout the world.

She never married, and with her Nobel Prize money she repurchased her childhood country home, Marbacka.

Monday, March 24 [1872]

As I sat down in the parlor to write today, a strange thing happened to Axel Oxenstierna*—but that I shall tell later on.

Yesterday we spent the entire forenoon at the Carolinian Institute—not Uncle and Aunt, of course, nor old Ulla, but Elin and Allan and I and the two maids. We went through the whole institution from attic to cellar.

When we left home we were elated because we were going to visit the Carolinian Institute. The air was clear and bracing, and the city looked enchanting, especially as I crossed Kungsholm Bridge. . . .

Aunt Georgian's cook has a paternal aunt who is married to the watchman at the Carolinian Institute, and every time the cook goes down to see her, she boasts of the marvellous sights she has seen there. She says that the Carolinian Institute is far more interesting than either the Royal Palace or the National Museum.

Since the cook had praised the wonders of the Carolinian Institute so highly, we children naturally were curious and begged her to ask her aunt if we could go along the next time she visited her.

The following morning the cook brought an invitation

---

* Her relatives had a portrait of a former king hanging in the parlor.

for Elin, Allan, the housemaid, and me to have coffee at the watchman's quarters of the Carolinian Institute. But as to seeing the Institute proper, the aunt said, that was out of the question, as it was strictly forbidden.

On hearing this, we were a bit dashed; but Cook assured us that, once we were there, she would arrange to have us see everything there was to be seen. First, of course, we had to ask permission of Aunt and Uncle, but they had no objection to us children, the housemaid, and the cook having coffee with the watchman's wife. They thought it very kind of her to invite us.

When we stepped into the watchman's quarters, we saw a large table already laid, and the watchman's wife asked us to be seated. We each drank two cups of coffee (think, if Auntie had known that!) and ate many small cakes. It all tasted awfully good. The cook's aunt was friendly and sociable, and a young niece who was learning to be a dressmaker was jolly. We would have had a most enjoyable time but for the fact that we were uneasy lest we should not be allowed to go through the Institute to see all the wonderful things to be found there.

For the longest time I wouldn't believe that the watchman's wife was serious when she said we would not be permitted to see the Institute; but when she made no move to rise from the table, and still sat talking, we grew more and more anxious. We nodded and blinked at the cook to remind her aunt of the hour. Otherwise we would not have a chance to see all the great halls before it was time to go home.

When Cook said that we were now well enough rested to bestir ourselves a bit, the aunt shook her head. She couldn't possibly allow such young children to go in, she said. They wouldn't know enough to keep mum. The cook assured her aunt that they would not talk. She believed that even if someone were to threaten them with branding irons, these children would still refuse to talk.

"Nor do I think it will be of any benefit to them," said the watchman's wife. "You see, I did not know they were so young."

"They can never see anything more useful to them than the things found here," said the cook. "Besides, it is a shame to disappoint the children when I have promised them that they will see a place that is more wonderful than the Royal Palace or the National Museum."

The cook was on the verge of tears, and we children were, too. I, at least, had been so sure that we would be allowed to go into a palace filled with beautiful paintings and statuary and fountains. I believed it was something of the same sort as the Lions' Garden at the Alhambra, which is pictured in the "Sketch Book" that lay on the parlor table at Marbacka. So I felt terribly disappointed. Now I know that the Carolinian Institute is nothing but a school for those who are studying to be doctors. But I had no suspicion of this when I went there yesterday.

The watchman's wife was very firm, and I do not think she would have yielded had not her dressmaker niece suggested showing us the lecture halls at least. Nothing dangerous was to be found there, she said.

The watchman's wife actually agreed to this, but anything more than the lecture halls was not to be shown.

Tuesday, March 25

. . . I must . . . finish with the Carolinian Institute.

We came into great halls, with benches and desks and blackboards. They were not unlike the public school at Ostanby . . . though there were many more and much larger rooms. . . .

Revelations

There was not the slightest resemblance to the Alhambra. Cook must have noted our disappointment.

"Just wait a bit," she said. "We'll soon come to the most remarkable thing."

In one hall a huge pile of colored plaques lay on a bench. The cook went at them in earnest. She set up one after another of these pictures against the blackboard and explained what they represented. This was the skeleton, that the heart and the circulatory system, the nervous system, and the digestive organism. They were large, fine plaques, and I should have liked to look at them, had I not expected to see marble halls and playing fountains.

The cook quickly put all the plaques back in their places. "Oh, these are nothing much!" she said, rather impatiently. "You children should see the ones they have upstairs! But we are not allowed up there."

She looked beseechingly at her aunt, but it was useless. No, we had to keep to the lecture halls.

"Every day I'll be ashamed," said the cook once again, "because I have said that this place is more remarkable than the Royal Palace or the National Museum."

The niece stood firmly on our side. It was a pity, she said, that these children, who have such good control of themselves, should not see the *real* Institute. "They will go away from here believing that the Carolinian Institute is only a primary school."

That about the primary school made an impression. The watchman's wife probably thought it would be unfair to her Institute if Elin and Allan and I were not permitted to see any of the wonderful exhibits they had here. So she took out the big bunch of keys from her belt and unlocked the door to another story.

Now we saw plaques of all sorts of misshapen limbs and malformed bodies, and also lifelike reproductions of every

318

known disease—cancer, smallpox, and horrible skin diseases.

"Don't you think, children, that this exhibit is simply marvelous?" said the cook. "It is something quite different from sitting in a theatre."

"Aye, this is real, you see!" said the watchman's wife. "The other is only play-acting."

She was just as anxious now as the cook and the other niece to show us everything. She actually feared we might miss some of the wonders.

We came to a room where the shelves and tables were covered with big glass jars.

"Look over here, Selma," said the watchman's wife. "Can you guess what this is? . . . Well, it is a child with two heads."

"And the hideous thing that lies in this jar has been dug from the belly of a human being," the young niece told us.

Next they showed us plaster casts of clubfeet and hands with articular nodes.

"I wish I were a man," said the cook, "so that I could be a doctor and go here day in and day out."

The last thing we saw was a closet in the attic where a row of skeletons had been set up. One of them was so huge that we had to ask whether it was the skeleton of a human being.

"Yes indeed," said the watchman's wife. "It is the skeleton of a woman known as 'Long Lapska.' She was the most discussed freak of nature of her time."

When we came down from the attic I was all tired out and did not want to see any more exhibits. But the cook said that the one we were coming to was the most interesting of all.

"It is down in the basement," she said. Turning to her aunt, she spoke in a lowered voice. "Have any come in today?"

Revelations

"Yes," said her aunt; "but not many—only four. But are you going down there alone? That's not for children to see, you know."

The cook said that, since we had seen everything else, we should also be allowed to see this; for this was something we could never forget. And so the kind wife of the watchman gave way.

She conducted us down the basement stairs, but here such a horrible stench assailed our nostrils that we stopped short.

"They are lying under water," said the watchman's wife; "but all the same, it's impossible to keep them fresh. There's no smell so penetrating as the odor of a cadaver."

We children were then told that all who had made away with themselves were brought here for the students who were learning to be doctors to dissect.

We stepped into a large cellar room which was well lighted, but where the stench was so overpowering that we had to hold our hands to our noses.

"I wonder if we hadn't better turn back," said the watchman's wife.

"Only for a moment," the cook said, as she opened a door.

I stood close beside her and looked into a dim oblong room. Along one side of the wall there was a wide bunk, and above it trickled a steady stream of water. On the bunk lay four bodies, their heads resting against the wall, their feet down in the bunk, as in a big double bed.

I saw them only for a second, but I remember exactly how they looked. The one nearest the door was an old man with a black beard streaked with gray and a long pointed nose. He wore a coat that reached down to his feet, but they were bare and full of knots and sores. But for the feet, the old man would not have been hard to look at.

320

Beside the old man lay a young woman (she was not so very young, though; I should say her age was about thirty). She was tall and dreadfully bloated; her clothes were worn threadbare in several places so that the dead-white skin showed through. The face was not so bloated as the body, and I could see that she had been beautiful.

At her side lay a boy of about five or six years. His cap was drawn down over his face, but one side of his body was bare, and through a large wound the entrails oozed out.

The fourth was only a bundle of black clothing. I think there was a man inside, but one couldn't be certain of that. A foot stuck out here, there a hand. The hair showed where the feet should have been, and the chin was thrust forward from under the elbow. He must have been ground to pieces and gathered up.

That much I saw before the watchman's wife came forward and shut the door.

As we went up the stairs our cook said that today the dead were rather a ghastly sight, to which the watchman's wife replied rather brusquely that they were about as usual. She evidently did not approve of their having been shown us children.

Though I had seen all the dead plainly, I had been moved most deeply by the woman, who had drowned herself. To think that she had been so unhappy that she had thrown herself into the lake!

I had heard of such things and read about them many times, but I had never before understood what they meant. No, I had not understood a single one of all the stories of unhappiness I had read about in books.

It was so terrible that this was real!

I thought of those who lay sick, and of cripples; but first and last of those who were so unhappy that they did not want to live.

Revelations

Could I ever be happy again now that I knew there was so much evil in the world? Never again, in all my life, would I be able to laugh or play or go to the theatre. Never again would I be the same as when I left home in the morning. Then, when we crossed the Kungsholm Bridge, I thought the view was beautiful. But I saw no beauty on my way back. Surely I could never again think anything in this world lovely.

As I walked home I thought that Stockholm was an ugly city; that the water under me was full of frogs and big slimy lizards. I thought that all whom I met on the bridge were rotting corpses.

March 26

I wrote last Monday that I would have to record a remarkable experience I had while looking at Axel Oxenstierna. But perhaps I'd better take that back, for when I think straight about the matter I know that it was only an illusion. But the illusion was so beautiful, while it seemed real and true, that just the thought of it fills me with awe. But now that I know it wasn't real, why write about it in my daybook? Yet surely it will do no harm to relate it, if at the same time I say the incident was only something I imagined.

On Monday morning when I was in the parlour ready to write in my diary about the Carolinian Institute, I sat awhile looking at the lovely painting of Charles X Gustaf at the deathbed of Axel Oxenstierna. It did my eyes good to rest upon this picture after all the gruesome things they had seen the previous day. But my joy was not for long. The canvas soon disappeared, and in its place was the bunk in the mortuary with the four bodies lying there so miserably poor and forsaken, the spray playing upon them all the while.

Sunday afternoon I saw them before me, and after I had

322

gone to bed that night, and when I awoke next morning. I felt terribly unhappy about them, so it was no wonder they were with me continually.

It would have been a comfort to me if I could have helped them in some way. The thought of what they must have suffered in life was so painful! If at least I could have decorated their last resting place a little!

But how could I help? For all I could do they would have to lie as they were. It was all so dreadful!

And then of a sudden I saw the beautiful painting with all its rich draperies and carpets, and I said to myself, "If one only had such lovely draperies to spread over them!"

It was a stupid thought. These were only painted draperies and could not be spread over anything. But all the same I went up to the painting and begged Axel Oxenstierna to let me have his beautiful bedcovers to spread over the four bodies that they would not have to lie there so wretchedly exposed. You see, he was dead, too, and he could do things, perhaps, that were impossible to us who are living.

I knew all the while that this was only fancy. Yet it wasn't altogether make-believe, either.

I told Axel Oxenstierna that I knew that in his lifetime he had been as a father to the Swedish people, and I implored him now to take pity on the four poor unfortunates; for they, too, were Swedes, though of a later age than his.

While I was asking the help of Axel Oxenstierna, I saw as it were before me the mortuary and the bunk where the four bodies lay. It was only an illusion, of course, but all at once I seemed to see a lovely shimmer envelop them.

I turned my eyes once more upon Axel Oxenstierna. He lay there, quiet as always; but the beautiful light grew more and more distinct as it spread over the four dead bodies on the bunk.

I stood still, not daring to move. For it was—how shall I

say? . . . Now, as I saw the mortuary before me, a wave of light lay over the four. They were entirely enveloped by the light, and I could see them no more.

I remembered them just as well as before, but I did not see them.

To be sure, I believe in the power of the dead, but I also know that Selma Ottilia Lovisa Lagerlöf is inclined to imagine things that are utterly impossible.

KATHERINE MANSFIELD
(1888-1923)

*K*atherine Mansfield's reputation as a short-story writer was earned during a life plagued with ill health. She died of tuberculosis at thirty-four. Her collections of stories, *Bliss* and *The Garden Party,* have widely influenced writers who followed her, while she herself was endebted to Anton Chekhov, whom she often mentioned in her diary. In 1911 she formed a relationship with John Middleton Murry, a writer and publisher whom she eventually married, and who was a strong support in her career. After her death Murry edited and published her letters and journals. We have excerpted sections which deal with her struggle to understand her illness.

She could not accept her tuberculosis as merely a physical disease. In fact, Murry states that she was convinced her heart was her weakness, and she discontinued treatments with a physician, Mamoukhin, in Paris, which Murry believed were helping her. She was convinced that her mind and spirit must be healed simultaneously with her body. Her friend A. R. Orage, a London journalist who became a psychologist, persuaded her that the treatment which orthodox medical science could not provide was available. He initiated her into the work of the Russian teacher G. I. Gurdjieff, and her journal tells of her life at his spiritual community in Fountainebleau, of which Orage was a member.

Parts of the journal written there were torn out to be sent to Murry but were not mailed (entry of October 14). Many of her last letters to Murry* reflect her hope of persuading him of the validity of the Gurdjieff method (in which she did not succeed).

"Jack" and "Bogey" refer to Murry.

(*December 19, 1920*)

Suffering.

I should like this to be accepted as my confession.

There is no limit to human suffering. When one thinks "Now I have touched the bottom of the sea—now I can go no deeper," one goes deeper. And so it is for ever. I thought last year in Italy: Any shadow more would be death. But this year has been so much more terrible. . . . Suffering is boundless, is eternity. One pang is eternal torment. Physical suffering is—child's play. To have one's breast crushed by a great stone—one could laugh!

I do not want to die without leaving a record of my belief that suffering can be overcome. For I do believe it. What must one do? There is no question of what Jack calls "passing beyond it." This is false.

One must submit. Do not resist. Take it. Be overwhelmed. Accept it fully. Make it *part of life*.

Everything in life that we really accept undergoes a change. So suffering must become Love. That is the mystery. This is what I must do. I must pass from personal love which has failed me to greater love. I must give to the whole of life what I gave to him. The present agony will pass—if it doesn't kill.

* See *Letters of Katharine Manfield to John Middleton Murry* (New York, Alfred A. Knopf, 1951).

It won't last. Now I am like a man who has had his heart torn out—but—bear it—bear it! As in the physical world, so in the spiritual world, pain does not last for ever. It is only so terribly acute now. It is as though a ghastly accident had happened. If I can cease reliving all the shock and horror of it, cease going over it, I will get stronger.

Here, for a strange reason, rises the figure of Doctor Sorapure. He was a good man. He helped me not only to bear pain, but suggested that perhaps bodily ill-health is necessary, is a repairing process, and he was always telling me to consider how man plays but a part in the history of the world. My simple kindly doctor was pure of heart, as Tchehov is pure of heart. But for these ills one is one's own doctor. If "suffering" is not a repairing process I will make it so. I will learn the lesson it teaches. These are not idle words. These are not the consolations of the sick.

Life is a mystery. The fearful pain of these letters will fade. I must turn to *work*. I must put my agony into something, change it. "Sorrow shall be changed into joy."

It is to lose oneself more utterly, to love more deeply, to feel oneself part of life—not separate.

Oh Life! accept me—make me worthy—teach me.

I write that. I look up. The leaves move in the garden, the sky is pale, and I catch myself weeping. It is hard—it is hard to make a good death . . .

September (1922)

My first conversation with Orage took place on August 30, 1922.

On that occasion I began by telling him how dissatisfied I was with the idea that Life must be a lesser thing than we were capable of imagining it to be. I had the feeling that the same thing happened to nearly everybody whom I knew and whom I did not know. No sooner was their youth, with the little force and impetus characteristic of youth, done, than they stopped growing. At the very moment that one felt that now was the time to gather oneself together, to use one's whole strength, to take control, to be an adult, in fact, they seemed content to swop the darling wish of their hearts for innumerable little wishes. Or the image that suggested itself to me was that of a river flowing away in countless little trickles over a dark swamp.

They deceived themselves, of course. They called this trickling away—greater tolerance—wider interests—a sense of proportion—so that work did not rule out the possibility of "life." Or they called it an escape from all this mind-probing and self-consciousness—a simpler and therefore a better way of life. But sooner or later, in literature at any rate, there sounded an undertone of deep regret. There was an uneasiness, a sense of frustration. One heard, one thought one heard, the cry that began to echo in one's own being: "I have missed it. I have given up. This is not what I want. If this is all, then Life is not worth living."

But I *know* it is not all. How does one know that? Let me take the case of K.M. She has led, ever since she can remember, a very typically false life. Yet, through it all, there have been moments, instants, gleams, when she has felt the possibility of something quite other. . . .

September 30.

"Do you know what individuality is?"
"No."
"Consciousness of will. To be conscious that you have a will and can act."
Yes, it is. It's a glorious saying.

October 3.

Arrived Paris. Took rooms in Select Hotel, Place de la Sorbonne, for ten francs a day per person. What feeling? Very little. The room is like the room where one could work—or so it feels. . . .

I have thought of M. to-day. We are no longer together. Am I in the right way, though? No, not yet. Only looking on—telling others. I am not in body and soul. I feel a bit of a sham. . . . And so I am. One of the K.M.'s is so sorry. But of course she is. She has to die. *Don't* feed her.

October.

Important. When we can begin to take our failures non-seriously, it means we are ceasing to be afraid of them. It is of immense importance to learn to laugh at ourselves. What Shestov calls "a touch of easy familiarity and derision" has its value.

What will happen to Anatole France and his charming smile? Doesn't it disguise a lack of feeling, like M.'s weariness?

Life should be like a steady, visible light.

What remains of all those years together? It is difficult to say. If they were so important, how could they have come to nothing. Who *gave up* and *why?*

Haven't I been saying, all along, that the fault lies in trying to cure the body and paying no heed whatever to the sick psyche? Gurdjieff claims to do just what I have always dreamed might be done.

The sound of a street pipe, hundreds and hundreds of years old. . . .

Revelations

I have been thinking this morning until it seems I may get things straightened out if I try to write . . . where I am.

Ever since I came to Paris I have been as ill as ever. In fact, yesterday I thought I was dying. It is not imagination. My heart is so exhausted and so tied up that I can only walk to the taxi and back. I get up at midi and go to bed at 5:30. I try to "work" by fits and starts, but the time has gone by. I cannot work. Ever since April I have done practically nothing. But why? Because, although Mamoukhin's treatment improved my blood and made me look well and did have a good effect on my lungs, it made my heart not a snap better, and I only won that improvement by living the life of a corpse in the Victoria Palace Hotel.

My spirit is nearly dead. My spring of life is so starved that it's just not dry. Nearly all my improved health is pretence—acting. What does it amount to? Can I walk? Only creep. Can I do anything with my hands or body? Nothing at all. I am an absolutely helpless invalid. What is my life? It is the existence of a parasite. And five years have passed now, and I am in straighter bonds than ever.

Ah, I feel a little calmer already to be writing. Thank God for writing! I am so terrified of what I am going to do. All the voices out of the "Past" say "Don't do it." Bogey says "M. is a scientist. He does his part. It's up to you to do yours." But that is no good at all. I can no more cure my psyche than my body. Less it seems to me. Isn't Bogey himself, perfectly fresh and well, utterly depressed by boils on his neck? Think of five years' imprisonment. Someone has got to help me to get out. If that is a confession of weakness—it is. But it's only lack of imagination that calls it so. And who is going to help me? Remember Switzerland: "I am helpless." Of course, he is.

One prisoner cannot help another. Do I believe in medicine alone? No, never. In science alone? No, never. It seems to me childish and ridiculous to suppose one can be cured like a cow *if one is not a cow*. And here, all these years, I have been looking for someone who agreed with me. I have heard of Gurdjieff who seems not only to agree but to know infinitely more about it. Why hesitate?

Fear. Fear of what? Doesn't it come down to fear of losing Bogey? I believe it does. But, good Heavens! Face things. What have you of him now? What is your relationship? He talks to you—sometimes—and then goes off. He thinks of you tenderly. He dreams of a life with you *some day* when the miracle has happened. You are important to him as a dream. Not as a living reality. For you are not one. What do you share? Almost nothing. Yet there is a deep, sweet, tender flooding of feeling in my heart which is love for him and longing for him. But what is the good of it as things stand? Life together, with me ill, is simply torture with happy moments. But it's not life. . . . You do know that Bogey and you are only a kind of dream of what might be. And that might-be never, never can be true unless you are well. And you won't get well by "imagining" or "waiting" or trying to bring off that miracle yourself.

Therefore if the Grand Lama of Thibet promised to help you—how can you hesitate? Risk! Risk anything! Care no more for the opinions of others, for those voices. Do the hardest thing on earth for you. Act for yourself. Face the truth.

True, Tchehov didn't. Yes, but Tchehov died. And let us be honest. How much do we know of Tchehov from his letters? Was that all? Of course not. Don't you suppose he had a whole longing life of which there is hardly a word? Then read the final letters. He has given up hope. If you de-sentimentalize those final letters they are terrible. There is no more Tchehov. Illness has swallowed him.

But perhaps to people who are not ill, all this is non-sense. They have never travelled this road. How can they see where I am? All the more reason to go boldly forward alone. Life is not simple. In spite of all we say about the mystery of Life, when we get down to it we want to treat it as though it were a child's tale. . . .

Now, Katherine, what do you mean by health? And what do you want it for?

Answer: By health I mean the power to live a full, adult, living, breathing life in close contact with what I love—the earth and the wonders thereof—the sea—the sun. All that we mean when we speak of the external world. I want to enter into it, to be part of it, to live in it, to learn from it, to lose all that is superficial and acquired in me and to become a conscious direct human being. I want, by under-standing myself, to understand others. I want to be all that I am capable of becoming so that I may be (and here I have stopped and waited and waited and it's no good—there's only one phrase that will do) *a child of the sun*. About helping others, about carrying a light and so on, it seems false to say a single word. Let it be at that. *A child of the sun.*

Then I want to *work*. At what? I want so to live that I work with my hands and my feeling and my brain. I want a garden, a small house, grass, animals, books, pictures, music. And out of this, the expression of this, I want to be writ-ing . . .

But warm, eager, living life—to be rooted in life—to learn, to desire to know, to feel, to think, to act. That is what I want. And nothing less. That is what I must try for.

I wrote this for myself. I shall now risk sending it to Bogey. He may do with it what he likes. He must see how much I love him.

And when I say "I fear"—don't let it disturb you, dearest heart. We all fear when we are in waiting-rooms. Yet we must pass beyond them, and if the other can keep calm, it is all the help we can give each other. . . .

And this all sounds very strenuous and serious. But now that I have wrestled with it, it's no longer so. I feel happy— deep down. May you be happy too.

I'm going to Fountainebleau on Monday and I'll be back here Tuesday night or Wednesday morning. *All is well.*

Dr. Young, the London man who has joined Gurdjieff, came to see me to-day and told me about the life there. It sounds wonderfully good and simple and what one needs. . . .

October 17.

. . . He [Gurdjieff] looks exactly like a desert chief . . .

To be wildly enthusiastic, or deadly serious—both are wrong. Both pass. One must keep ever present a sense of humor. It depends entirely on yourself how much you see or hear or understand. But the sense of humor I have found true of every single occasion of my life. Now perhaps you understand what "indifferent" means. It is to learn not to mind, and not to show your mind.

October 18.

In the autumn garden leaves falling. Little footfalls, like gentle whispering. They fly, spin, twirl, shake. . . .

[Katherine's work with the community involved her in physical and spiritual activities to which she was not accustomed, from dancing to milking cows. Some say that the experience shortened her life. She wrote Murry; "Here it is part of the 'work' to do a great many things, especially things which one does *not* like . . .

It's the same principle as facing people whom one shrinks from and so on. It is to develop a greater range in oneself. But what happens in practice is that no sooner do the people begin doing those things they don't like than the dislike changes. One feels it no longer." And of the dancing, she wrote: "There is one [dance] which takes about seven minutes and it contains the whole life of woman . . . Nothing is left out. It taught me, it gave me more of a woman's life than any book or poem . . . Mysterious . . . I remember I used to think—if there was one thing I could not bear in a community, it would be the women . . . It does seem to me there are certain people here who are far beyond any I have met—of a quite different order."

But despite the confidence of her letters, she did not survive. In January Murry was allowed to visit her. He arrived and found her "pale," "radiant," "transfigured by love, absolutely secure in love." Several days later she had a final hemorrhage and died.]

LORAN HURNSCOT

oran Hurnscot is a pseudonym for Gay Stuart Taylor, a woman who took part in the sexual revolution in England in the twenties, and then later in the thirties turned to the kind of inner search we have seen in Katherine Mansfield. Her pseudonym is an anagram on what she considered her besetting sins: Sloth and Rancour. She published her diaries as a book in two parts under the title *A Prison, A Paradise,* the first part dealing with a tormented love affair, the second with her spiritual awakening.

The diary written as a young wife records a sexual experiment undertaken at her husband's suggestion, an open affair with a mutual friend, the writer A. E. Coppard, with whom the couple ran a small publishing operation. The husband soon discovered a raging jealousy in himself and punished her for their adventure for the rest of his life—in fact, after that: he left his small income in someone else's trust.

The poet Kathleen Raine, in her introduction to Hurnscot's book, speaks of the attempts made in the twenties to "realize perfection through sexual love, a sort of religion in that decade, that demanded . . . an effort of positive idealism, no mere moral inertia." Hurnscot was surely moved by moral integrity when eventually she chose to follow "the way of the solitary, the way of the mystic," studying privately, occasionally meditating with friends and others whom she knew to be truly religious without orthodoxy. The process, as her diary discloses, was slow and lonely, with occasional false inflation and discouraging periods of aridity. It is a revealing study of the steps an intelligent woman went through in order to overcome the subjective emotionality of earthly life. She died in 1970. In a recent letter about her, Kathleen Raine says, "Since her death her stature has somehow increased. She used to laugh at a famous psychologist who had once said to her 'unearthly woman.' And she was. Death has not diminished her."

Our excerpt, from the second part of her book, finds her early in her study, at the opening of the second part of her book, when she is attempting to work with a group led by the Russian P. D. Ouspensky. Ouspensky taught a psychological system closely linked to that of Gurdjieff. Hurnscot later strongly rejected Ouspensky's system as mechanistic. After leaving the group, she went into a suicidal period, and it is here we see the longing for death transformed into a recognition of the divine. Her re-creation of the English landscape and people has been compared to Thomas Hardy's. It was in such country that she found the path of what she calls the "tilted spiral" to paradise.

May 26, 1936.

Went to the first Ouspensky lecture, at a house in Warwick Gardens. Two sad-looking, worn, rather severe women in neat navy-blue suits sat at a table in the hall, checking people as they came in. My slightly feather-headed but charming sponsor left me in the lecture-room and I went and sat in a corner. The room filled up. Intelligent-looking men. Uncouth-looking men. Several very attractive women. The room is papered in a depressing purplish-grey; purplish Sundour curtains at the windows; on the two mantelpieces there are brass ash-trays and pots with bare branches ornamented with mother-of-pearl leaves. Before the lecturer's chair is a small table covered with an orange cloth.

A fattish greasy-skinned Scotsman sat beside the table and asked people to ask any questions that were in their minds. No one spoke. After a long pause he suggested that people might write down questions and hand them in . . . At last Ouspensky came in. He looked like a short stout benign Buddha, with a dash of Erik von Stroheim and an air of having just come back from a long sea voyage, which as he had been lecturing last Thursday was impossible.

The fat Scotsman began to read the questions. Ouspensky said that many were irrelevant to the System he taught, and that some could only be answered at a later stage. The first one he answered (What principle makes the process of growth painful?) was mine. "Effort," he said. "Without effort there is no growth, and to man effort is always painful."

An elderly woman asked a question about God. He frowned. "This is *not* a religion. This is a system of psychology."

Another man, with an agreeable voice, began to read the lecture. It was not very new to me, after reading Ouspensky's books: man as a machine; as a collection of "I's" with no permanent or controlling "I"; psychology as an incomplete and misleading science in our time: not much else. When it was over there was hardly a pause. Questions showered. The room seemed charged with vitality. Ouspensky answered with a certain benignity, encouraged the questioners; looked like a sun surrounded by its planets. Nobody was abashed. One or two silly women felt rather too much at home. Ouspensky did not accuse his audience of sleeping but at least admitted they were awake. "Are we conscious now?" asked one woman. "For a moment," said O., smiling kindly. . . .

337

Revelations

. . . Nobody could spend two years in attempting to follow the teachings of Ouspensky and remain quite unchanged. He himself has said that the man who taught him what he now teaches us instructed his disciples, after a few months, to ask their friends whether they had noticed any difference in them. In every case the answer was the same. Yes, they had become very hard and very dull. "You see," said Ouspensky, suddenly beaming on his by now rather lifeless audience, "they had all begun to lie less."

But lying is one of the few faults I don't possess, and I don't particularly want to grow any harder and duller than I am. Are these the fruits of the spirit? . . .

February 1939.

Tried to leave Ouspensky and the System—perhaps a suicidal longing to start cutting all the links? But to my very great surprise I got a note from him (in green ink) saying I was making a mistake. I thought this more than possible, so I went back, and again they surprised me by their uncondemning attitude. Though if I go on, it will have to be differently . . .

Return of suicidal thoughts. What has this cold System to give, that might hold one back? Self-observation and self-remembering. Two dead words to me. "Charity is something we cannot have. St. Paul had it, therefore he thought others could have it too. No, in our present state we cannot have charity." Is it possible that my joining so cold and loveless a thing as the System has been in effect another sort of self-destroying? . . .

LORAN HURNSCOT

Undated.

There are times when I feel I can no longer bear that grey room where I go once a week or fortnight in order to discover (presumably) how to turn from one sort of person into another sort of person.

People arrive at the gate, exaggeratedly quiet and self-contained, turn in under the dark hood of the hawthorn tree, enter the room with an unnatural look and subside into an unnatural silence. What we learn here is something that does not enrich but desiccates the universe, and by heaven you can tell as much from our faces. Here we collect: the hoaryheads, the three or four beauties, the professional men, the Victorian-Gothic-Insurance men, the young women that look like Girl Guides and the less young ones that look like police women; the very few genuine oddities—for it is quite intentionally that Ouspensky draws the dull rather than the odd, and the three Voices of Protest that belong to two men and to me.

Yet I go on hoping . . . for something I have not got so far . . . from this System. My soul's tongue is hanging out for water, and Ouspensky says, in effect, "Have a biscuit." . . .

Tonight Ouspensky himself presented me with a loophole through which to vanish. Until now I had had the impression that this grey room was the only alternative to a bed of spikes, a nunnery, or a journey to India with a very difficult goal at the end of it. But even he has admitted that there is another way, a way of the solitary, a way of the mystic, for those who through weakness or some other incapacity cannot go the way of a number of deadened-looking people in a grey room . . .

July 9.

I've quietly left the Ouspenskians. . . . I left for serious reasons. But now that I can admit all the niggling annoyances, well, I can admit them. Russian (I am told) has no definite or indefinite article, so to Ouspensky the System is, "System." And in this his flock follow him. "System says, System says," they parrot. I believe that minds of some rare quality have, from time to time visited that grey room. And that they have also gone again.

Another thing, I grew to know very well Ouspensky's appearance when lecturing to my own group: no longer a little Buddha, but merely grey, bored, codfishy and liverish. "You know, the further you get on in the System, the less you see of Ouspensky. He's more interested in the new groups," someone once told me. It was startling to hear that he is more interested in the ignorant beginners than in those who may be on the way to developing Higher Consciousness. I feel sure that with the real Masters, the reverse is true. Once I was put back into a quite new group, to hear an early lecture I had missed. With this group Ouspensky, I observed, wore the same revitalized, well-nourished look that he wore the first time I saw him. I began to wonder whether, after all, he was a kind of psychological vampire.

[After leaving the Ouspensky group, Loran became more suicidal, and by 1941, against a background of war and national disturbance, she found herself so personally disturbed that she decided to seek out a river a friend had once told her about in the north country, a "river that never gave up its dead . . . for below the water were limestone caves, into which the bodies of those who fell or jumped in were swept and never found." Leaving all money and identification behind, she took a train to the remote town, aware that "one cannot seriously plan suicide without becoming mad." She heightened that sense of madness by going for three nights without sleep. Arriving at her destination early in the day, she realized that she must wait until darkness fell to approach the river. Somehow the day wore on . . .]

In the afternoon I called for some tea at a farmhouse. There were two young girls there, and they were gauche and grudging. And yet, it was in that flagged kitchen that the first misgivings arrived. They knew their place in creation, as I had never known mine. A kind of doubt crept like a snail through my mind.

But just at dusk, I was there on the rocks by the river. I'd had to wait in the woods for people to go. There was silence at last. I burnt a card—the nine of diamonds—that I had seen in a street in Bloomsbury and picked up, out of some queer whim, wondering why it was not the nine of spades. The subcurrents of lunacy had been swaying through me for a long time.

The sheer evil of the place was growing. The water was still and oily below the spume. "If a man fell in there by sheer accident, he'd be damned for a thousand years," I thought. I felt the presence of past suicides, evil and despairing, all round me. "Is that the company I'm going to keep?"

The last light died out on the grey-green woods. I sat on, on the rocks. It was time. Was it time? And suddenly I knew that if I did this thing, I should be making an unbreakable link between myself and all the evil in the world. It came over me, blindingly, for the first time in my life, that suicide was a wrong act, was indeed "mortal sin." In that moment, God stopped me. I did not want my life, but I knew I was suddenly forbidden by something outside myself to let it go.

I cried hopelessly for a long while. I looked again at the water, and thought of the Dial in my bag, that I'd meant to swallow to deaden consciousness. A tremendous "NO" rose—within me? outside me? I don't know. "I can't do it—I'm held back—I know beyond all doubt that it is absolutely *wrong.*"

Some blind instinct made me pull off my "disguise." It began to rain. There were seven shillings in my bag, dark was falling, and I was two hundred miles from home. I walked back to the village in the darkness, sobbing and talking to God. There was no earthly help for me anywhere, but I knew I was no longer alone; that God was there. It had always been pride that had held me off from Him. Now it was broken the obstacle was gone. One is never simple enough, while things go well.

"I'm in Your hands," I kept whispering. "You stopped me. You must show me what to do." I got back as far as the hotel, and asked about a bus to Sherston. They had all gone. "You might get a lift," someone said. I stood in the rain, on the bridge, crying, utterly down and out, praying in my heart all the time. Out of the rainy darkness a voice called out, "Mrs. Mitchell might put you up—first house on the left, over the bridge."

I went and knocked at the door. She was full up, but her next-door neighbour could. There, I explained that I had been out the whole day, walking, had lost my way and got stranded. No, I did not want any supper, was very tired, would go to bed at once. So at twenty to ten I went to bed. I slept and slept and slept, a deep natural sleep, the first for six months. In the morning I prayed again. "Tell me what to do." I thought of the Quakers, whose meetings I had been frequenting for about a year. But I had always felt, about them, that their goodness was too "natural": none of them had been out on the seventy thousand fathoms as I had. None of them would understand what I was going through. And then the answer came, quite distinctly, "Go to S—— and see a priest."

I was given a pleasant breakfast. The bill was four and six, so I left five shillings and went out into the misty morning. I had slept all night to the murmur of the river outside the windows. I walked up a hill, and a lorry-driver loaded up with sacks of flour gave me a lift to a village I have not since been able to find on the map. I went into the church, but God

was not there. Another lorry took me to Chayley, and from
there I got a bus to S——, which cost eightpence.

There, the predicament grew comic. I went to the
cathedral and found a charwoman washing the chancel. The
priests were all out. No one would be in till six o'clock. I
asked if there was another R.C. church. Yes, St. Dunstan's, in
Lincoln Road. At noon I walked in. It was a terribly ugly
ornate interior. A young priest was putting booklets in a rack.
I went up to him and said I wanted to speak to a priest.
"What's the trouble?" he said. I said, "You believe that suicide
is mortal sin, don't you?" "Yes," he said. "Don't you?" I told
him where I had been, and that I had gone there in order to
kill myself. "A beautiful place," he said. "I was up there last
week." "A sinister place," I said. "Other poor souls have
committed suicide there before," he said. "If that was in your
mind, you might well feel it sinister."

He asked if I had ever been to see a priest before and I
said no. I told him that I had no means of proving my story, or
even who I was; that I had only one and fourpence in my bag.
That I felt God had stopped me, and when I prayed to be
shown what to do I had been told to come to S—— and see a
priest. That I had had to come to someone who understood
sin.

"Well, that's what we're ordained for," he said. He was
young, dour, north-country, with grey stony eyes that were
deeply intent. He said, "You must go and have something to
eat—you can get it at the restaurant belonging to the work-
men's flats opposite. Come back and talk to me at four o'clock.
I have to go out till then." So I went. I was still terribly
distracted. All the elements were broken up, waiting to take a
new form. I had some soup. Then I thought that if it wasn't
"meant" that the little priest was to help me, I'd go to see
someone in the town that I slightly knew. But it was a relief
to find her house shut up. I felt that the fare for the journey

back from death to life had got to be handed to me by some-one who represented God, so that I could know it was truly God and not my own cowardly courage that had held me back.

Shortly before four o'clock I went back to St. Dunstan's, and presently he came in. I was sitting in a pew, empty and quiet. "Can't you telegraph for your fare home?" he said. "Or wouldn't any friend lend you the money?" I said it would be too late, I'd have to stay the night in S——, which would mean my going to a Travellers' Aid Society or something, and lying to them.

"Yes, if you told them what you told me they would only be suspicious of you," he said, suspicious himself. I waited, knowing I was in God's hands. Presently he said, "I'm going to help you. We aren't supposed to, or people would always be coming to us for money. How much would see you safely back to London?"

He lent me two pounds. I gave him my name and address, and the names of two people who knew me—"In case I don't hear from you," he said. "You *will* hear from me—don't you know that?" I said. "I'm trusting you, mind," he said. But most of him wasn't doing so. In a way, he was under God's compulsion, I felt. When I said I didn't know how to thank him, he said, "Don't try. Just kneel down before you go, and ask God to forgive you for your intention and show you what to do."

The train left at ten o'clock. I rang him up, meaning to try to reassure him. A young startled Irish maid answered. "Father Ransome's out. He's gone to the police station." Comedy and tragedy raced together. "Oh—why?" "His bi-cycle's been stolen. It went about eight o'clock tonight." "His faith's being tried hard," I thought. "I'm certain he thinks I'm dishonest. Perhaps even that I took his bicycle."

I telephoned again, but he had not come in. Just before

the train left, I rang up once more, after having had a hot bath. I told him I was just leaving, wanted to tell him everything was all right, that I would post the cheque to him before noon, and how sorry I was to hear of the loss of his bicycle.

Again, I forget the journey. Perhaps I slept. Once more I went to Robin's basement, retrieved my property, posted the cheque and sent a telegram. Then I went down to Wellbridge, where Bee and Angus met me. It was lovely to see her good kind face at the station, after all I'd gone through. They were very sweet to me and I spent a happy ten days there, mostly out in the hopfields, getting well. The old persecution-complex melted away; a bad dream. A little money was promised me till Christmas, so that I could just live. Everything in me was very quiet, waiting. And when I came back to Tripoly, the peace of God seemed to enter my heart.

I feel that it all had to happen, and happen in just that way. Nothing else would have removed the suicide-obsession I've cherished secretly, ever since I was a child. Those hours by the northern river had to be, when I was beyond all human help, and knew at last that God was there.

The future looks most uncertain. But my faith is certain, now. "You've been given a very great grace," said that little priest, "to have been stopped on the last edge like that." And I knew he understood.

October 2nd.

The present is being a sort of holiday, a holy day. Life won't go on like it—it may be the best that I shall ever know. There is a radiance within. The screen my bitter "outcast" pride put between God and me has gone, and I know both in spirit and (in a strange inexplicable way) even in body that it is true that God is love.

345

Revelations

Mist and cold, after yesterday's Indian summer. It was one of the perfect days—the high tide of this present time. I went out for a walk, then picked blackberries on Periton Hill, in that far clump at the edge of the downs. For a long time I sat out on the crumbling turf, sheltered from the wind, with the blue distances below, and warm sun lying over this lovely autumn land. And suddenly I was swept out of myself—knowing, knowing, knowing. Feeling the love of God burning through creation, and an ecstasy of bliss pouring through my spirit and down into every nerve. I'm ashamed to put it down in these halting words. For it was ecstasy—that indissoluble mingling of fire and light that the mystics know. There was a scalding sun in my breast—the "kingdom of God within"—that rushed out to that All-Beauty—its weak rays met those encompassing ones and the bliss of heaven filled me.

JOANNA FIELD

A diary used for self-analysis provided the basis for *A Life of One's Own*, by an English psychologist who used the pseudonym Joanna Field. In the 1930's, when she started her self-exploration, she was in her mid-twenties, promising in her work, surrounded by friends, loved and loving, and not as happy as she had expected.

Her purposes in putting her personal discoveries into a book were to outline a method available to anyone, even though it might well yield completely different results for others. In her own case, she found her way back to an acceptance of a personal God she had been trained to doubt. The excerpts we have made of the diary and text center around that realization, during which she came to accept what she called a "wide focused," receptive way of thinking, as opposed to the analytical, concentrated method which had been the goal and result of formal education.

Joanna Field had entered a career designed for the method of thinking she had been trained for, which more women are now able to do than ever before. If discontent comes with such attainment, it may be that an individual quest must follow, sometimes a more difficult undertaking than professional training. For Joanna Field demonstrated through her own self-study that her problems are recognizably shared by many men as well as women in contemporary society. The Afterword to this book deals further with some of her findings.

Because the nature of *A Life of One's Own* is to offer both the diary and an analysis of it alternately, we are reprinting passages from her retrospective text. Her explanation and the diary together demonstrate her two ways of thinking, in which she brings her scientific habits to bear upon subjective insights.

––––––––––

About this time I came upon many new experiences. Up to now, I had been determined to examine my experience in order to find out where and why it was inadequate. Now, when new things were beginning to happen to me, I seem to have felt, for a time at least, that the experience was enough in itself and that it was better simply to live it, since looking at it too deliberately might spoil it . . .

Some of my new experiences were physical ones, and I think I was particularly reluctant to record these for two reasons. First, I found words so hopelessly inadequate to convey the quality of what happened, and that they even sometimes had the power to destroy what they could not express. Second, these moments of physical happiness were emerging from a new direction. Up to now the incidents which I had felt impelled to select for each day's record had been moments of clearer consciousness, whereas physical sex experience was a plunge into a darker region. Yet although I could not bring myself to observe this new awareness, I did feel there was a tremendous amount to be learned in it, and in some curious way I seem to have understood that by persisting in my study of the moments of clear-headed happiness I would eventually reach a more real understanding of the passionate ones.

JOANNA FIELD

June 7.

We have been camping by the Thames . . . I smelled the young corn in the evening and the dusty road and nettles in the hedge. In the mornings I lay beside D. and sometimes slept or watched the swifts circling high up against a pale sky, their wings gold-bronze when catching the early sun. D.'s touch soothed me, giving peace through my body. . . . All this time since Easter I have felt life flowing all around me and over my head—and I am happy being immersed.

June 8th.

I want us to travel together, exploring, seeing how people live, talking to queer people by the roadside, sleeping at country inns, sailing boats, tramping dusty roads . . .

. . . to learn to understand the intricacies of his personality, like a piece of music—fitting the bits together—the connecting themes and central purpose.

Then to have him as a support and buttress to rely on for judgment and understanding, and someone to contend with . . .

To give up to the creative chemistry and live among things that grow—a child, a garden and quietness.

FEARS AND DRAWINGS-BACK

Of being tied up, of limiting my will, no longer a "mobile unit" to come and go as I choose.

Of limitations in future friendships . . .

I used to trouble about what life was for—now being alive seems sufficient reason.

June 18th.

I want—

Time, leisure to draw and study a few things closely by feeling, not thinking—to get at things.

I want a chance to play, to do things I choose just for the joy of doing, for no purpose or advancement.

To understand patiently the laws of growing things. I feel there is no time for these because I am driven by the crowd, filling my days with earning money, and keeping up with my friends—like a ping-pong ball. . . .

September 17th.

Today several of us walked through Golders Hill Gardens. There was a swan on the pond. Then I felt a sudden immense reality with D. The swans and reeds have a "thusness," "so and no otherwise" existing in an entirely different sphere from the world of opinion.

September 20th.

Yesterday I saw quite clearly (but now my head swims when I try to think of it) that the realness I feel with D. is because we supply mutual needs. Apart from my need for a man and his for a woman, we can understand each other, and he can give a certain vigor, headstrongness . . .

I feel by having him I can plunge more into life and take part in the business of living, home-making, money-making, discovery. Even a suburban existence would be exciting, experimenting to see what we could make of the universal problems. . . .

And I think I have got things to give him. I can help him to adapt, to co-ordinate his energies, to achieve more poise without losing vigor. Sometimes I have been angry with his arrogances—just as I have been angry when people are ill—and think I have only to tell him and he will change as I please. But I think I can learn to understand what he is getting at—often blindly, in spite of his insight. I feel now sometimes that I am inextricably bound up with his growth. I feel we have picked each other from the crowd as fellow-travelers, for neither of us is to the other's personality the end-all and the be-all. We are both after something (God knows what) and feel instinctively we can help each other toward it. I would like the relationship to give the greatest possible freedom to both of our personalities. . . .

I feel we are young together, immensely young.

September 21st, 12 P.M.

My last night alone in bed for many a day. It seems "putting off childish things" to have someone to love. Yet I was hoping together we might be more childlike, less oppressed with cares and heavy expediencies. It all feels very inevitable—like the spring following winter. . . .

October 10th.

We shall arrive in New York sometime tomorrow morning. Last night there was a moon over the sea and clouds, so that fields of silvery whiteness showed unexpectedly far away in the distance. The *Majestic* steamed steadily through a quiet sea, with a gentle hissing from the margin of white foam swirling past the hull, and white foam from the bow wave widening out to sea, the water dark between the whiteness. This isn't just an attempt to describe the picturesque. It was my first realization of the sea, its spaces and the depths below us where queer things grow and swim silently. The hissing foam was again that of "perilous seas" . . . I saw our funny little desires and lusts against the background of this endless sea and gloried in realizing things so overwhelming of myself. . . . It was almost the same when D. and I lay together this morning. We became conductors for some terrific current of life and here in this little cabin is the center of an immense reality. . . .

I began to try and observe what happened when I wrote my thoughts freely without any attempt to control their direction . . . Only the first sentence or two were concerned with the present and then I plunged into memories of fifteen or twenty years ago, memories of things I had not consciously thought of for all those years, memories that I never knew I had remembered. . . . It seemed that I was normally only aware of the ripples on the surface of my mind, but the act of writing a thought was a plunge which at once took me into a different element where the past was intensely alive.

Although my glimpses of the inhabitants of these deeper waters of the mind were rather disquieting, suggesting creatures whose ways I did not know, I found the act of writing curiously calming, so that I gradually came to use it whenever I was over-burdened with worry. . . .

. . . I seemed to have two quite different selves, one which answered when I thought deliberately, another which answered when I let my thought be automatic. I decided to investigate further the opinions of the automatic one, to ask it questions and write answers without stopping to think.

So one day when I was feeling particularly under a cloud of apparently causeless anxiety I wrote:

Why this uneasiness? foreboding? . . . a black man holding you, a baby, in his arms, up in a tree—black man—father—he must have nursed me as

a baby—I remember his study with the sparking coil
and his singing me to sleep—"Now the day is over."

Although I could not then tell what all this meant, it
was clear that my automatic self was busy with happenings in
my remote past and was perhaps bringing over into my
present concerns emotions which had no real connection with
adult life. Certainly I had not seen the electrical machine in
my father's study since before I was three years old.

(It was only after considering the theory described in
the Epilogue [of Psychic Bisexuality] that I came to understand what this flood of emotionally tinged ideas from childhood might mean. Then I saw that these feelings of guilt and
futility towards my father might be, not expectation of punishment as a result of experience of punishment, but a more
*simple and primitive female impulse towards power and sym-
bols of power.*)

It next occurred to me to study my dreams in the same
way. At that time I used very often to dream of the sea, of
wanting to bathe and being in various ways prevented. I
therefore chose the word "sea" as a starting point.

SEA . . . mother—perhaps derived from
"mer"—feeling ashamed when they laugh at Miss
R.'s and they said I'd painted the sea blue—why did
I feel such accusations always unjust, a hot fighting
to deny and escape—to bathe in the sea. What does
it mean? Deep cool green water to dive into, but
often no bathing-dress and people watching and I
never would bathe naked and damn the people?
God—is that what the sea means?—lose myself—this
is just maundering—fear of the sea . . . fear to go
in farther than up to my ankles . . .

I was surprised at God coming into it. At that time if anyone had asked me what I thought about God I would have probably given a non-committal agnostic opinion, taking into account the latest fashion in science. I would have assumed that I had thus satisfactorily dealt with the question, taking it for granted that emotional troubles about it were things of the past, no doubt quite suitable during adolescence, but no concern of the twentieth-century adult. But since the word had cropped up in my free ideas about the sea, it now occurred to me that my automatic self might not hold the same views as my deliberate self, so I sat down to write freely, taking the word "God" as starting point:

GOD . . . happiness—wrong—damnation— those who do not believe shall be damned—as soon as you are happy enjoying yourself, something hunts you on—the hounds of heaven—you think you'll be lost—damned, if you are caught—no never stop—God is wicked, cruel—the Old Testament God, who commands whole cities to be put to the slaughter—a jealous God, visiting the sins—Oh God —what a God! Hell—blasted, you'll be annihilated, puffed out—they said you'd be raped by tramps on the grassy hills—I cried—Oh God, is it come to this —Lord save us—what from? Our own idea of thy nature . . . the God of my learning—trees, grass, wind and sea—"I give thanks and adore thee, God of the open air"—crawling worms and mud-blind sea worms—white worms—intestinal worms—enemas—beastly, hateful—menstruation—the hellish smell of blood—the end of everything—prison—foul smells—sweaty bodies—my God is better than. . . .

Not a little surprised at the effects of an ordinary Church of England upbringing, I tried again, after an interval of three months, in order to see whether this first effusion was not perhaps the result of a temporary mood:

> God—rod—sod—this is absurd—go on, go on—
> God—Almighty—spread over the sky—God help us
> . . . Trees lashed by the storm—"But the Lord was
> not in the wind"—"Lord" more intimate but less
> personal to one than "God"—What else does God
> mean? Holy—this is rot—rot—rotting—decay—death
> Devil—Duty—disease—putrefaction . . . God help
> me . . . God is a spirit—a spirit—spirits—gin—grog
> —spiritual . . . I hate God—God doesn't want me
> to be happy—*Why* must I do it?—"Because I say so"
> —and who are you?—why should I obey you? I won't
> I won't I won't—child—"before I spake as a child,
> understood as a child—now face to face"—love,
> love is of God.

Once more I tried, this time six months later. I had not read through what I had written on the two previous occasions and could not remember at all what I had put down. This time, however, I did not begin with the word God, but with the phrase "I believe."

> I BELIEVE . . . in God, etc.—that's no use
> —God—something large up in the sky rather like a
> canopy—and a shrinking fear inside me—memory of
> pain, when I have said: "Oh God," the ache of
> foreboding and fear of consequences—dread—when
> I have said: "God help me"—the God of Moses with
> piercing eyes that burned one's face—no, it was a

burning light, the face of God, that blinded one—
St. Paul was also blinded—and God, no, the Lord
was not in the fire—yet I feel he is very much fire—
the queer awe and terror and excitement of watching a heath fire and fighting it—the living fury of
the flames—this is as God—fierce, destructive, beautiful, inhuman—the sun also blinds one—I cannot
look upon his face—he is joyful and strong and
aloof . . . a queer thing sometimes glowing inside
oneself—sometimes a little flickering flame—God—
the woods and forest stand aloof—great beeches on
the Downs with a brooding life of their own—rain,
persistent, uncontrollable, wind—sometimes male-
volent howling, furious seas, personal but inhuman,
having purposes apart from men's little affairs—a
vast brooding existence—more than a mass of water
—the Earth, a gentler being, bearing fruit, more
man's slave than the sea and the wind and the fire—
when these are tamed it is more on sufferance. . . .

All this puzzled me a great deal. I thought—"What is
the good of imagining I accept what the scientists are saying
about the nature of the universe if all the time part of myself
is believing something quite different?"

Might not these apparent beliefs of my automatic self,
although I had had no notion of their existence, possess the
power to influence my feelings and actions? And was it not
important that I should find out how to control the beliefs of
this part of myself, since they seemed to take so little account
of what my deliberate self thought?

. . . For this discrepancy between the views of my
deliberate and automatic selves gave me an idea of what

356

might be the reason why I found it so difficult to make up my mind what I liked or what I thought about a thing. For as a rule I had tried to make decisions without stopping to hear what my automatic self had to say, assuming that my deliberate opinions were all that mattered or even all that existed. So my decisions were made on a basis of only part of the facts, with the result that I never quite felt sure of my conclusions and was liable to reverse them on the slightest provocation. Dimly realizing this, I began to use this free writing of my thoughts as a means for making important decisions . . . Also it seemed to me that perhaps my previous ignorance of the ways of this self might be sufficient reason why I had felt my life to be of a dull dead-level mediocrity, with the sense of real and vital things going on round the corner, out in the streets, in other people's lives. For I had taken the surface ripples for all there was, when actually happenings of vital importance to me had been going on, not somewhere away from me, but just underneath the calm surface of my own mind. . . .

I began to have an idea of my life, *not as the slow shaping of achievement to fit my preconceived purposes, but as the gradual discovery and growth of a purpose which I did not know.* I wrote: "It will mean walking in a fog for a bit, but it's the only way which is not a presumption, forcing the self into a theory." . . .

I (often) felt a desperate need to protect my ego by keeping the walls of my selfhood intact. Occasionally, in clear moments, I could see what I was doing. . . .

On the downs above Ashbury, walking past Wayland Smith's cave. I felt I ought to be thinking about something, getting the most out of the Downs, and yet constantly preoccupied with thoughts. Then I said, "The self in all these things does not know, it just is. I will sink down into my heart and just be." Walking over the thyme on the earthwork slope, for a moment I lost my personal self. Then I found that I was afraid that if I didn't think, do something, according to my own little plan, I'd be lost, sink into a coma of inaction. (There flashed in my mind a picture of a lunatic I had seen, sitting, all day and always, like a Buddha.) So I can't sink down and let the tide of my real being take me, for if I try and for a moment can see no direction, cannot tell where I am going, I am filled with panic, scared of emptiness. I must be doing something, doing something for my own salvation . . . The answer to "What shall I think about? then seems to be "Watch and wait . . . wait patiently for the Lord," keep still, silent, not only look but listen. . . . I tried, walking along the Ridgeway. Soon, instead of feeling I ought to be in touch with the landscape but couldn't. I found colors and shapes appearing of themselves . . . I began to exult, to see the cornfields and hedge and downs as exultant . . . Did the Stone Age people walk this road exulting? Singing exultant songs? All religion is not dirges and beseechings, one forgets sometimes . . .

If the self is what they say it is, surely it does not need my little plannings and purposes to tell it what to do . . .

It struck me as odd that it had taken me so long to reach a feeling of sureness that there was something in me that would get on with the job of living without my continual tampering. I suppose I did not really reach it until I had discovered how to sink down beneath the level of chattering thoughts and simply feel what it meant to be alive. . . . And once I had made contact with my own source of life, then belief or doubt about "everlasting arms" was quite irrelevant, just as one does not *believe* that the apple one eats tastes good, it *is* good.

358

One day the phrase, "Thy will, not mine, O Lord," rang in my head. I stopped to consider what it might mean.

"Thy" as this insistent reality which comes back at me; wells up from inside, frightens me by its nearness, shocks me by its inclusiveness because it's in the things I love, the lustiness and vigor and lavish things, and abandon—which before I had put as outside, not God.

This isolated thought reminded me of some of my earlier experiments of six years ago, and I decided to try again to find what my automatic self thought about God, to see whether blind thinking might perhaps have changed its ideas in the interval:

GOD . . . "of our father, known of old," God, God help me, God, not what I'm discovering, not Tao, too near, God, rod, sod, same old things! sod, sodden, drunken sod, looking down from heaven, blessed damosel, warm breast . . . God, oh God, not you, not anything so near, You are something remote, "beyond and yet again beyond," but you are not beyond . . . brooding over everything, like a mother chicken, brooding in everything, genesis, the conception, I am the seed, the pattern, the pull and tenseness of the Early Purple Orchis, the Meadow Crane's Bill, the whirl of a dandelion head seeded, the stresses and strains that keep a plant upright, what else? sex, isn't it that? the dark sea, the dark stream, thought-less, the apple leaf's becoming, being, not thinking . . . you playing, you absorbed, you like a child playing having your own concerns, beyond me, your own designs, that's the word, design, not purposes or intentions but design, like a drawing, every part holding together, a crispness, a wholeness, precise like a formula, like a dance, a crystal . . . yes, a crystal, forming a pattern out of nothing . . .

Apparently, then, this part of my mind has got over some of its fears and hatred in the intervening years, and I thought that this might perhaps be connected with my growing ability to recognize my own unwitting thoughts.

I came to the conclusion then that "continual mindfulness" could certainly not mean that my little conscious self should be entirely responsible for marshalling and arranging all my thoughts, for it simply did not know enough. It must mean, not a sergeant-major-like drilling of thoughts, but a continual readiness to look and readiness to accept whatever came. The worst sin, then, was to refuse to accept any thought, for it was only by scrutinizing everything that I could wean my blind thinking away from its childish preoccupations and make it assist my real present-day problems. Certainly whenever I did so manage to win its services I began to suspect that thought, which I had always before looked on as a cart-horse to be driven, whipped and plodding between shafts, might be really a Pegasus, so suddenly did it alight beside me from places I had no knowledge of.

FLORIDA
SCOTT-MAXWELL

lorida Scott-Maxwell was born in Florida in 1883. Her education was mainly through private lessons at home. At sixteen she went on the stage; at twenty she began another career as a writer of short stories. After her marriage she went to live in Scotland and worked for women's suffrage, wrote plays and raised her children. At fifty she began still another career by entering training as an analytical psychologist, studying under Carl Jung. She practiced in psychology clinics in Scotland and England.

At eighty-two, living alone, she kept a private notebook in which she recorded her strong reactions to being old and her feelings of being at variance with her times. At first the notebook was not intended for other eyes, but she finally decided she wanted to share her insights with others, and in 1968 her entries were published as *The Measure of My Days*.

Her notebook is not a dated record of events because, as she says, there are few external happenings in old age. Instead, it is a place where she is justified in "thinking two ways at once" as she continues her inner journey of growth, exploring the nature of love and work and the power born of claiming the self, a process that makes her "fierce with reality."

Revelations

Age puzzles me. I thought it was a quiet time. My seventies were interesting and fairly serene, but my eighties are passionate. I grow more intense as I age. To my own surprise I burst out with hot conviction. Only a few years ago I enjoyed my tranquillity, now I am so disturbed by the outer world and by human quality in general, that I want to put things right as though I still owed a debt to life. I must calm down. I am far too frail to indulge in moral fervour.

I love my family for many reasons; for what I see them to be, for the loveliness they have been, for the good I know in them. I love their essence, their "could be," and all this in spite of knowing their faults well . . .

No matter how old a mother is she watches her middle-aged children for signs of improvement. . . .

As I do not live in an age when rustling black skirts billow about me, and I do not carry an ebony stick to strike the floor in sharp rebuke, as this is denied me, I rap out a sentence in my note book and feel better. If a grandmother wants to put her foot down, the only safe place to do it these days is in a note book.

Fool that I am, I worry at the combat of life like a dog with an old shoe. It is differentiation in action, it is what the competitive nature of man forces him to do whether he will or no. It is the creation of quality, good and bad. Most women only half understand it and they tend to dislike it, for they feel the human price is too high. It is high. Good may lose and bad may win. The public view and the private differ. It could make unexpected history if wives wrote what they saw work—its efforts and its achievements—doing to their husbands; telling honestly how much of the husband is left for human purposes and how good the human quality remains.

My kitchen linoleum is so black and shiny that I waltz while I wait for the kettle to boil. This pleasure is for the old who live alone. The others must vanish into their expected role.

When a new disability arrives I look about to see if death has come, and I call quietly, "Death, is that you? Are you there?" So far the disability has answered, "Don't be silly, it's me."

Age is a desert of time—hours, days, weeks, years perhaps—with little to do. So one has ample time to face everything one has had, been, done; gather them all in: the things that came from outside, and those from inside. We have time at last to make them truly ours.

When I was a child I went with my grandfather when he hunted wild turkey, or quail, driving through the roadless woods under great water oaks shining as though newly washed by rain. Once on reaching a river I jumped from the wagon and running into the deep shade sat down on a large alligator, taking it for a half-buried log. I was also the child who walked out on a plank placed as a pier to reach the centre of the dark pool, then knelt, plunged in her hands to scoop up a drink, and saw that fatal snake, a water moccasin, dart between her closing hands.

You need only claim the events of your life to make yourself yours. When you truly possess all you have been and done, which may take some time, you are fierce with reality. When at last age has assembled you together, will it not be easy to let it all go, lived, balanced, over?

A note book might be the very thing for all the old who wave away crossword puzzles, painting, petit point, and knitting. It is more restful than conversation, and for me it has become a companion, more a confessional. It cannot shrive me, but knowing myself better comes near to that. Only this morning—this mild, sunny morning that charmed me into happiness—I realized my cheer was partly because I was alone. I thought for an awful moment that perhaps I was essentially unloving, perhaps had never loved; but years of absorption, and of joy, yes I have loved, but enough? Is there any stab as deep as wondering where and how much you failed those you loved? Disliking is my great sin, which I cannot overcome. It has taken me my entire life to learn not to withdraw.

I wonder why love is so often equated with joy when it is everything else as well. Devastation, balm, obsession, granting and receiving excessive value, and losing it again. It is recognition, often of what you are not but might be. It sears and it heals. It is beyond pity and above law. It can seem like truth. But what is truth? Oh this mysterious world in which we know nothing, nothing. At times love seems clarity, beyond judgment. But this is a place that can also be reached alone, an impersonal place, found and lost again.
Love is asked to carry intolerable burdens, not seen from outside. Love can be hard service, giving your all, and it may be finding your all. It is sometimes a discipline enabling you to do the impossible. It may be your glimpse of transcendence. It is even agreement. But it is all the pains as well, the small pains as well as the great. It is baffling to be loved by someone incapable of seeing you. It is pain to have your love claimed as a cloak that another may hide from himself. Love tested by its indulgence to weakness, or its blindness to unworthiness can turn to scorn. Love may have blind facets in its all-seeing eyes, but it is we who are blind to what we ask it to bear. Of course it is the heights and the depths, the follies and the glories, but

being loving is not always love, and hate can be even more cleansing. Why are love and hate near each other, opposite, and alike, and quickly interchangeable?

My only fear about death is that it will not come soon enough. Life still interests and occupies me. Happily I am not in such discomfort that I wish for death, I love and am loved, but please God I die before I lose my independence. I do not know what I believe about life after death; if it exists then I burn with interest, if not—well, I am tired. I have endured the flame of living and that should be enough. I have made others suffer, and if there are more lives to be lived I believe I ought to do penance for the suffering I have caused. I should experience what I have made others experience. It belongs to me, and I should learn it.

If I suffer from my lacks, and I do daily, I also feel elation at what I have become. At times I feel a sort of intoxication because of some small degree of gain; as though the life that is in me has been my charge, the trust birth brought me, and my blunders, sins, the blanks in me as well as the gifts, have in some long painful transmutation made the life that is in me clearer.

The most important thing in my life was the rich experience of the unconscious. This was a gift life gave me and I only had the sense to honor and serve it. It taught me that we are fed by great forces, and I know that I am in the hands of what seemed immortal. It hardly matters whether I am mortal or not since I have experienced the immortal. This makes me at rest in much of my being, but not in all. It is almost as if the order in me is barely me, and I still have to deal with the chaos that is mine. . . .

It has taken me all the time I've had to become myself, yet now that I am old there are times when I feel I am barely here, no room for me at all. I remember that in the last months of my pregnancies the child seemed to claim almost all my body, my strength, my breath, and I held on wondering if my burden was my enemy, uncertain as to whether my life was at all mine. Is life a pregnancy? That would make death a birth.

I am re-reading after fifty years Henry Adams's *Mont-St.-Michel*. One of the pleasures of age is reading books long forgotten, with only the enlargement they once brought remembered. As Henry Adams tells of that great flowering of trust in the Virgin, of glorious building in her honour, of the consummate artistry and rich humanity that burgeoned on every hand, I was so moved by the abundant beauty that I was almost healed of a wound that has ached in me all my life; the inferiority of women. It lamed me as a child. I still do not see why men feel such a need to stress it. Their behaviour seems unworthy, as though their superiority was not safe unless our inferiority was proven again and again. We are galled by it, even distorted by it, mortified for them, and forever puzzled. They have gifts and strengths we lack, achievement has been theirs, almost all concrete accomplishment is theirs, so why do they need to give us this flick of pain at our very being, we who are their mates and their mothers?

I was entranced by the Virgin whom Henry Adams deduced. She was loved, loved for her mercy, for her love of beauty and gift of inspiring its creation in others; loved above all for her generosity and power. She both gave and forgave. Then to honour the feminine enhances life. That is an arresting fact, often forgotten. But this great feminine symbol is a pattern that women do not follow, and could we? It is man's concept, and it is above all an appeal for mercy, and an appeal for bounty.

366

As long as men had this vision they could project on to her the creative heights in their own natures. They could represent their aspirations and the profound depths of their being in buildings that achieved miracles in stone, solving mathematical problems of weight and balance with the beauty of complete mastery.

It intoxicates, heals and shames me, and very humbly I ask myself what relation can ordinary women have to this divine feminine figure? Can we, should we, even attempt to serve this vision? We try to live her a little, we are expected to, and that is a great honour. We would try to live her more if we could, but the truth is we also execrate, desecrate, and rail at her while we do our chores. There is a smallness in us, a justified resentment perhaps, that makes us tend to reduce life to chores as though to refute this great ideal. It may be the contrast between the ideal and the real that makes so many women hate being women. Here we are caught, and here we struggle.

The selfless, tireless one, the rich giver and the meek receiver, with life-giving energy flowing like milk from the breast, costing her nothing, is too, too much. Looked at in the grey light of daily living the concept is the demand of the ravening child, and we cannot respond to such a claim in man or child. Our protest at the human enactment of the ideal may be why we are not worshipped, but belittled. Or is man's scorn a cry for help, and one to be met? Does he need us to be wiser than we are? He well might. Perhaps life needs it too.

We do not often live with the superior side of the man— that is generally expressed in his work—but more habitually with his weak, tired, shadow side. We indulge him, restore him, and though we exploit him (that is a mutual game) it often seems to us our role and fate to deal with his inferiority, and conceal it from him. We may do it with wisdom and grace, but usually we project our faults onto each other, all can be beneath comment, and there are times when only mutual forgiveness makes us fit to face each other once more.

Here is inferiority indeed, but it belongs to both and needs both to deal with it. It demands honesty and mercy, and these are not easy to summon; they may be beyond us, but when they answer our mutual cries of what can be despair, they are good enough to call divine. There can seem no connection between the great impersonal concepts and the problem of living our personal lives. Yet when men and women truly love each other they project their greatest possibilities onto the loved one. When love vanishes for a while the woman does not see the god in the man, he seldom lives it, and if he never sees the goddess in the woman it is never there.

Her failure may be the greater, as she is the midwife of the profound forces stirred by love, and it is for her to join the ideal and the human, but she cannot do it alone. The intimacy that exists between men and women can seem the confrontation between good and evil, the place where there is the greatest chance of their being resolved by compassion and insight. It is here that souls are bared. Here in the welter of complete exposure we meet our glories and our sins, and we can see when we should have accused ourselves not the other: here too we may find the mutual support to enable us to say, "I see myself." . . .

So I still care! At my age I care to my roots about the quality of women, and I care because I know how important her quality is.

The hurt that women have borne so long may have immeasurable meaning. We women are the meeting place of the highest and the lowest, and of minutia and riches; it is for us to see, and understand, and have pride in representing ourselves truly. Perhaps we must say to man . . . "The time may have come for us to forge our own identity, dangerous as that will be."

I am uncertain whether it is a sad thing or a solace to be past change. One can improve one's character to the very end, and no one is too young in these days to put the old right. The late clarities will be put down to our credit I feel sure.

It was something other than this that had caught my attention. In fact it was the exact opposite. It was the comfortable number of things about which we need no longer bother. I know I am thinking two ways at once, justified and possible in a note book. Goals and efforts of a lifetime can at last be abandoned. What a comfort. One's conscience? Toss the fussy thing aside. Rest, rest. So much over, so much hopeless, some delight remaining.

One's appearance, a lifetime of effort put into improving that, most of it ill judged. Only neatness is vital now, and one can finally live like a humble but watchful ghost. You need not plan holidays because you can't take them. You are past all action, all decision. In very truth the old are almost free, and if it is another way of saying that our lives are empty, well—there are days when emptiness is spacious, and nonexistence elevating. . . .

I wish I could remember that Blake said, "Any fool can generalize." I generalize constantly. I write my notes as though I spoke for all old people. This is nonsense. Age must be different for each. We may each die from being ourselves. That small part that cannot be shared or shown, that part has an end of its own.

Again a day that is so empty that I cry inside, a heavy weeping that will not stop. I cannot read, the papers depress me, reviews are written from points of view so outside my experience that I wonder if I ever understood anything. The grey sky seems very grey, but I finally soothe myself by small duties, putting away freshly ironed linen, watering plants. Order, cleanliness, seemliness make a structure that is half support, half ritual, and if it does not create it maintains decency. I make my possessions appear at their best as they are my only companions. Some days it is the only improvement I can bring about. I remember a beautiful girl of seventeen with destructive parents; unable to improve her position in any way she burst out with the surprising phrase, "I could neaten the stars." With less need I neaten my flat.

Old people can seldom say "we"; not those who live alone, and even those who live with their families are alone in their experience of age, so the habit of thinking in terms of "we" goes, and they become "I." It takes increasing courage to be "I" as one's frailty increases. There is so little strength left that one wants shelter, one seeks the small and natural but where to find it?

A garden, a cat, a wood fire, the country, to walk in woods and fields, even to look at them . . . Here in a flat, I must make the round of the day pleasant, getting up, going to bed, meals, letters with my breakfast tray: can I make it total to a quiet heart? I have to be a miracle of quiet to make the flame in my heart burn low, and on some days I am a miracle of quiet. But I cannot conceive how age and tranquility came to be synonymous.

My youngest grandchild uses silence as well as he does sound. He is consummate in making soft confiding noises that bind the heart of the hearer to him. But for long periods he prefers to keep his own counsel. Then he looks forth on the world unblinking, unhurried, and with a dignity that should be the rite of Kings.

At times he gazes at me without interest; above self-doubt he yawns, a wide, slow, complete and uncovered yawn. He removes his gaze from me so that I wonder if I was seen, if I was present. With grave deliberation he discovers a hole in the arm of his chair so small that no one else could have had the calm to take it in, and he gives it his undivided attention. He gives all of himself to that hole which just fits the tip of his minute first finger, and I know that all hope of further conversation with him is over. I also know that I have been in the presence of perfect naturalness, and I feel chastened and uplifted.

EMILY CARR

(1871-1945)

The work of the artist Emily Carr is little known outside her native Canada. We have not been able to see her paintings in the Vancouver Art Gallery collection, but the reproductions in her published journal *Hundreds and Thousands* indicate a powerful talent that deserves wider recognition. Her subject was the raw Canadian wilderness she loved, and in one painting in particular, "Houses Below Mountains," the human element of clustered houses is beautifully reconciled with the mysterious awe of mountains looming above in a pictorial metaphor of her own life.

She was wonderfully human herself: "unvarnished Emily," full of spunk and humor; crotchety, outspoken and often depressed; culturally isolated from the artistic companionship she craved; but always sustained by a sense of larger purpose as grand as her beloved mountains.

Her childhood was not happy. Her mother died when she was twelve, and when her authoritarian father died two years later, she was left in the care of a sister whose discipline was equally harsh. She left Canada to study painting in San Francisco, London and Paris and then returned to her home in Victoria, British Columbia, where she painted steadily with little recognition for many years. Not until 1927, when she met the Canadian Group of Seven, particularly Lawren Harris, did she receive the support of other artists. They recognized her fervent absorption in nature, her rhythms, and the dynamics of her painting as religious experience. Critics eventually came to agree, and when she was in her sixties her gifts were widely acknowledged. By then her health had declined and she had to curtail her work in art. She devoted more time to her writing, continuing the diary she had begun when she was fifty-six, working on her autobiography, *Growing Pains* (published posthumously, 1946) and several children's books, among them *The Book of Small.*

She never married and was extremely close to her family, particularly to two sisters in later life. Emily didn't worry about being thought eccentric, delighting in escaping in a cumbersome van with her pet monkey, rat and puppies to paint her challenging mountains. Her sense of the relationship between small delights and larger mysteries informed a courageous and remarkable life. The title of her diary, *Hundreds and Thousands,* derives from a never-forgotten memory of childhood. She explains that "Hundreds and Thousands are minute candies made in England—round sweetnesses, all colors and so small that separately they are not worth eating. But to eat them as we did in childhood was a different matter. Father would take the big fat bottle off the shelf in his office and say, 'Hold out your hands.' Father tipped and poured, and down bobbed our three hands and out came our three tongues and licked in the Hundreds and Thousands, and lapped them up, lovely and sweet and crunchy.

"It was these tiny things that, collectively, taught me how to live. Too insignificant to have been considered individually, but like the Hundreds and Thousands lapped up and sticking to our moist tongues, the little scraps and nothingnesses of my life have made a definite pattern. Only now, when the river has nearly reached the sea and small eddies gush up into the river's mouth and repulse the sluggish onflow, have they made a pattern in the mud flats, before gurgling out into the sea. Thank you, tiny Hundreds and Thousands. Thanks, before you merge into the great waters."

Revelations

Yesterday I went to town and bought this book to enter scraps in, not a diary of statistics and dates and decency of spelling and happenings but just to jot me down in, unvarnished me, old me at fifty-eight—old, old, old, in most ways and in others just a baby with so much to learn and not much time left here but maybe somewhere else. It seems to me it helps to write things and thoughts down. It makes the unworthy ones look more shamefaced and helps to place the better ones for sure in our minds. It sorts out jumbled up thoughts and helps to clarify them, and I want my thoughts clear and straight for my work.

I used to write diaries when I was young but if I put anything down that was under the skin I was in terror that someone would read it and ridicule me, so I always burnt them up before long. Once my big sister found and read something I wrote at the midnight of a new year. I was sorry about the old year, I had seemed to have failed so, and I had hopes for the new. But when she hurled my written thoughts at me I was angry and humbled and hurt and I burst smarting into the New Year and broke all my resolutions and didn't care. I burnt the diary and buried the thoughts and felt the world was a mean, sneaking place. I wonder why we are always sort of ashamed of our best parts and try to hide them. We don't mind ridicule of our "sillinesses" but of our "sobers," oh! Indians are the same and even dogs. They'll enjoy a joke with you, but ridicule of their "reals" is torment.

When I returned from the East in 1927, Lawren Harris and I exchanged a few letters about work. They were the first real exchanges of thought in regard to work I had ever experienced. They helped wonderfully. He made many things clear, and the unaccustomed putting down of my own thoughts in black and white helped me to clarify them and to find out my own aims and beliefs. Later, when I went East this Spring, I found he had shown some of my letters to others. That upset me. After that I could not write so freely. Perhaps it was silly, but I could not write my innermost thoughts if *anybody* was to read them, and the innermost thoughts are the only things that count in painting. I asked him not to. He saw my point and said he wouldn't. I trust him and can now gabble freely. Still, even so, I can't write too often, hence this jotting book for odd thoughts and feelings.

July 16th, 1933

Once I heard it stated and now I believe it to be true that there is no true art without religion. The artist himself may not think he is religious but if he is sincere his sincerity in itself is religion. If something other than the material did not speak to him, and if he did not have faith in that something and also in himself, he would not try to express it. Every artist I meet these days seems to me to leak out the fact that somewhere inside him he is groping religiously for something, some in one way, some in another, tip-toeing, stretching up, longing for something beyond what he sees or can reach.

I wonder will death be much lonelier than life. Life's an awfully lonesome affair. You can live close against other people yet your lives never touch. You come into the world alone and you go out of the world alone yet it seems to me you are more alone while living than even going and coming. Your mother loves you like the deuce while you are coming. Wrapped up there under her heart is perhaps the cosiest time in existence. Then she and you are one, companions. At death again hearts loosen and realities peep out, but all the intervening years of living something shuts you up in a "yourself shell." You can't break through and get out; nobody can break through and get in. If there was an instrument strong enough

375

to break the "self shells" and let out the spirit it would be grand. . . .

July 23rd

Dreams do come true sometimes. Caravans ran round inside of my head from the time I was no-high and read children's stories in which gypsies figured. Periodically I had caravan fever, drew plans like covered express carts drawn by a fat white horse. After horses went and motors came in I quit caravan dreaming, engines in no way appealing to me and my purse too slim to consider one anyhow. So I contented myself with shanties for sketching outings, cabins, tents, log huts, houseboats, tool sheds, lighthouses—many strange quarters. Then one day, plop! into my very mouth, like a great sugar plum for sweetness, dropped the caravan.

There it sat, grey and lumbering like an elephant, by the roadside—"For sale." I looked her over, made an offer, and she is mine. Greater even than the surprise of finding her was the fact that *nobody* opposed the idea but rather backed it up. We towed her home in the dark and I sneaked out of bed at 5 o'clock the next morning to make sure she was really true and not just a grey dream. Sure enough, there she sat, her square ugliness bathed in the summer sunshine, and I sang in my heart.

Now she's just about fixed up. She has no innards, that is works, so I'll have to be hauled. I've chosen the spot, Gold-stream Flats, a lovely place. I'm aching to be off but not yet as nobody wants to go with me. I've asked one or two. I thought it would be nice to have someone to enthuse to, just for the first trip. With one accord they all made excuses except Henry. Poor Henry, who has lived twenty years and only developed nine when sleeping-sickness overwhelmed him and arrested his progress, like a clock whose hands have stuck though it goes on ticking—Henry *wants* to go along.

July 27th

Oh, these mountains! They won't bulk up. They are thin and papery. They won't brood like great sitting hens, squatting immovable, unperturbed, staring, guarding their precious secrets till something happens. At 'em again, old girl, they're worth the big struggle.

July 28th

. . . I have wiped out the village at the foot of the mountain. Now I shall paint the little cowed hollow that the village sits in and maybe toss the huts in last of all. It is the mountain I *must* express, all else subservient to that great dominating strength and spirit brooding there.

August 12th

. . . I thought my mountain was coming this morning. It began to move, it was near to speaking, when suddenly it shifted, sulked, returned to obscurity, to smallness. It has eluded me again and sits there, mean, puny, dull. Why? Did I lower my ideal? Did I carelessly bungle, pandering to the material instead of to the spiritual? . . .

August 19th

My van elephant is now a reality. While she sat there in the lot she was only a dream shaping itself. She was bought so suddenly after long years of waiting. It is two months from the morning that I got out of bed at 5 A.M. to peep out of the studio window and see if she was really there in the lot beneath. Then came all the fixings, meat safe, dog boxes and monkey-proof corner. And when she was ready, equipped in full, the hauler came and said that it was impossible to get her out of the lot because she was too low, and he was horrid and I was mad. "Well," I said, "if the man brought her 3,370 miles across the Rockies, surely she can be taken twelve miles to Goldstream Flats." And she was, but not by that old fool. The third who inspected ventured. The family sat on the creature crates and watched the tugging, heaving and wrenching. Sweat and cussings poured! Poor rat Susie was aboard and must have got severely jerked. The lid was off her box when we got there but Susie sweetly asleep within.

Henry and I and the animals drove in the truck. Whew, it was hot at the wood yard! The jacking-up blocks weren't ready. Then we stopped for the tires to be winded. We lumbered right through Government Street. Mercy, it was hot! And the delays were so numerous I patted my wallet and wondered if she was fat enough but they only charged the original $3.50 agreed upon. I was so thrilled that I "coned" and "ginger-popped" the man liberally when we got to the pop shop on the Flats.

It wasn't the spot I had picked, but the Elephant found it to her liking. The Elephant is a grand sitter but a heavy traveller.

Henry went all to pieces when we got there, not a steady nerve in his body. He hopped and wiggled and shook and stuttered. I ran hither and thither getting blocks and bricks and stones to aid the man in hoisting the Elephant off her tires. It was almost 5 P.M. when he left. The Elephant had chosen a favourite cow spot and much raking was necessary. This was accomplished with the aid of a row of rake teeth absolutely devoid of a handle. Everyone on the Flats collected to see us unpack, the monkey, of course, being the centre of attraction. The tent fly tormented me but I got it stuck up at last unaided. I made up the beds and prepared supper. Black fell down among the great cedars before I was nearly out of the mess.

Neither of us slept. I could hear Henry groaning and tossing under the tent. The creatures were all in the van with me and very good. The monkey is housed in a hollow cedar tree, cuddled into its very heart. Surely I have at last found her a habitation she *cannot* wreck. She'd have made matchwood of the Elephant. I ship-shaped up next morning and we are spick and span, very comfortable and very happy. Henry's nerves torment and wrack him a little less. There's a great peace under these magnificent cedars and the endless water sings its endless sound not a stone's throw off. I've made a range to rival any "Monarch" or "Canada's Pride" ever invented. The ingredients are a piece of automobile frame, the leg of a stove, a pile of rocks, scraps of iron, tin and wire, and parts of a gridiron. It's a peach!

Last night we slept like babies. Each creature has dropped into its own niche. The spirit of freemasonry and intimacy among us all is superb. It's wonderful to watch the joy of the pups playing tag among the cedars. There is a delicious little breeze humming among the leaves without bluster or vulgarity. Today I love life, so do the four dogs, the monkey and the rat. And poor Henry; this must make up to him a little for all that he hasn't got in life.

Last night when the pop shop was shut and everyone was in bed I slipped into a nondescript garment and tumbled into the river. It was wonderful. I lay down on the stones and let the water ripple over me, clear, soft water that made the skin of you feel like something namelessly exquisite, even my sixty-year-old skin. When I had rubbed down and was between the sheets in the Elephant's innards, I felt like a million dollars, only much cleaner and sweeter and nicer. The precious pups were asleep all round, and rat Susie, Woo just outside the window in her hollow cedar, Henry in the tent lean-to. The cedars and pines and river all whispered soothingly, and there was life, life, life in the soft blackness of the night.

Today is wonderful again. Henry has found companionship with the pop lady's small boys. They are playing ball, all laughing. . . .

August 31st

A wet day in camp. The rain pattered on the top of the Elephant all night. Mrs. "Pop Shop" and I went for our nightly dip in the river. It was cold and took courage and much squealing and knee-shaking. Neither of us has the pluck to exhibit the bulges of our fat before the youngsters, so we "mermaid" after dark. I dare not *run* back; the footing among the cedars is ribbed with big roots. One's feet must pick and one's eyes must peer through the dim obscurity of the great cedars and maples. Once inside the Elephant, scrubbed down with a hard brush and cuddled up to a hot bottle, I thought I loved the whole world, I felt so good. But last night as I stood in my nightie and cap, a male voice made a howl and a male head thrust into the van. Well, all the love and charity fled from my soul. I was red hot and demanded his wants. By this time the dogs were in an uproar and I couldn't hear his answer. Finally I caught, "Can I get any bread?" "No," I replied tartly, "the shop is shut out there." He disappeared in the night and then I felt a beast and ran to the door to offer him what I had in camp but he had vanished, swallowed up in the black night. I might have been more tolerant, but I hate my privacy being torn up by the roots. I thought of that one word "bread" every time I awoke. . . .

380

September 5th

It started to rain last night and has rained all day. I packed Henry off home because his shelter was too slim. Anyhow he has had two good weeks. I had spent all day rearranging the camp for rain and snugging it up. I moved the "Monarch" range up close in front of the awning. The great cedar hangs over it and sheds off the rain. Woo in its innards is dry and cosy. She loves her cedar home. The woods are delightful in the rain, heavily veiled in mystery. They are delicious to *all* the senses but most to the smell. An owl came and sat on my cedar beside the fire. How I love it when the wild creatures pal up that way! The van is cosy, come rain, come shine, and all is well. Now Henry is gone I hope to try and work. Perhaps it wasn't Henry; maybe it was me. I care much too much for creature comforts and keeping the camp cosy and tidy. It seems necessary, especially with all the creatures. Mrs. Giles, the nursery woman, said that when her small boys went home and reported that there was a lady in the Flats in a house on wheels, with four dogs, a monkey and a rat, and a hopping boy, she thought it must be a section of a circus or travelling show. They also reported that when they came into my camp I chased them all off with a broom. I believe I was considerably tormented that first morning. How different you sound when described to what you feel!

September 8th

. . . I had thought this place somehow incongruous, the immensity of the old trees here and there not holding with the rest but belonging to a different era, to the forest primeval. There is no second growth, no in-between. It is too great a jump from immensity to the littleness of scrub brush. Today I see that I am what Whitman would call "making pictures with reference to parts" not with reference to "ensemble." The individual mighty trees stagger me. I become engaged with the figures and not the sum and so I get no further with my reckoning of the total. Nothing stands alone; each is only a part. A picture must be a portrayal of relationships. . . .

September 14th

I have found winter grazing for the Elephant after much tramping. It has settled in to pour. Mrs. Hooper supped in my camp and by the fire we sat long, talking. There is a straight-from-the-shoulderness about her I like. She does what comes to her hand to help people—reared a worse than parentless girl, looked after and helped old poor sick women. Through her conversation (not boastfully) ran a thread of kindness and real usefulness. I feel wormy when I see what others do for people and I doing so little. I try to work honestly at my job of painting but I don't see that it does anyone any good. If I could only feel that my painting lifted someone or gave them joy, but I don't feel that. I enjoy my striving to express. Another drinks because he enjoys drinking or eats because he enjoys eating. It's all selfish.

The rain is thundering on the van top. The creatures are all folded down in sleep, the park blackly wrapped about in that dense dark. There is a solidity about the black night in this little valley, as if you could cut slices out of it and pile them up. Not a light anywhere. The stream gargles as if it had a perpetual sore throat. A car passes up on the Malahat highway with a swift flash of light on this and that up above us and is gone like an unreality.

September 16th

After living for a whole month, or thereabouts, in a caravan and then to return to a two-storey house with six rooms all to oneself makes one feel as if one had straddled the whole world. The Elephant is bedded down opposite the Four Mile House in a quiet pasture. It is hard to settle down. The house feels stuffy and oppressive but the garden is joyful . . . I have uncovered "The Mountain." It makes me sick. I am heavy in spirit over my painting. It is so lacking. What's the use? Sometimes I could quit paint and take to charring. It must be fine to clean perfectly, to shine and polish and *know* that it could not be done better. In painting that never occurs. . . .

October 5th

Oh, that mountain! I'm dead beat tonight with struggling. I repainted almost the whole show. It's still a bad, horrid, awful, mean little tussock. No strength, nobility, solidarity. I've been looking at A. Y. Jackson's mountains in the C.N.R. Jasper Park folder. Four good colour prints but they do not impress me. Now *I* could not do one tenth as well but somehow I don't *want* to do mountains like that. Shut up, me! Are you jealous and ungenerous? I don't think it is that.

October 6th

My mountain is dead. As soon as she has dried, I'll bury her under a decent layer of white paint and top her off with another picture. But I haven't done with the old lady; far from it. She's sprawling over a new clean canvas, her germ lives and is sprouting vigorously. My inner self said, "Start again and profit by your experience." Oh, if I could only make her throb into life, a living, moving mass of splendid power and volume!

Revelations

October 17th

The mountain is finished, and the Brackendale landscape and the tree with moving background will be coffined
tomorrow and away. They ought not to go out as pictures,
finished. I feel them incomplete studies, just learners not
show-ers. Will I ever paint a show-er, forgetting the paint and
remembering the glory? I will not berate them. I have
wrestled with them honestly, now I put them from me and
push on to the next, carrying with me some bit of knowledge
and growth acquired through them—on, up! Oh, the glory of
growth, silent, mighty, persistent, inevitable! To awaken, to
open up like a flower to the light of a fuller consciousness! I
want to see and feel and expand, little book, you holder of my
secrets.

December 12

Emily Carr, born Dec. 13, 1871, at Victoria B.C., 4
A.M., in a deep snow storm, tomorrow will be sixty-two. It is
not all bad, this getting old, ripening. After the fruit has got
its growth it should juice up and mellow. God forbid I should
live long enough to ferment and rot and fall to the ground in a
squash. . . .

April 6, 1934

. . . I'm a bit ashamed of being a little depressed again.
Perhaps it is reading the autobiography of Alice B. Toklas—
all the artists there in Paris, like all the artists in the East,
jogging along, discussing, condemning, adoring, fighting,
struggling, enthusing, *seeking* together, jostling each other,
instead of solitude, no shelter, exposed to all the "winds" like a
lone old tree with no others round to strengthen it against the

buffets with no waving branches to help keep time. B-a-a-a-, old sheep, bleating for fellows. Don't you know better by now? It must be my fault somewhere, this repelling of mankind and at the same time rebelling at having no one to shake hands with but myself and the right hand weary of shaking the left. . . .

August 3rd

It's a long week since I told you anything, little book. Here's a secret first. Others might say it was silly. For the second time a soul has kissed my hand because of a picture of mine—once a man, once a woman. It makes one feel queer, half ashamed and very happy, that some thought you have expressed in paint has touched somebody. Today I sold a sketch and gave another, though of my very most recent. They always pick the newest and leave the old frowses. One's glad, in a way, that the recentest should be approved above the older. It looks like progress. One would rather like to keep one's latest, but there's always the hope that there'll be better ones than the latest by and by, so scoot them off before they grow too drab. . . .

August 12th

I haven't one friend of my own age and generation. I wish I had. I don't know if it's my own fault. I haven't a *single thing* in common with them. They're all snarled up in grandchildren or W.A. or church teas or bridge or society. None of them like painting and they particularly dislike my kind of painting. It's awkward, this oil and water mixing. I have lots more in common with the young generation, but there you are. Twenty can't be expected to tolerate sixty in all things, and sixty gets bored stiff with twenty's eternal love affairs. Oh God, why did you make me a pelican and sit me down in a wilderness? These old maids of fifty to sixty, how dull they are, so self-centred, and the married women are absorbed in their husbands and families. Oh Lord, I thank Thee for the dogs and the monkey and the rat. I loafed all day. Next week I must step on the gas.

June 30th, 1935

The wind is roaring and it is cold. I revolted against wrestling with the campfire and shivering over breakfast in the open field, so I breakfast in the van. It is a day to cuddle down. Even the monkey pleaded to come back to her sleeping box, tuck her shawls about her and watch me. . . .

I did two sketches, large interiors, trying to unify the thought of the whole wood in the bit I was depicting. I did not make a good fist of it but I felt connections more than ever before. Only three more whole days of this absolute freedom and then I have to pack up and get back to the old routine, though it will be nice to get back to those two dear sisters who plod on, year in and year out, with never a break or pause in their monotonous lives. But it would not give *them* a spacious joy to sit at a little homemade table writing, with three sleeping pups on the bunk beside me, a monk at my shoulder and the zip and roar of the wind lifting the canvas and shivering the van so that you feel you are part and parcel of the storming yourself. That's living! You'd never get that feel in a solid house shut away securely from the living elements by a barricade!

Christmas eve, 1935

We have just had our present-giving at Alice's, just we three old girls. Alice's house was full of the smell of new bread. The loaves were piled on the kitchen table; the dining-room table was piled with parcels, things changing hands. This is our system and works well: we agree on a stated amount—it is small because our big giving is birthdays. Each of us buys something for ourselves to our own liking, goods amounting to the stated sums. We bring them along and Christmas Eve, with kissings and thankings, accept them from each other—homely, practical little wants, torch batteries, hearth brooms, coffee strainers, iron handles, etc. It's lots of fun. We lit four red candles in the window and drank ginger ale and ate Christmas cake and new bread and joked and discussed today and tomorrow and yesterday and compared tirednesses and rheumatics and rejoiced that Christmas came only once per year. We love each other, we three; with all our differences we are very close.

Christmas Day, 1935

. . . Two would-be art critics came to the studio. They were "pose-y," waved their paws describing sweeps and motions in my pictures, screwed their eyes, made monocles of their fists, discoursed on aesthetics, asked prices, and expounded on technique. One paints a little and teaches a lot, the other "aesthetics" with I do not quite know what aim. Both think women and their works beneath contempt but ask to come to the studio on every occasion. Why?

February 9th, 1936

. . . Lover's letters I destroyed years back; no other eye should see those. But there was a note, written forty years and more after the man had been my sweetheart and he loved me still. He married as he told me he should. He demanded more than I could have given; he demanded *worship*. He thought I made a great mistake in not marrying him. He ought to be glad I did not; he'd have found me a bitter mouthful and very indigestible and he would have bored me till my spirit died. . . .

April 16, 1937

. . . I have been thinking that I am a shirker. I have dodged publicity, hated write-ups and all that splutter. Well, that's all selfish conceit that embarrassed me. I have been forgetting Canada and forgetting women painters. It's them I ought to be upholding, nothing to do with puny me at all. Perhaps what brought it home was the last two lines of a crit in a Toronto paper: "Miss Carr is essentially Canadian, not by reason of her subject matter alone, but by her approach to it." I am glad of that. I am also glad that I am showing these men that women can hold up their end. The men resent a woman getting any honour in what they consider is essentially their field. Men painters mostly despise women painters. So I have decided to stop squirming, to throw any honour in with Canada and women. It is wonderful to feel the grandness of Canada in the raw, not because she is Canada but because she's something sublime that you were born into, some great rugged power that you are a part of.

December 13, 1937

Sixty-six years ago tonight I was hardly me. I was just a pink bundle snuggled in a blanket close to Mother. The north wind was bellowing round, tearing at everything. The snow was all drifted up on the little balcony outside Mother's window. The night before had been a disturbed one for everybody. Everything was quieted down tonight. The two-year-old Alice was deposed from her baby throne. The bigger girls were sprouting motherisms, all-over delighted with the new toy. Mother hardly realized yet that I was me and had set up an entity of my own. I wonder what Father felt. I can't imagine him being half as interested as Mother. More to Father's taste was a nice juicy steak served piping on the great pewter hotwater dish. That made his eyes twinkle. I wonder if he ever cosseted Mother up with a tender word or two after she'd been through a birth or whether he was as rigid as ever, waiting for her to buck up and wait on him. He ignored new babies until they were old enough to admire him, old enough to have wills to break.

March 6, 1940

. . . I used to wonder what it would feel like to be sixty-eight. I have seen four sisters reach sixty-eight and pass, but only by a few years. My father set three score years and ten as his limit, reached it and died. I, too, said that after the age of seventy a painter probably becomes poor and had better quit, but I wanted to work till I was seventy. At sixty-four my heart gave out but I was able to paint still and I learned to write. At sixty-eight I had a stroke. Three months later I am thinking that I may work on perhaps to seventy after all. I do not feel dead, and already I am writing again a little.

I used to wonder how it would feel to be old. As a child I was very devoted to old ladies. They seemed to me to have faded like flowers. I am not half as patient with old women now that I am one. I am impatient of their stupidity and their selfishness. They want still to occupy the centre of the picture. They have had their day but they won't give place. They grudge giving up. They won't face up to old age and accept its slowing down of energy and strength. Some people call this sporty and think it wonderful for Grannie to be as bobbish as a girl. There are plenty of girls to act the part. Why can't the old lady pass grandly and grudgingly on, an example, not a rival? Old age without religion must be ghastly, looking forward only to dust and extinction. I do not call myself religious. I do not picture after-life in detail. I am content with "Eye hath not seen, nor ear heard" . . . but I cannot imagine anything more hideous than feeling life decay, hurrying into a dark shut-off.

The days fill out. They are happy, contented days. I am nearer sixty-nine than sixty-eight now, and a long way recovered from my stroke. There is a lot of life in me yet. Maybe I shall go out into the woods sketching again, who knows? . . .

December 13th, 1940

. . . Life has been good and I have got a lot out of it, lots to remember and relive. I have liked life, perhaps the end more than the beginning. I was a happy-natured little girl but with a tragic streak, very vulnerable to hurt. I developed very late. Looking back is interesting. I can remember the exact spot and the exact time that so many things dawned on me. Particularly is this so in regard to my work. I know just when and where and how I first saw or comprehended certain steps in my painting development. Of late years my writing has shown me very many reasons for things. I do not resent old age and the slowing-down process. As a child I used to say to myself, "I shall go everywhere I can and see and do all I can so that I will have plenty to think about when I am old." I kept all the chinks between acts filled up by being interested in lots of odd things. I've had handy, active fingers and have made them work. I suppose the main force behind all this was my painting. That was the principal reason why I went to places, the reason why I drove ahead through the more interesting parts of life, to get time and money to push further into art, not the art of making pictures and becoming a great artist, but art to use as a means of expressing myself, putting into visibility what gripped me in nature.

February 21, 1941

. . . It is the ugliness of old age I hate. Being old is not bad if you keep away from mirrors, but broken-down feet, bent knees, peering eyes, rheumatic knuckles, withered skin, these are *ugly,* hard to tolerate with patience. I wish we could commune with our contemporaries about spiritual stuff. With death getting nearer it seems to get harder. We think of it often but rarely mention it, then only in stiff, unnatural words.

[The final entry of her diary:]

March 7 (1941)

Today Miss Austie took me for a drive round the park and to the Chinese cemetery. The sun was powerful, the Olympics strong, delicate blue, Mount Baker white. The cat bush is already green and the weeping willows round the lake droop with the weight of flowing life, but there are no leaves yet. Everything was splendid. The lend-lease bill has gone through in the States. The war is staggering. When you think of it you come to a stone wall. All private plans stop. The world has stopped; man has stopped. Everything holds its breath except spring. She bursts through as strong as ever. I gave the birds their mates and nests today. They are bursting their throats. Instinct bids them carry on. They fulfil their moment; carry on, carry on, carry on.

AFTERWORD

"Psychic Bisexuality" by Charlotte Painter

*W*omen now enjoy a frank articulation of their inner lives, at least in my local bookstore, where I may buy accounts by the newly divorced, recycled and resexed, by the impregnated and the aborted, by the hooker and the hooked, and by the unhinged. This delightful new freedom, suggesting that secrecy is at a low ebb, has an intriguing counterpart—diary-keeping is on the rise. Only ten years ago, I was the only diary keeper among my friends; now we are legion. Ten years ago, Anaïs Nin had only begun to publish her vast and influential diaries; now she is more widely read than Taylor Caldwell. This shift in activity suggests to me that while the diary may have lost its former use, a cache for words for the unspeakable, it has gained a new use that may have some relevance not only to the writing of books but also to the living of life.

As Emerson told us in his essay "Books," a book is important, but it is not what it stands for. Literature is not life, but I personally developed an early confusion about the two, possibly because of a singular intimacy with the school series *Literature and Life* during those trying junior-high-school years our educational system likes to set apart like a contagion. Since puberty I have always been, as my mother once put it, "among the books," and have written much of my life down in diary form, and published as much of that as was readable. I make this little biographical discursion because I suspect this new use the diary is finding may relate somewhat to my own early confusions. To a lover of literature, life tends to will o'wisp on either side of the poem, the story, the play. The source and the ballad, like the chicken and the egg, are enigmatically linked, and we find evidence of that in the plots and devices of public life, which frequently seem bent on surpassing any fare invented for mass consumption. The melodrama of the 1973–74 political arena, and before that the realizations of outer-space exploration have boggled the imagination. The imitation of art by life may no longer be an academic question of aesthetics, but simple fact. And so, to those of us who are concerned more about quality than sensation, and particularly about the quality of our own inner space, the diary is a simple, direct means of exploring it. I also have a creeping persuasion that this exploration of consciousness may be evolving into an art form. But I think we can at least argue that many women are using it in ways that might tend to threaten the professions that thrive on the human psyche.

One psychologist, writing under the pseudonym Joanna Field, presumed as long ago as 1934 to undertake her own analysis through the use of a diary. The book that came of it was *A Life of One's Own,* published five years after Virginia Woolf's *A Room of One's Own,* and bearing a relationship to Woolf's book, which I'd like to discuss here.

The publication history of Field's book supports the belief that evolution is not a linear process, a notion that Field herself expresses in a footnote: "Sometimes the meaning of an experience would only begin to dawn on me years afterward, and even then I often had to go over the same ground again and again, with intervals of years between. In fact, I came to the conclusion that the growth of understanding follows an ascending spiral rather than a straight line." First published in England in 1934 and not at all in this country, the book was revived in 1952 in a Penguin edition that had some distribution here. Now after another twenty years, although out of print, it is, I believe, enjoying an underground life. It has been recommended to me from three unrelated sources, and I know of one group which has xeroxed copies of the book for their friends. Such currency, unrewarding as it may be financially to its author, suggests that what she learned about herself has taken another turn on its spiral, this time for the common good.

On the face of it, her book offers some fare that has recently become familiar—the exercise of free association in diary form for gaining access to one's unconscious, meditation, relaxation, body awareness, the use of "active imagination" in sketching and daydream—many of the techniques advanced by the humanistic psychology movement. However, in an analysis of what she discovered about her mind, Field takes a refreshing turn, one that is relevant not only to psychology but to the women's movement, and to anyone concerned with the creative process.

Attempting to ignore her professional familiarity with psychological theory and to concentrate solely upon what her diary and personal exploration provided her, she eventually distinguished two mental functions in herself, both of which were impeded by what she called "blind thinking." Blind thinking was an either-or reactive process, familiar to all of us who have responded with purely emotional conditioning. It is the polarizing thinking that alienates those one might reasonably be disposed to like, that meanly or jealously judges others, and creates heroic fantasies for oneself. But it was also a surprisingly superficial process, once she established contact with deeper levels of her own thought. Then she was able to see that those "surface ripples of childish thinking" were dominating the two mental functions in herself that needed to be more fully developed, the masculine and the feminine. These two ways of thinking became clear to her, not through what she had read about such possibilities in literature and psychology, but unexpectedly through a consideration of biology. She found herself reading about the male and female egg cells, that the female gamete is slow-moving, enduring, receptive, occupies itself with the storage of food for the purpose of creation, that the male is active, self-assertive, courageous, questing. And she found that cell activity was no mere metaphor but rather that the "bi-polarity of attitude shown in the characteristics of the spermatozoid and the ovum might permeate the whole of life." And as far as the individual mind was concerned, she decided that the two aspects "do not grow at an equal rate, and it is the conflict between these two sides of the personality, and the relation of this to the physical sex, which is at the root of a great amount of psychological difficulty in both children and adults." She concluded that she might state her own difficulties in terms of psychic bisexuality and say that "it was the conflict between my ideas of the male and female attitudes themselves which prevented me from reaching the fullness of either." She was able then to see that her happiness depended entirely upon developing skill at balancing these two sexes within her mind, at learning how to distinguish when one or the other needed to be brought into play, and as the demands of life's ever changing situations arose, she could call upon the rational, narrow-focused, analytical, "masculine" side of her mind, or the wide-focused, yielding, receptive, "feminine" side. In such a context, this familiar terminology, which has angered feminists who do not wish to be stereotyped, now becomes disarmed; it is merely descriptive, not restrictive. We need only discover within ourselves how and when to call upon either of the functions we need—a task that may, like the *via longissima* of the alchemists, take more lives than one.

However, some of those lives may already have been lived for us, if we look back over the thought in literature and philosophy of the notion of the union of male and female in one. Considering her resolve not to refer to psychological texts, in order to find herself in the present pragmatic experience, Joanna Field's search demonstrates the power of the collective unconscious. She is continually approaching the shores of what Carolyn Heilbrun has called the "hidden river of androgyny."* Heilbrun's very eloquent and scholarly work argues for an interpretation of the Antigone in which the male-female roles might be reversed, for a recognition that Shakespeare thought every human power "quickened when 'masculine' and 'feminine' forces are conjoined," and for an androgynous reading of the life of Christ and the elevation of Mary. Field eventually came to relate her findings to other Eastern religions; the ying-yang sign may well be the oldest of symbols for her personal discovery. I can imagine that even though Field may have consciously borrowed from Virginia Woolf's title, *A Room of One's Own,* it is quite possible she had not read what Woolf had written five or six years earlier, in her by now famous metaphor of the mind, where a man and a woman enter a taxi which Woolf imagined as a brain, in a natural fusion and out of a man-woman desire to cooperate.

> But the sight of the two people getting into the taxi, and the satisfaction it gave me made me also ask whether there are two sexes in the mind corresponding to the two sexes in the body, and whether they also require to be united in order to get complete satisfaction and happiness. And I went on amateurishly to sketch a plan for the soul so that in each of us two powers preside, one male, one female, and in the man's brain the man predominates over the woman, and in the woman's brain the woman predominates over the man . . .

Their parallel ideas, written at very nearly the same time, are now both enjoying revival. As Heilbrun has said, "Ideas move fast when their time comes." Clearly these were ideas ahead of their time.

And now in 1974, as we find these ideas taking hold, there are concurrent notions being entertained in the realm

---

* Heilbrun, Carolyn, *Toward a Recognition of Androgyny* (New York, Knopf, 1973).

of science. Two research centers, the California Institute of Technology and the Langley Porter Neuropsychiatric Institute, have announced this year the results of brain studies that suggest close correlation of the physical brain with male-female functions. By measuring the waves from both hemispheres of the brain, scientists have found that each hemisphere has its specialties, which the other hemisphere does not take part in. On tests involving intuition, the right side of the brain was found to function while the left side rested; in tests involving analytical tasks, the left side went to work. The separate functions may be altered by the use of biofeedback, the term that has come to signify a mechanical control of the brain's alpha waves. Whether science provides a means to shortcut the process of self-discovery, or whether that is even desirable, we can imagine how scientific sanction of psychic bisexuality can move the idea of it along even faster.

As I am more bemused than activated when science catches up with imagination (as Freud did with Dostoevsky), and tend to move rather more like that slow and enduring female gamete, I want to go back now to the task that gave Joanna Field her impetus toward psychic bisexuality, the writing of a diary.

To me the diary has been not only a tool for self-exploration—used without Joanna Field's steadfastness, to be sure—but also a basis for finding the imaginative writing I wanted to do. And I am wondering, since the diary has (at least) this twin capacity, if we can consider it momentarily as a kind of double-minded entity, too.

If we can distinguish between specialized art, as designed for an intellectual, educated group, and primitive art, as created through a group's unconscious symbols, then perhaps we can talk about some diaries as primitive. Several come to mind (are here in this collection), and have been edited and studied by scholars and biographers, just as musicologists went to the Southern states a few years back with their tape recorders to capture the last strains of black spirituals and the origins of jazz. We find a tribute to that untutored musical art in the diary of Mary Boykin Chesnut, written about the time it was being created, when she speaks of the "soul-stirring Negro camp-meeting hymns. . . . the saddest of all earthly music, weird . . . beyond my powers to describe." A similar feeling moved Georges Bernanos to envy when he wrote Helena Morley that he felt sure the "mystery" of her diary would always elude him. It was the unconscious spirit in both cases, the inspiration of a collective symbology no individual can quite create by himself. A volume could be put together of these purely un-self-conscious diaries, and would include such pieces from childhood as the diaries of Marjory Fleming and Helena Morley, and such vigorous pioneers as Martha Martin. If we can believe that primitive art is an unconscious process, and acknowledge that painters, architects and composers turn to such art for inspiration, then we can perhaps appreciate the use a writer aspiring to specialized art might eventually make of his or her own diary. The process might take some time for some growth of consciousness on the part of the writer, or with luck recognition might come as the words drop onto the page. In *A Writer's Diary*, Virginia Woolf suggested for herself a year or two before that the diary might have "sorted itself and refined itself and coalesced, as such deposits so mysteriously do, into a mould, transparent enough to reflect the light of our life . . ." If the diary *is* a mine, a depository, a refinery, and self-operative at that, we have to believe the changes we find in turning back to it are refinements of consciousness. This is assuming that the writer has inside a primal self, one that is reactive on an unconscious level to experience, as well as the so-called civilized self that has endured the process of education that helps him attain a higher consciousness than his primal self. It might be argued that the writer, by virtue of literacy, is never primitive, has no escape from the sophistication language implies, but I think we need only pause a moment to consult our own angers or sudden accesses to passion to realize that education is only a functional barrier between these two selves. Moreover, the levels of the unconscious mind are yet to be counted.

Using the diary to lower the barrier to the primal self does not exorcise that self as if it were some expungeable evil, but instead enables it to function positively as part of the total being. Joanna Field, in fact, defines the happiness she was searching for as that which includes the daemonic, the joy of finding as well as the pain of losing. I believe that this integrating process of the primal and civilized selves is the concern of writers like Sylvia Ashton-Warner and Evelyn Scott, whose diaries are obviously rewritten. It is what I am concerned with in my own published diaries, to "get it together." And if "it" is together, then it may have some metaphorical sense for others.

The search for such metaphors is what Joseph Campbell had in mind in speaking of imaginative work as a quest, and the artist as a quester. "In all the myths of adventure the hero starts out innocently looking for something lost or following an animal into the forest, and before he knows it he is in a place nobody has ever been before that is filled with monsters or demons that may destroy him." And having entered the regions of the unconscious, the artist responds "to the need to escape from this danger and chaos . . . and deals with his 'interior difficulties' by organizing his life on a higher level than before."* If an artist is making that attempt at reorganization through the experience in a diary, then we have a meeting place for the primal self and the tutored self.

In the courtyard of a mental hospital in Malaga, my notebook was the repository of some untidy drawings that reflect a quest very similar to Joanna Field's, in that I came up with unconscious symbols of my own mind's search for a male-female balance, the male symbol bearing a forbidding sign: NO HAY PASO (No Entry). Getting through that impasse was a primal experience.

To the writer questing after art, working with the sub-

* *Psychology Today* (July 1970), p. 89.

stance of a diary offers another double possibility, both imme-
diacy and distance. For the instantly recorded experience,
un-analyzed, can later come together with the recollections
of a more tranquil time.

Distance is important to any art, as Virginia Woolf
warned us in *A Room of One's Own,* in urging women to
forgo anger if they want to create lasting literature. Perhaps
then it was not quite clear just how much anger there was,
and perhaps its usefulness in prompting social action has not
yet been exhausted, and perhaps we have not fully understood that anger is a secondary emotional cover for hurt.
(Righteous indignation feels good; hurts do not.) But whatever the reason, women (and men) have a way to go before
we have "consumed all impediments" to the free transmission
of emotion in art, so that our prose can attain an incandescence
and clarity that is distant from our intrusive selves. But I take
the freedom of expression that is available in my corner bookstore as a hopeful sign; even if anger has prompted much of
it, a collective process of self-discovery underlies it. As Joanna
Field said after becoming acquainted with the dual activity of
her mind, "I must give myself the opportunity and not be
ashamed to practise crude attempts at maleness, even the
crude assertiveness of the noisy little boy, before I can expect
to use the more mature form." But as much permission as we
may grant ourselves as persons to practice such newfound
powers, those of us who write must eventually realize, with
Woolf, that "it is fatal for anyone who writes to think of their
sex," but rather to search within for some collaboration in the
mind between the woman and the man.

Anger aside, I think it is the collective process of inner
exploration that has determined the shift we have seen in
imaginative writing in recent years, which places more em-
phasis on essential truth than on factual realism. Long ago we
realized that an imaginative work need not be *all* imaginary.
Now we may accept that facts are irrelevant if the truth gets
told. Emerson, who did not care for fiction, observed that

"these novels will give way by and by, to diaries or autobiographies, captivating books, if only a man knew how to choose among what he calls his experiences that which is really his experience, and record the truth truly." Our reconstructions may involve us in a mingling of fact and fantasy, if necessary for our metaphor to be accessible.

I suggest we look upon these "captivating" books Emerson spoke of in the original sense of the word "capture," to hold captive, a portion of one's life in motion. They are a plastic art, one that is changing, not final, one that the writer is not obliged to stand upon except for the moment during which it is given, not even in the moment during which it is received. They are a part of the drive to self-completion everyone alive has, whether we write of it or not. One friend, a good reader, told me of trying to understand what I was about in my last book. Her first reaction, a primary one, was: "Ugh, such appalling admissions!" Then some months later she went to the trouble to read the book again and said her attitude during the first reading had prevented her from receiving it. "I missed the universality" was her inflated tribute. Whether universal or not, I was making an attempt to appeal to another than the primal person in rewriting my diary, just as I was trying to reconstruct something above the primal in myself. The writing of the book objectified the experience. It would please me for readers to recognize that, as awareness increases, the need for personal secrecy almost proportionately decreases. If such books can be seen as a "search for truth," then we can also see need for a somewhat revised attitude toward how to hear the truth. One shouldn't have to read a book twice in these days of communication overload. But if readers begin to see that a writer's reconstructed experience is a metaphor for the reconstruction of their own inner life, then the writer has some cooperation.

The success of Carlos Castaneda's books, in which he is clearly using himself metaphorically, gives hope that the audience is ready. His books, incidentally, draw upon primi-

tive knowledge in somewhat the way I meant when speaking
of the uses specialized art can make of primitive art. It has
been rumored that he is his own Yaqui Indian, is Don Juan
himself, a possible mingling of fantasy and fact in the interest
of truth. My reading of his dialogues with Don Juan is that
they demonstrate precisely the capacity of a single individual
for more than one way of thinking. His intuitive, mystical
mentor is his own rejected "female" self (no matter what the
fact, which I hold to be irrelevant, might be), and his task
is similar to Joanna Field's, to balance the two, to take possession again of the rejected self. In that sense his books can
be seen as a metaphor for the modern dilemma of the western
mind.

Here is Field again:

> I now saw that just as I, although searching for the
> feminine, had feared it as a spiritual death, so the
> average Westerner fears the Eastern glorification of
> the female attitude to life, and fears that if he is not
> perpetually active and efficient everything he knows
> and clings to will cease to exist. So he fears and
> hates the power of passive resistance, and makes a
> mystery of the *jiu-jitsu* skill which conquers by
> giving way.

And as we know, since that writing in 1934 the collective spiral of knowledge has taken another turn and swept
up with it a fresh appreciation for eastern physical skills and
philosophy, creating a generally receptive ambience for such
books as Castaneda's.

That the strongest example of the kind of writing I am
endorsing comes from a man may give some spark to argument
for the differences between men and women writers. But I
suggest it is only historically significant. My hope is that
women are ready to abandon the block-making notion that there
is a "female" voice or a sexual style to be attained. Finding

the way to "tell the truth truly" may definitely involve both faculties of the mind. There is no need, however, to abandon certain habits we have lived with. Habits do not like to be abandoned, and besides they have the virtue of being tools. One in particular is the habit women have of fragmenting their activity. In the *Subjection of Women* John Stuart Mill, aside from expressing doubts that men and women have any essential differences, spoke of the capacity women apparently have of "passing promptly from one subject of consideration to another," as far more valuable than the "male capacity for absorption in a single subject." Women "perhaps have it from nature," he says, "but they certainly have it by training and education; for nearly the whole of the occupations of women consist in the management of small but multitudinous details . . ." Further, he expresses the opinion that "the mind does more by frequently returning to a difficult problem than by sticking to it without interruption." These are supportive observations for a woman writer who has borne up under that habit of a conditioned fragmentation of life. Since the diary allows for that fragmentation, thrives on it, there may be less need to alter our style than there is to accept and re-create what we have not yet used of ourselves. Or do even more generations need to spiral around before we know what we know?

In her enlightened anthology, *Psychoanalysis and Women,** Dr. Jean Baker Miller speaks of there being no psychoanalytic model for growth for women. As a scientist, she must, I suppose, be purposive in her thinking, and seek some definitive model. Among the diarists it seems to me we have many models of women who made individual strides toward self-realization—Ruth Benedict in her decision against marriage, Käthe Kollwitz in her continuing creativity within marriage, Fanny Kemble in her move to place morality above the satisfactions of maternity, Emily Carr in her continuing activity as a painter in old age. The understanding that Joanna

---

* Baltimore, Md., Penguin Books, 1973.

Afterword

Field came to about growth strikes me as more useful than a "psychoanalytic model" might be, for she realized that she could not *decide* to grow but could only discover conditions that made her own individual growth possible, and try to encourage them. The diary becomes a way for the individual to uncover design as opposed to purpose, and the design she discovered of psychic bisexuality may be useful to us all.

Field found that her own female element was held down —as she expressed it, "raped"—because she had been trained to have specialized purposes and "think like a man." Perhaps the more common complaint among women is the opposite, a want of occasion to develop the capacity for concentrated work. But in "psychic bisexuality" each of us finds the balance suitable for his or her mind. One is not trapped into "thinking like a man" or "developing a feminine approach." One is doing something completely different, freeing the total power of the individual mind.

Psychic bisexuality is a de-conditioning process, which can eventually eliminate sexist limitations for both men and women. In psychic bisexuality the mind is not blinded by childish responses or cluttered with taboos. Capacities are aroused that allow for greater receptivity to others, deeper responses, and, alternately, sharper penetration of thought, more heightened and courageous activity.

That Joanna Field's book is being read at the same time that Virginia Woolf's ideas about women and literature are enjoying new life seems altogether just. They both lead us to accept the unity of all things and to perceive that as human beings we reflect that unity within ourselves, just as cellular life does, and that responsibility for one's own growth is a voluntary support of the whole.

SOURCES

ALCOTT, LOUISA MAY, see CHENEY, EDNAH D.

ANONYMOUS, *A Woman's Diary,* from *Kotto* by LAFCADIO HEARN. New York, The Macmillan Co., 1902; Boston, Houghton Mifflin Co., 1922.

ASHTON-WARNER, SYLVIA, *Teacher.* New York, Simon and Schuster, 1963.

———, *Myself.* New York, Simon and Schuster, 1967.

BASHKIRTSEFF, MARIE, *Marie Bashkirtseff: The Journal of a Young Artist,* trans. by Mary J. Serrano. New York, E. P. Dutton & Co., 1923.

CARR, EMILY, *Hundreds and Thousands.* Toronto, Vancouver, Clarke, Unwin & Co., Ltd., 1966.

CHENEY, EDNAH D., ed., *Louisa May Alcott, Her Life, Letters, and Journals.* Boston, Little, Brown, and Co., 1919.

CHESNUT, MARY BOYKIN, *Diary from Dixie.* Boston, Houghton Mifflin Co., 1949.

DE JESUS, CAROLINA MARIA, *Child of the Dark, The Diary of Carolina Maria de Jesus,* trans. by David St. Clair. New York, E. P. Dutton & Co., 1962.

ELIOT, GEORGE, *The George Eliot Letters,* Gordon H. Haight, ed. New Haven, Conn., Yale University Press, 1955.

———, *George Eliot's Life as Related in Her Letters and Journals.* New York, Thomas Y. Crowell & Co., 1900.

FIELD, JOANNA, *A Life of One's Own.* London, Chatto & Windus, 1934, Penguin Books, 1934, 1952, 1955.

FLEMING, MARJORY, *The Complete Marjory Fleming,* Frank Sedgwick, ed. London, Sedgwick & Jackson, Ltd., 1934.

Sources

FRANK, ANNE, *Diary of a Young Girl*. Garden City, N.Y., Doubleday & Co., 1952.

HURNSCOT, LORAN, *A Prison, A Paradise*. New York, The Viking Press, 1959.

JAMES, ALICE, *The Diary of Alice James*, Leon Edel, ed. New York, Dodd, Mead & Co., 1964.

KEMBLE, FRANCES ANNE, *Journal of a Residence on a Georgian Plantation in 1838–39*, John Scott, ed. New York, Alfred A. Knopf, 1961.

KOLLWITZ, KÄTHE, *Diaries and Letters*, Hans Kollwitz, ed. Chicago, Henry Regnery Co., 1955.

KOTELIANSKY, S. S., trans. and ed., *Dostoevsky Portrayed by His Wife, The Diary and Reminiscences of Mme. Dostoevsky*. New York, E. P. Dutton & Co., 1926.

LAGERLÖF, SELMA, *The Diary of Selma Lagerlöf*, trans. by Velma Swanston Howard. Garden City, N.Y., Doubleday Doran, 1936.

MANSFIELD, KATHERINE, *Journal of Katherine Mansfield*, John Middleton Murry, ed. New York, Alfred A. Knopf, 1927.

———, *Letters of Katherine Mansfield to John Middleton Murry*. New York, Alfred A. Knopf, 1951.

MARTIN, MARTHA, *O Rugged Land of Gold*. New York, The Macmillan Co., 1952.

MEAD, MARGARET, *An Anthropologist at Work, Writings of Ruth Benedict*. Boston, Houghton Mifflin Co., 1951.

NIN, ANAÏS, *Diary of Anaïs Nin*, Volume I. New York, Harcourt, Brace & World, 1966.

PAINTER, CHARLOTTE, *Confession from the Malaga Madhouse*. New York, Dial Press, 1971.

PTASCHKINA, NELLIE, *Diary of Nellie Ptaschkina*, trans. by Pauline D. Chary. London, Jonathan Cape, 1923.

SAND, GEORGE, *Intimate Journal*. New York, John Day, 1929.

SANTAMARIA, FRANCES KARLEN, *Joshua: Firstborn*. New York, Dial Press, 1970.

Sources

SCOTT, EVELYN, *Escapade*. New York, Thomas Seltzer, Inc., 1923.

SCOTT-MAXWELL, FLORIDA, *The Measure of My Days*. New York, Alfred A. Knopf, 1972.

SEI SHONAGON, see WALEY, ARTHUR.

SENESH, HANNAH, *Her Life and Diary*. New York, Schocken Books, 1971.

STEIN, GERTRUDE, *A Diary* from *Alphabets and Birthdays*. New Haven, Conn., Yale University Press, 1957.

TOLSTOY, SOPHIE A., *The Diary of Tolstoy's Wife, 1860–1891*, trans. by Alexander Werth, London, Victor Gollancz, Ltd., 1928.

WALEY, ARTHUR, ed., *The Pillow Book of Sei Shonagon*. Boston, Houghton Mifflin Co., 1929.

WOOLF, VIRGINIA, *A Writer's Diary*, Leonard Woolf, ed. New York, Harcourt, Brace, 1954.

WORDSWORTH, DOROTHY, *Journals of Dorothy Wordsworth, The Alfoxden Journal, 1798, The Grasmere Journals, 1800–1803*, Mary Moorman, ed. New York, Oxford University Press, 1971.

SOME FURTHER RESOURCES
FOR WOMEN'S DIARIES

ANDREAS-SALOMÉ, LOU, *The Freud Journal of Lou Andreas-Salomé*. New York, Basic Books, 1964.

ANDREWS, E. W., *Journal of a Lady of Quality*. New Haven, Conn., Yale University Press, 1919.

ANONYMOUS, *Diary of a Nursing Sister on the Western Front*. Edinburgh, Blackwood, 1915.

BAGNOLD, ENID, *Diary Without Dates*. New York, William Morrow, 1935.

BIRD, ISABELLE, *A Lady's Life in the Rocky Mountains*. New York, G. P. Putnam, 1885; New York, Ballantine Books, 1973.

BREMSER, BONNIE, Troia. Millerton, N.Y., Croton Press, 1969.

BROWNING, ELIZABETH BARRETT, *The Diary of Elizabeth Barrett Browning*. Athens, Ohio, Ohio University Press, 1969.

CARRINGTON, DORA, *Carrington, Letters and Extracts from Her Diaries*, David Garnett, ed. New York, Holt, Rinehart and Winston, 1970.

CLIFFORD, ANNE (PEMBROKE), *The Diary of the Lady Anne Clifford*, with an Introductory Note by Vita Sackville-West. London, William Heinemann, Ltd., 1924.

COLETTE, *Earthly Paradise*. Robert Phelps, ed. New York, Farrar, Straus and Giroux, 1966.

DALY, MARIA, *Diary of a Union Lady, 1861–1865*. New York, Funk & Wagnalls, 1962.

Sources

DAWSON, SARAH MORGAN, *A Confederate Girl's Diary*. Bloomington, Indiana, Indiana University Press, 1960.

DAY, DOROTHY, *On Pilgrimage: The Sixties*. New York, Curtis Books, 1972.

DOSTOEVSKY, FEODOR, *The Gambler with Polina Suslova's Diary*, trans. by Victor Terras. Chicago, University of Chicago Press, 1972.

FORTEN, CHARLOTTE, *The Journal of Charlotte L. Forten; Free Negro in the Slave Era*, Ray Allen Billington, ed. London, Collier-Macmillan, 1969.

GAG, WANDA, *Growing Pains*. New York, Coward, McCann, 1946.

HATHAWAY, KATHARINE B., *Journals and Letters of the Little Locksmith*. New York, Coward, McCann, 1946.

JAMES, WINIFRED, *A Woman in the Wilderness*. London, Chapman and Hall, 1916.

JEFFERSON, LARA, *These Are My Sisters*. Tulsa, Vickers Publishing Co., 1948.

KELLER, HELEN, *Helen Keller's Journal* (1936–1937). Garden City, N.Y., Doubleday Doran, 1938.

LAWRENCE, FRIEDA, *Not I But the Wind*. New York, Viking Press (Curtis Brown), 1934.

LINDBERGH, ANNE MORROW, *Bring Me a Unicorn*. New York, Harcourt Brace Jovanovich, 1971.

———, *Hour of Gold, Hour of Lead*. New York, Harcourt Brace Jovanovich, 1973.

MALINA, JUDITH, *The Enormous Despair*. New York, Random House, 1972.

MALLET-JOURIS, FRANÇOISE, *Letter to Myself*. New York, Farrar Straus, 1965.

McKEE, RUTH KARR, *Mary Richardson Walker: Her Book, The Third Woman to Cross the Rockies*. Caldwell, Idaho, Caxton Printers, Ltd., 1945. (Includes extracts from MRW's diaries.)

SOURCES

MUMEY, NOLIE, *Calamity Jane (1825–1903): A History of Her Life and Adventures in the West*. Denver, Colo., The Range Press, 1950.

OMORI, ANNIE SHEPLEY, *Diaries of Court Ladies of Old Japan*. Tokyo, Kenkyusha Co., 1935.

PAINTER, CHARLOTTE, *Who Made the Lamb*. New York, Mc-Graw-Hill, 1964, 1965.

POTTER, BEATRIX, *Journal*. London, Frederick Warne, 1966.

LADY SARASHINA, *As I Crossed the Bridge of Dreams: Recollections of a Woman in Eleventh Century Japan,* trans. by Ivan Morris. New York, Dial Press, 1971.

SHELLEY, MARY WOLLSTONECRAFT, *Mary Shelley's Journal,* Frederick L. Jones, ed. Norman, Oklahoma, University of Oklahoma Press, 1947.

SPRAGUE, WILLIAM FORREST, *Women and the West, A Short Social History*. New York, Arno Press, 1972. (Includes extracts from Narcissa Whitman's diary.)

STANTON, THEODORE and BLATCH, HARRIOT STANTON, *Elizabeth Cady Stanton As Revealed in Her Letters, Diary and Reminiscences*. New York, Harper and Row, 1922.

WEIL, SIMONE, *First and Last Notebooks*. Oxford, Oxford University Press, 1965.

ABOUT THE EDITORS

Mary Jane Moffat worked from the age of ten as an actress, married, had two sons, then later trained for another career. She received an M.A. in Creative Writing at Stanford University, and afterward taught there. She now teaches courses in writing, literature and women's diaries for the University of California, Santa Cruz.

Charlotte Painter has also taught at Stanford and at the University of California, Berkeley and Santa Cruz. She is the author of *Confession from the Malaga Madhouse* and *Who Made the Lamb* and has had stories and poetry published in many magazines. She now lives in the San Francisco Bay Area with her son.

DATE DUE

F			
OC 15 '80			
GAYLORD			PRINTED IN U.S.A